S0-AGD-623

Leadership Development in Balance

MADE
Born

Leadership Development in Balance

MADE

Born

Bruce J. Avolio
University of Nebraska

LEA
LAWRENCE ERLBAUM ASSOCIATES, PUBLISHERS
2005 Mahwah, New Jersey London

Lawrence Erlbaum Associates, Inc., Publishers
10 Industrial Avenue
Mahwah, New Jersey 07430

Cover design by Kathryn Houghtaling Lacey

Library of Congress Cataloging-in-Publication Data

Avolio, Bruce J.
Leadership development in balance : MADE/born / Bruce J. Avolio.
p. cm.

Includes bibliographical references and index.
ISBN 0-8058-3283-1 (cloth : alk. paper)
ISBN 0-8058-3284-X (pbk. : alk. paper)
1. Leadership. I. Title.

HM1261.A95 2004
303.4—dc22 2004050625
CIP

Books published by Lawrence Erlbaum Associates are printed on acid-free paper, and their bindings are chosen for strength and durability.

Printed in the United States of America
10 9 8 7 6 5 4 3 2 1

Dedication

I am dedicating this book to my wife, Beth. Since we first met, she has enhanced my numerator each and every day of our relationship. She has done so in her words, through her actions, with her kind thoughts and by the addition of three people to our world's population, Casey, Jake, and Sydney. I know I would be a much smaller fraction of myself without her in my life stream, and because of her I have the chance to get my number above 1.

Contents

Preface

When I set out to write this book, I had four major goals in mind. The first goal was to provide the reader with a broader and deeper understanding of what constitutes authentic leadership development. Specifically, I view leadership development as much more than a program, and more than just developing a single individual. At the very least, it should include a focus on the leader, follower, and the context in which they have been, are, and will be interacting. Second, I wanted to challenge a very basic notion that leaders are born versus made. As you will soon see, this notion may limit the full potential of one's leadership development. Stated simply, if you believe that leaders are born, you will probably not develop your full leadership capacity. Third, I wanted to talk about the elements that comprise leadership development efforts, so that you would be informed to ask the many providers of leadership development the right questions. There are so many programs out there that profess to develop leadership and so few that have any evidence to support their claims. I wanted you to know more about authentic leadership development, so that you could challenge the field of leadership development to raise the standard on how such programs are evaluated and marketed to you. Fourth, I wanted to help you develop your full leadership potential and in turn all those who you influence through your leadership.

Each of the chapters in this book addresses a core concept that comprises the overall leadership development process. I have tried to write each chapter integrating my own experience, the experiences of others, research, and my understanding of a broad range of models pertinent to the development of leadership. However, rather than cite specific studies or theory within a particular chapter, I have tried to distill other people's work and then present that work to you based on my own interpretations. At the end of the book, I have highlighted some of the research and theory that informed my thinking about leadership development. So, if you are interested in exploring the research base for my discussion of leadership development, you can go to these alternative sources for a more in-depth discussion of the various topics.

There are times throughout my discussion that I will return to earlier points in the book. I try to use strategic redundancy in revisiting points that we ought to go back through and reflect on, sometimes again and again. When I come across a complex idea for the first time, I generally do not understand it fully the first time through, and for me strategic repetition is helpful to learning what constitutes its true meaning. Please keep in mind that most great leaders repeatedly made mistakes before they got it right, and became what we now read about in terms of their insightful and inspiring leadership. If it took them more than one time to learn something important, modeling their behavior probably is a good thing for us to do. Repetition can help enhance awareness and deepen our understanding of the core concepts of leadership, although I must admit most smart people abhor repetition. Effective leadership development is rife with repetition.

To develop leadership means that we must engage in a relationship with each other at a distance and, of course, virtually. This means I need your active participation in the thinking and reflection process, so I will from time to time send out a wake-up call to you, in order to promote self-talk. I will also share information about my own observations, doubts, experiences, and life events, because I assume that by doing so, I can help you to reflect on your own life events.

Now, I need to introduce you to the first concept, which I have called the life stream. I view all leadership development efforts as entering into some point in an individual's respective life stream. If it is a team and we are discussing shared leadership, then we may refer to the collective life stream of team members. The timing and the purpose of a leadership development intervention is usually to change the course of the stream to go in some new direction. By using this metaphor, I want you to envision where your life stream comes from, where it is now, how fast it is flowing, and in what direction, if any, it is heading. So an obvious question that I must now ask is where am I in your life stream today ... rapids, waterfalls, quiet pools, or somewhere in between? Who has had the greatest influence on setting its course other than you?

I believe exemplary leadership is earned by how much effort we put into developing it. I think the magic of leadership derives from the perseverance of working hard at being a more effective individual, who works with people to make them more effective to induce positive change. People certainly come into the world with predispositions and talents that make it easier for them to influence others, which we can use as the core definition of leadership—*influencing people to achieve some particular targeted objective*. Yet, leadership is not preordained, in that it can take many courses across different life streams. Take the best predispositions and place them in the worst context, and I am sure that leadership development will take longer to evolve than in an environment that is generally supportive of the best leadership development.

Fundamental to leadership development is stopping to reflect on what happened, what is happening, and what you think will be happening given certain actions taken by you and others. So throughout this book, I also need to talk about reflection as an essential component in the leadership development process. If you do not step back to reflect on significant events, you will certainly never achieve your full potential as a leader.

1

Stretching Views of Leadership Development

"The surest way to lose the truth is to pretend that one already wholly possesses it."

—Gordon Allport (1955)

Have you ever had the experience of someone saying to you that she had met a person who was a natural born leader? It has happened many times to me in interviews, consulting projects, and/or interacting with students in my university classes. You meet someone who seems to fit that description, someone who seems to be a natural at influencing others to achieve certain objectives. And it is easy to say, "She is a natural born leader." It's easy because we can simply attribute the individual's leadership to something we may not understand, as opposed to digging in and trying to understand its source. It's much more efficient to say it is born into the individual and use that as my basis of truth. Why? Because once we say leadership is *made*, we have to systematically examine every aspect of the individual's life course to try and understand what contributes to a person's leadership development. Perhaps more vexing, is the possibility that certain events and experiences may contribute differently to the leadership development of different individuals. Can you see why it is easier to simply say it is *born*, and leave it up to the bio-geneticist to solve this mystery?

ARE LEADERS BORN VERSUS MADE?

One of the truths held by many people about leadership is that leaders are born to lead, made by some mysterious confluence of events, or both. In every workshop on leadership development that I have either led or attended, someone will ask the question: "Are leaders born or are they made?" If asked, I simply respond now by saying, YES! If leadership is not made, I oftentimes wonder why they are attending a workshop on leadership development. Perhaps, they were asked to come to the workshop by a manager or someone from Human Resources. My initial reaction usually does not satisfy people in the workshop, especially those in the workshop who would like to believe that leadership is fixed at birth. It represents their truth, or what may be considered their mental image or model of what they believe explains why some people emerge as leaders, while others do not. Many authors have addressed this issue, but none so directly as John Gardner in his book entitled *On Leadership*.

Gardner (1990) noted: "Many dismiss the subject with the confident assertion that 'leaders are born not made.' Nonsense! Most of what leaders have that enables them to lead is learned. Leadership is not a mysterious activity ... And the capacity to perform those tasks is widely distributed in the population" (p. xv).

Developmental Readiness and Your Possible Self

I have come to realize that what people are asking me may be a very important signal of their developmental readiness to learn about leadership development. For some people, it is simply less effort both intellectually and emotionally to accept leadership is born into some people, but not others, including themselves. They learned at some point in their *life stream,* that leadership is inborn and it became a truth for them and part of their mental image or model about leadership.

I will use a term called one's *possible selves,* which comes from work in cognitive psychology, to describe the model of leadership people have developed during their life stream. I would also like to discuss how such models set artificial boundaries on people's readiness for leadership development at different points during their life stream.

The mental model that each of us builds defines who we are, who we believe we can become down stream, and what we fear and avoid trying to change. Inevitably, unless we can expand this model to enlarge the boundaries of what we view as constituting our possible selves, all of the training, feedback, or personal coaching in the world is likely to fall short of achieving its objectives of developing a person's full leadership potential. If you truly believe leaders are born to lead, you may avoid engaging in situations and experiences that trigger your full leadership potential. You may even engage in those situations and experiences, but fail to derive the deep meaning from those events that can enhance your leadership development. Your beliefs about leadership can become self-fulfilling and self-limiting.

To be in a state of becoming in terms of one's leadership development, you must believe that certain things are not fully programmed in advance. Thinking in terms of becoming, is an essential part of the mental model that provides each of us with a greater readiness to assume new roles and responsibilities en route to redefining our relationships with others. I therefore suggest that leadership is by no means irrevocably fixed by genetics. I am challenging you to consider this possibility right now wherever you are in your own life stream before you come across the next set of events and experiences that might contribute to enhancing your leadership potential. Now, we need to spend some time discussing why I believe this challenge is worth pursuing.

THE LEADERSHIP DEVELOPMENT EQUATION

I have chosen the title of this book to consider that leadership development is indeed made and born. The base of the equation is clearly one's predispositions, our genetic base, and what we are born into this world with and hopefully fully utilize. The "made" in the numerator is underestimated if you simply believe leadership is born. It is underestimated if you fail to accumulate and learn from life experiences that have already been shown to have an impact on leadership development. Let us be clear, even if you are predisposed to be a leader by some favorable combination of genetics, you are not preordained, and learning and leading must go hand in hand for anyone to achieve his or her full leadership potential.

For the moment, let me suggest a more flexible strategy, whereby you assume that much more can be developed in terms of your leadership potential, as a starting point for your leadership development. I am specifically asking that you inflate your estimate of what you feel you are capable of accomplishing in developing your full leadership potential. Give yourself the flexibility to explore possibilities for development as a starting point. Inspiring leaders create possibilities. I am asking you to expand your strategy to provide some additional space for your own leadership development and what will in turn effect the development of people around you. As you limit yourself, so too will it affect the development of others. You cannot change the denominator, at least at this point in the genetic revolution, so we only have to focus on the top half, above the genetic bottom line so to speak.

Having asked for a delay in judgment in how much you believe leadership can be developed, let me be completely transparent with you regarding my next point. I believe that leadership development is by far one of the most complex human processes in that it involves leaders, followers, dynamic contexts, timing, resources, technology, history, luck, and a few things we have not thought of yet. However, it is in many ways like other complex phenomena, models, and processes in that once we break it down into its essential parts, or get the code, we can begin to understand how the various pieces fit together into the whole. We are currently at the same point with the human genome project, understanding all of the code but not yet how it all fits together. In leadership, a lot of the code has been identified, but it has not been integrated into a comprehensive framework for development. For example, we know that leaders with narcissistic personalities will do more for themselves, ruining their organizations and institutions in the process. Alternatively, we see those leaders who are at higher stages of personal development usually evolve their followers and institutions to higher levels of development. We have learned what components of a vision motivate people to the highest levels of potential. We also know that a leader's actions and behaviors are not necessarily seen as they have occurred, but how they are interpreted by followers. Throughout this book, I provide specific examples of what we know, and how it can contribute to your development as a leader, and I hasten to add, to being an effective follower as well.

AN ARCHITECTURAL RENDERING OF LEADERSHIP DEVELOPMENT

Let us try another example in terms of understanding the leadership development process. An architect develops a complex model for a building, and when the model is complete we are able to see what that building will eventually look like or become. It is in a state of becoming, as envisioned and drawn by the architect. It will continue to be in a state of becoming as contractors begin work, and as the owner moves in to designing the desired look and feel of the new building. Over time the building will change as new materials are added, walls are moved around, members come and go, and so forth. What seemed like an inert object is in a state of becoming or emerging over time. Indeed, the new smart homes currently being built, are based on the very premise that our homes are constantly in a state of becoming and adapting to our needs. By actively making sense of life's experiences you can continuously enhance your development. You also remain in a state of becoming if you seek out events that can influence your development.

Let us extend our analogy one more step. The model for the building started out as a picture in the architect's head, albeit limited by what the architect considered a proper building should look like. Before Rudolf Buckminster Fuller came along, the idea of putting together triangles to construct buildings was not very common. There are truisms and limitations to mental models in all fields that get shattered. The building ends up as a detailed drawing we can observe and eventually touch, feel, and occupy in a virtual sense. Today, we can even walk through the building in simulations of its design, and make alterations before the first brick is ever laid. For architects and leaders, the model shows the range of possibilities that will work, and the structure and boundaries developed based on those possibilities. The depth and breadth of the design will eventually provide the framework in which we live with ourselves, and how we go about influencing others.

Leadership follows patterns similar to the previously mentioned architectural example. An autocratic leader builds very strict boundaries within which he or she wants followers to live as opposed to a more inclusive, enabling leader who expands boundaries for followers. The intent of the autocrat's design is to control the behavior of followers, and the designer's intent becomes the basis for interactions, as well as retarding development of both leader and follower. We know that autocratic leadership limits the scope and creativity of followers. Followers are controlled in their behavior based on compliance as opposed to commitment and this over time can disable the leader as well, who is far less informed by followers.

I know some colleagues would say that 360-survey feedback (where leaders are rated by supervisors, peers, and followers) partly serves the function of building a model of who the leader is at a point in time based on follower, peer, and supervisor views of his or her leadership. Assessment centers may also provide a close approximation to a model of oneself, where each individual receives feedback on how they think, decide, solve problems, and relate to others. Yet, each of these forms of assessment and feedback provide a limited one-dimensional view as opposed to the three-dimensional video cam-walk one can take through a house when visiting a local real estate broker who is selling a house.

I believe we can do much better in terms of offering people a three-dimensional view of their established model of leadership potential, which they carry in their heads, as well as their emerging or future potential model. It is not just getting feedback on tests or surveys, it is being able to step back and see one's own complete model through reflective learning, and then to choose where changes are desired in the model. Choosing to move forward represents part of the self-discovery process. It represents self-leadership and it can positively impact on the numerator. Or, you can simply choose to be passive and let someone else determine your boundaries for leadership development.

Let us use the analogy of a personal web page as a guiding framework to build your own model for leadership development. The web page is designed with a specific model in mind, and it also allows for customization of input relevant to the model. Like your leadership model, if you set up your web page to only include a very narrow set of information or experiences, then the web page, like your own development, may very well be prematurely limited. The same is true for the architectural design of a home, which may conform to other designs, rather than being designed to the lifestyle of the house's future occupants.

THE DEPTH AND BREADTH OF LEADERSHIP DEVELOPMENT

My overarching goal for writing a book about leadership development was to help people see the model that guides their leadership development in more depth and breadth. Once viewed in this way, you can take advantage of that knowledge to enhance what you believe is possible. As a leader, what you believe is possible determines what your followers believe is possible. It creates the model in their minds that either limit or expand their possible selves. As a follower, I want you to consider what you can do to take greater responsibility for leadership, and to challenge the constraints and boundaries in your mind of what constitutes traditional followership. By doing so, challenge the traditional boundaries of leadership as well. To best measure leadership, you must look at it in the reflection created by your followers.

This book encompasses what I consider to be essential components comprising a universal model of leadership development, which you can use to develop your own personal model and mental picture of leadership. I say your own model because everyone I have talked to across many different cultures and organizations appeared to have a model of leadership they were able to visualize and describe once asked to do so. These descriptions came from very senior executives in government, industry, at universities, not-for-profit agencies, military, and even eighth and ninth graders in middle schools in the United States. What's on your drawing board right now?

Allport said about personality development, " ... for it is knowledge of our own uniqueness that supplies the first, and probably the best, hints for acquiring orderly knowledge of others" (p. 23). Knowing the unique model one has in their head about leadership development is key to building greater leadership potential for yourself and the followers who choose to follow you. This is at the core of the self-reflective learning process that facilitates self-discovery and ultimately the development of greater levels of leadership potential.

I was reading about Kofi Annan, who is from Ghana and at this writing, the leader of the United Nations. He is described as being a man of high moral values, who believes there is goodness in people and that through his work he can make evil leaders the exception in the world. He was described by his wife, a Swede, using a Swedish word she translated as "cast whole." Sounds a bit like a born leader. Later on in the article, Annan described himself in the following way, "If someone knew me when I was young, they would say, 'We should have known that you were a leader.' But perhaps once we are really challenged, you find something in yourself. Man doesn't know what he is capable of until he is asked" (Cooper, 2000, p. 42). Have you been asked yet?

Born to Lead?

In September, 2001, Rudy Giuliani, mayor of New York City at the time, was called to leadership during and following the 9/11 terrorist attacks on the World Trade Center. Many felt his leadership during this critical and unique period of time was essential in getting New York City to move beyond the early moments of the disaster, to rebuild both physically and emotionally. Was Rudy born to lead? In a recent interview with Tim Russert, he was asked what helped him lead through that catastrophic period. He said his dad always emphasized when things get chaotic get quiet. When the situation is too quiet, he said, it is probably time to be loud! Again and again, the mayor was described as providing a sense of reassurance to New York City and in many instances the nation. He also said that after being Mayor for nearly 8 years, he had the experience and confidence to lead through this crisis. What if the attack started a day after he took office? Born or made?

THE COMPONENTS OF LEADERSHIP DEVELOPMENT

Many of the components contained in the model of leadership development to be presented here have already been tested in terms of their links to effective leadership performance. However, these links have never been tested in total. That remains a challenge for all of us to pursue in the field of leadership development. The model is a prototype for you and I to build on together to maximize leadership development. In fact, with almost all of the concepts, there is an adequate base to warrant their inclusion in a comprehensive model of leadership development. Yet no one has attempted to put them together in an integrative way, and by saying this, I may be vulnerable to attack. However, being vulnerable and transparent is part of being an authentic leader, and right now, as most leaders have to do, I have to make a choice on what arguments or positions to put forth so early in our relationship. My choice is to tell you where the boundaries are in terms of what we know and what yet needs to be explored. I make that choice realizing the risk to our relationship, since some people may want to be told the single best way to develop leadership.

The truth is there are many ways to develop your full leadership potential based on your unique talents, strengths, and experiences. There are many avenues to explore. There simply is no one best way, and even if there was, it would change as the dynamics of leadership change. For example, can we consider leadership as being the same pre and post the Internet? Now that leaders can lead at a distance and have personal contact with each and every follower, is there anything about our leadership models that should be changed? The fastest growing structure in organizations today is teams and now many are virtual teams. What are the implications for leadership development with this change in structure? How will the development of leadership change, when leadership is shared or horizontal as opposed to vertical and based on one individual?

We often describe leaders as those people who explore the frontiers of science, technology, space, geography, and understanding. So let us explore leadership development with a new map that will be updated along the way. Your leadership and the field are both in a state of becoming, if you believe it is so.

I have 20 years of research and training experience in the field of leadership development, and can offer my experience to enhance your understanding of how to use this model of leadership in terms of your development. And you have … wait a second, who are you?

Are we in some leadership training program together? Run. Just kidding! If the instructor had the wisdom to select this book, then … well … she's probably a former student of mine getting a percentage of the royalties. Relax, I don't give former students cuts on royalties! Are we in your office or a quiet library or on a plane together? If a plane, then go ahead, and stand up and say, "Ladies and gentleman, the book I hold here contains the answer to what it takes to be an inspiring leader! I stand before you at the dawn of a new era, unlimited by its possibilities, united with you, my fellow passengers, in a glorious endeavor—one that is unrivaled in humankind." Okay, you'd better sit down, as the flight attendants and air marshal are getting nervous.

One thing is very clear to me right now, and that is I do not know you. And you do not know me. A basic lesson in leadership development is that *one should try to know one's followers before attempting to develop them into leaders*. And the next lesson is that *you should know everything you can about your leader, his talents, strengths, mental model, and aspirations*. Assume you do not know your leader, and learn who she is and what she needs from you to be successful. There is a leadership lesson right in front of you to observe each and every day, and that is your leader in action.

Why review training tapes when you can watch your own leader in action? Is your leader aware of your needs? If not, he is probably not fully developing you. Does your leader know what your favorite form of recognition is? In most organizations, leaders do not know what employees value in terms of recognition. Unfortunately, this is all too common in many organizations around the world. Your leader needs to know her followers fully, and the followers need to know her, what she stands for, what she values, and what she hopes for in the future. (Take a look at the STAARR report at the end of this chapter. It outlines how to observe and reflect on leadership moments, which in my opinion is one of the essential bases of leadership development.) What we see and understand in others, we can potentially incorporate or avoid in our own behavior.

Leadership development is reciprocal and involves followers. It cannot be done alone! It is important to tell people who you are without overwhelming them with a long and glorious history of yourself. Try to err in the direction of conveying who you are as a leader, through your behaviors and actions. Use the 80/10/10 rule where you convey your beliefs and values 80 percent of the time through the consistency of your actions and espoused values. Ten percent of the time you reaffirm your beliefs and values in what you say. And with the remaining 10%, you convey what you value and believe in through the description of you by others and through their own behavior—where you have created a ripple or cascading effect. By the way, this last 10% grows over time; as people around you come to trust what you say to them, it is a reflection of yourself.

PROMOTING SELF-REFLECTION

Since the current medium restricts my ability to get to fully know you, I suggest we try some alternatives. First, let me become on a temporary basis the voice in your head about leadership development. Consider me a reflective voice prompting you to think about your model and I hope emerging model of leadership. I encourage you to think about areas that can be developed in yourself. View me as a virtual coach if you will. I in turn try to anticipate what you might not understand, and offer alternative examples and methods for your consideration. I use strategic redundancy to make sure you heard what I said. And, I practice reflective learning myself, offering you what I thought, in order to encourage you to do the same.

Now, if you have read this far in the book, I assume we have a very loose deal. The deal is simple. I take the lead in presenting portions of the model for your consideration and simply ask you to reflect on how to try out some suggestions for expanding your internal model of leadership and its development. As part of the deal, I expect and encourage you to challenge the model as it emerges in your mind. Development does not occur without challenging the "as is" for the "what could be." So, please challenge it and how it might best apply to your own development as part of your self-discovery process.

DESIGN AND OUTLINE OF BOOK

In thinking about the basic design for this book, I wanted to first provide the deep structure or components of a model that we can use as a basis for leadership development, while helping you learn something that you could apply to your own development. I wanted this book to be more than a simple "how to be a more effective leader" guide because I believe the development of authentic leadership is much more profound than simply listing "do this and do that and you will be a great leader." Of course, I ultimately rely upon you to be the best judge of whether I am able to provide the structure that underlies leadership development, balanced with the necessary practical applications that make your efforts to read through this book worthwhile, interesting, and I hope sometimes fun.

In each chapter following chap. 1, I discuss one main concept that makes up an overall model of leadership development. From your perspective, you can think of each chapter as a component of the leadership development process, in some cases a guiding concept that leads us to a specific point in leadership development, or both. As we work through the components that make up the leadership development process, my hopes are that you begin to see the complexities of leadership development in a different light, and realize you have much more control over your leadership development than you previously believed before reading this book. By the way, when I say "realize" here, you can assume that I mean the difference between your model of leadership development you entered this book with and the new one you are now forming in your mind.

Leadership's Special Effects

Let me try approaching our discussion of leadership development from a different angle. Do you recall seeing a movie where you had not a clue how they were able to show some special effect during the movie? Then one day you were watching a show about the making of that movie, and there was the special effect, which took 15 steps to create and 40 camera angles. That "aha" experience you had there is what I would like to create for you here regarding the special effects associated with leadership development.

Leadership is not all smoke and mirrors nor is it simply special effects. The point here is that we typically do not understand something when it is all put together, but if we can break it down into meaningful chunks, then we have a chance of understanding the whole picture of events without losing the whole. The human genome project contains 3.5 billion letters, which are now deciphered. Scientists must now figure out what it all means. Hence, my goal is to compartmentalize leadership development in a way that does not trivialize the process, while at the same time making it understandable enough for you to fully use in your own leadership potential, whatever that might be. Let us say we are building the leadership development periodic chart together.

Many of the base concepts that I cover with you are linked to a model of leadership that my colleagues and I have described in other sources in more extensive detail, which we have called a "full range model of leadership development" (see Avolio, 1999; Bass, 1998). You see, the concept of full range is one of those base concepts that can facilitate how you go about developing your leadership potential, regardless of where you are in your own life course or stream.

The question I would like you to begin thinking about now, is what you currently consider to be your full range of leadership ability and potential? How broad and deep is your range of leadership ability and potential? What areas are currently underdeveloped? I will explain in much more detail what I mean by "full range" shortly.

I approach the partitioning of leadership, using what I consider to be main concepts underlying the leadership development process. While going through each concept, I highlight how each concept can be applied to one's development as a leader, thus turning concept into practice. At the end of each chapter, I provide a description of a situation or case to help you visualize the concept in action, to help you understand its special effects.

THE LIFE STREAM

We begin our discussion with an overarching concept that goes back to the issue we first began with, and that is whether leaders are born versus made. The concept is what I called a person's life stream. Simply defined, the *life stream* represents events you accumulate from birth to the present that shape how you choose to influence others and yourself. Dramatic life events can force an individual to reconsider who he is, what he stands for and the model that guides his thoughts, behaviors, and actions. Of course, there are also less dramatic life stream events that one accumulates and may place you at the same point down stream, as compared to someone who had a more difficult route. Not knowing a person's life stream and its impact on leadership development is one of the reasons why people simply say, "Ah, leadership ... it's born." Keeping in mind the concept of one's life stream helps to keep leadership development in a state of becoming, until all of our streams, so to speak, run dry.

Two people will experience similar if not identical events in their respective life streams at the same point in development, but end up being very different in terms of their leadership potential. One person may become devastated and unable to ever fully recover, while the other becomes inspired, and goes on to change the world. I am sure other Indians went to South Africa before Ghandi. If so, why did Ghandi translate his experience with discrimination into a vision for peace and nonviolent protest?

For now, I am going to take the lead in presenting the main concepts to you which make up leadership development. However, if you simply become a passive reader, then developing your full leadership potential will not work. To be successful in enhancing your full leadership potential, you MUST attack these concepts, twist them around, try them on, question them, and leave each chapter feeling you have taken on a debate with your own model of leadership.

WORKING WITH WHAT WE'VE LEARNED

Over the next several days, take some time to complete the STAARR report below. This report is used as a basis for starting the process of reflective learning. What I am asking you to do is to identify one positive and one negative incident of leadership that you have observed in your organization and to complete a STAARR report. The purpose of asking you to complete this report is to get you to be a more structured observer of leadership moments that occur within your life stream. Oftentimes, we fail to take the time to notice and then review such events, which can hamper our development. There is a leadership development program unfolding around you.

STAARR REPORT

INSTRUCTIONS: Use a separate form for each leadership incident.

Situation: Examine how a follower or followers have had influence on the evolving L-F relationship or task outcome. Briefly tell when, where, how, why they assembled, and other relevant aspects of the situation.

*T*ask:	State the task of the named leader; include the larger goal or mission if relevant.
*A*ction:	What did the leader do that was positive (negative)? Describe each L behavior & follower response in a single sentence.
*A*nalysis:	Why did you consider the behavior or incident (positive or negative)? Was it in terms of the impact on the follower, the situation, the task, or some other facet in the situation?
*R*elationships:	How did the positive (negative) relationship affect the relationship between the leader and follower in both the short-term and long-term?
*R*esults:	What happened as a consequence of the leader's positive or negative behavior?

2

One's Life Stream

"The drama of human life can be written largely in terms of the friction engendered."

—Allport (1955, p. 28)

I have always been amazed to find out what has happened in leaders' lives to make them who they have become. Meeting Lech Walesa in Korea was a very profound experience for me. When he told us that he was a boxer growing up, it made so much sense to me in terms of how he dealt with the former Soviet Union. Great boxers know when to go in and fight and when to cover up. He was a master of this trade. Then when I read Nelson Mandela's biography I discovered that he too was a trained boxer. I was convinced with a sample of just two, that I had my boxer theory of leadership. Both of these men stood toe to toe with awesome regimes that had all of the institutional power, and yet they took the punches and survived.

One stream we have no choice of jumping into is our life stream. From the moment of our birth, we are embedded in our life stream, and quickly become embedded in others, oftentimes by our own choosing. After birth is where leaders evolve beyond their genetic predispositions, thus forming the numerator of development potential. Some of us enter life in an easy way. Some struggle for their life almost from the very start. In these very early moments, there can be huge differences in how one begins life.

HOW DIFFERENCES MAKE A DIFFERENCE

The complexity to keep in mind is that not even the same events for two people will necessarily produce the same leader. The same events experienced by someone who is extremely intelligent will not be processed in the same way as someone who is of average to below average intelligence. Or someone open to experiences in terms of their personality will certainly derive different meaning from unexpected events, versus the individual who has no desire to experience anything remotely different from the norm. How meaning is attached to significant life events, and then what we do with that meaning, determines what we learn and incorporate into our own developmental potential.

Many will miss great opportunities along the way to learn from events, reflect on them, and enhance their models of leadership potential. This may have prompted the noted psychologist Erich Fromm to comment generally on the development of people by saying, "Some people die before they are fully born."

There is a point worth reemphasizing here for reflection. Two people have nearly identical life streams, but one ends up as a very successful leader and the other never holds down a job, nor is seen as being someone who can be respected or trusted. The common attribution is to say that the one individual must have been naturally born to be a leader. Although this is always true in part, it is the interaction of events with the individual that may actually help explain why only one individual became an effective leader. For example, let us add in some details. The successful leader had a very high energy level. This is a facet of the human personality that many consider to be inherited. Someone with a high energy level will be more likely to engage in a broader array of events, put the time and effort into learning from them, and incorporate what she has learned into a renewed leadership style. They have the energy to work at it, until they have achieved success.

Someone who has a low energy level may over time become overwhelmed by events leading to a partial or total breakdown of their life system. The predisposition of high versus low energy level may have been a key difference in explaining why two individuals went down very different life streams.

Of course, there are many other factors that may result in these two individuals following a very different course. Perhaps most important is the support that an individual has to go back and learn from events. That facet is usually labeled exemplary parenting, teaching, coaching, and supervision. Mayor Rudy Guiliani's father's words rang through his mind that horrible day in September, "to get calm." He had heard those words and advice many times before in his life stream.

So let us ask the obvious question, "What if we intervened to provide some support for the less energized individual?" Could we make a difference in the end result? The river guide can make suggestions on how to easily move from the eddy or to avoid getting in one. Can't we do the same in coaching leadership development? By intervening we become an event, and that is very central to understanding how leadership development evolves. It is event-driven whether those trigger events occur naturally or are inserted in a more strategic or systematic sense. The choices you make from here on out can help determine, in part, how your leadership development emerges. For example, if you choose not to complete a STAARR report, you are choosing one event over another in your development process. Every event is by no means critical, but the accumulation of many events over time give us choices that can shape how we develop as leaders in terms of the numerator.

LIFE IS THE TRAINING PROGRAM IN WHICH LEADERSHIP DEVELOPMENT IS EMBEDDED

Unlike most training programs, we typically have less control over the sequence of training events in life, although what you choose to try, engage in, learn from, or walk away from, all shape the training events that you confront in life and in turn your leadership development. When we intervene with the typical leadership development training program we are consciously trying to alter the life stream in a direction that will result in more effective leadership. It can be as simple as getting managers to set more specific goals and contracts with their employees, provide more frequent feedback or praise, and take time to understand the needs of their followers. It can also be as complex as thinking about what constitutes an inspiring vision, how to communicate that vision both verbally and nonverbally, and how to follow up the vision with personal actions and determination to make sure it is fully understood.

The life stream metaphor provides a framework for us to discuss events that accumulate to shape an individual to emerge as a leader. Specifically, certain events, their timing, number, and accumulation can influence the course of leadership development.

I do not know if you do this, or have seen or read about it, but one thing I have observed in outstanding leaders is their ability to squeeze out of every life event as much as they can learn for their personal development, and the development of others. During the event, or after it has concluded, you can reflect on what was important, what caused the event, how you dealt with the event while it was happening, and how you could have avoided this event. If the event was positive, how could future similar events be replicated and continue to add value? Such leaders do not move away from failures without learning something significant. Not learning from failures is yet another compounded failure.

There are many life events that we have little if any control over. These events could include moving every year from one location to another as a child; losing one or both parents before graduating high school; having a teacher in elementary school that displayed every positive attribute of leadership ever discussed; having one or both parents that were exemplary role models of leadership and ethical conduct; being given a particular challenge during school that everyone else overlooked, and turning out to be successful at it; having a first manager who could have written the book on how to be either the very best or worst manager, and so on. What you have more control over is what you can learn from these events and in some cases the events you choose to experience yourself. This process involves self-reflection, after-action reviews, full debriefs, and ultimately self-discovery.

LIVING AND LEARNING FROM THE EVENT

There are some obvious applications that I am sure you have already observed. For example, what have you learned from the worst decision you made in the past year? How has what you learned changed the direction your life stream took over time? Did you reflect on the decision and go back to it several times? Did you understand the sequence of actions that unfolded as a consequence of the decision? Did you debrief this decision with others to get their reactions? Did you try to see what would have happened if you never made any decision?

Let us be even more proactive. By exploring alternatives in the future of what you dream about in terms of what you can accomplish, you can begin to configure events and experiences that can shape the course of your life stream. This could be properly described as self-defining leadership. Many leaders are described as seeing the future in the evolving present. A guide on the river will describe the types of rapids ahead by her observations of the water around her. You can think in advance of how to prepare for them, even avoid them if they are too treacherous. We know the future by carefully observing the present in which we are embedded. This is one reason why I think reflective learning and debriefing what just happened are so important to developing one's leadership potential.

A classic example of how life events can shape the person is the one I mentioned earlier regarding Ghandi going to South Africa, and seeing up front and close the discrimination against races including his own. Or, how about the countless number of women Mary Kay Ash has affected in terms of boosting their pride in being women? Take Mary Kay out of the lives of these women, and what would their life streams have looked like over time and their accomplishments? Leaders can be a profound event in one's life stream, and events are what shape our leadership development.

One has to wonder whether President Gerald Ford learned something about the power of healing from his mother or stepfather, which prepared him to assume the Presidency after Nixon resigned. When he was just an infant Ford was taken by his mother to escape from a physically abusive husband. She never returned to her husband and Ford's biological father. She met another man, who was caring, loving, and an exemplary role model for Ford. Was he born to lead, or did events provide him with the training he would need later in life to help the nation to heal during one of the most uncertain times in the history of the United States?

The life streams associated with the previously mentioned people represent individuals who made a positive contribution to their communities, organizations, and in some cases nations. Of course, there are many people who have been in leadership roles whose life streams took them down a very different course. How did the life stream of Josef Stalin, Idi Amin, Adolf Hitler, and Pol Pot, shape the leaders they were to become? What significant life events comprised their life leadership training? Were they all born to destroy their communities, or were there some trigger events that shaped these leaders and what they became to their nations and more importantly where they fell short? Can we intervene right now, to avoid such destructive leaders from gaining power again in the future?

Most people see these benevolent and horrific leaders once they have assumed a leadership position. However, it is critical to tease apart the events that contributed to the emergence of these leaders we have all come to love and those we revile. Taking into consideration each individual's life stream is a way of understanding how leaders emerge over time beyond genetics.

APPLYING THE LIFE STREAM TO THE LEADERSHIP TRAINING PROCESS

I have come to imagine that each individual entering leadership training workshops is trailing behind some life stream. At what point have I entered? Is it at a moment of quiet reflection? Is it when everything about life appears to be falling apart, or is it somewhere in between? Like many leadership development workshops, I used to routinely move forward with my lesson plan intent on developing better leaders, regardless of each individual's developmental readiness. Can you do the same when you meet your next follower? What is that follower's life stream and how has it shaped his development as a leader?

In good conscience, I can no longer proceed with this "one size fits all" strategy of leadership development. I have learned that some people engage leadership development workshops in a very deep and serious way. The feedback they receive from others concerning their leadership styles forces them to reconsider the actions they have taken at work prior to the training workshop. For some, it is a walk in the park, nothing ventured and nothing gained. While for others, they come to a realization that this workshop does apply to them, but there are just other things on their mind and the training is simply a distraction they have to put up with for a short period of time. No wonder Avi Kluger and Angelo DeNisi found that after receiving personal feedback one third improved, one third stayed the same, and one third did worse!

We can and should be more systematic than life in the design of our development efforts, because we do not have as much time as life! Consequently, our efforts must be more exacting and carefully measured so that we introduce as many of the right events that can help develop an individual's full leadership potential as possible. No one in his or her right mind is giving us a lifetime to develop leadership, and we are often lucky to get 3 days!

MAKING SENSE OF ONE'S PERSPECTIVE

I have been discussing what constitutes the life stream, perhaps in a rather general sense, indicating that it is the accumulation of certain events determined by the life we live. However, we need to drill down now to a more specific level of analysis, to include a very important component in the leadership development process called interpretation, perspective, understanding, or all of the aforementioned. Stated differently, it is how we make sense of events.

In terms of different interpretations, one person with what psychologists call high internal locus of control will take the time to try and understand why certain things went wrong in her life, and what she could have done to change those things in retrospect. This person could have conducted her own personal debrief trying to understand how the course of events in her life stream placed her where they did over time because the locus of her control is on the inside versus saying it is something she could not control. This debrief may involve a simple ordering of events to see which event started the chain of event reactions. I hasten to add that such debriefs can be very challenging, the more difficult and emotional the events become. Indeed, there are times that an external coach or consultant in this process, or peer mentor can help provide invaluable insights into one's development.

The person with an external locus of control may have simply felt that things happen and a lot of it happened to them at some particular point in time, which he or she could not control. He perhaps just chose to move on downstream in life, with the learning and interpretation of events suffering. There were no personal debriefs, no after-action reviews, and no sense of personal reflection.

THE LIFE MODEL IN STREAM

Each of us constructs what she or he interprets to be the significance or meaning underlying various events. The interpretation of events builds in each of us a unique life construct or internal model, which becomes the lens that we use to view the world around us. The internal model is the deep structure upon which our leadership is developed. We can say the model includes our core value system and beliefs. It also includes mechanisms for weighting the importance we give to certain information and events that we experience in stream.

When we refer to a person's moral compass, it means the personal model that an individual has created. We each build our model from events we experience and they over time become the mechanism for selecting which events we will choose to experience subsequently, when the choice is ours. The model is a dynamic mechanism that can make us optimistic, calculating, a life learner, controlling, prejudiced, cynical, positive, or vengeful. The person we become is in large part a function of the model we create and use over time to interpret events. I have said "we" purposefully, because at some early point in our life stream, it is our choice that shape who we are becoming. Also, unless we can evolve the model, we cannot evolve leadership development.

Depending on one's life stream, the model can become very narrow and resistant to any change. Some people define early on what the model of the world is for them, and then use the lens created to interpret all subsequent events. In the extreme, their model becomes fixed at a point in time and fails to take advantage of new events that could help grow and broaden the individual's view of the world. The person's life learning stream has run dry! You have met such people I am sure, who are always lamenting about how things were, and how today, blah, blah, blah doesn't make any sense to them. Would you be interested in being led by someone whose life model was not evolving anymore? Ask yourself when was the last time you directly and significantly altered your model? For me, it oftentimes occurs when I travel to a different culture, and realize how simplistic I was in my conceptualization of what that culture meant in terms of actions and behaviors. I have seen in Asia how hard it is for people to question those in authority, while observing in North America that to not question leaders is nearly failing to be alive! How can I lead followers in these very different cultural contexts, without expanding my model about what constitutes deference to authority?

A friend recently sent me an article about making U-turns in Singapore. The article pointed out that in Singapore if a sign is not there prohibiting a U-turn you should assume it is there. In our culture, if there is no sign, then go for it! This simple example portrays the challenge of leading followers in the Singapore culture to be part of a thinking nation that supports challenges to the current way of thinking.

I wonder to what extent the events of 9/11 in the United States have significantly altered many people's models of our world. On an individual level, we need to come to grips with how others perceive us around the world in order to prevent such attacks from happening again. Someone dislikes us enough to want to sacrifice their life while killing us. In the long term, we are certainly more aware of our collective vulnerabilities than we were on 9/10/2001 in the United States. What impact will these events have on our next generation of leaders, as I am sure what has happened is now shaping their individual and collective life models? Some data collected by the Gallup organization indicates that many Muslims believe we do not respect their culture.

How do we alter that perception and the part of our personal models that might be contributing to that perception?

Now, at the other extreme, we witness certain people who seem to be able to continuously adapt their personal model of life over time, which guides them into the many new courses they choose to follow. They view it as a learning center for incorporating new information that can be revised, as new and significant events are both experienced and interpreted. In the former case, the individual who continues to work with *Life Model Version 1.03* versus the latter case where the individual is using *Life Model Version 5.0*, 5.0 represents an individual who continuously replenishes the life model with new ideas, information, facts, and interpretations. The newer versions are upgrades as opposed to changes for change sake. These people are life learners and they seek out information to help improve their understanding of people, events, and their interaction. They are intrigued by the next generations' trends. They find it possible to reinvent who they are and how they are perceived by others. Yet, their core values may remain solid year after year after year. Think of someone you labeled resilient, and probably that person had a very viable life model that was growth oriented. Meeting an 80-year-old woman who was fascinated by how the Internet was affecting everyone's life and its potential is the type of resilience we can find in this thing called a life model.

As we look at people's life model today, it will become increasingly important that we examine those models with greater attention to the cultural forces that have shaped the model. Today, much of business crosses all sorts of cultural boundaries within and between countries. Understanding how people evolve from their culture in terms of core values, treatment of different ethnic groups, gender differences, views of family, and so forth will be increasingly important to the full development of leaders.

I recall observing a senior officer in the South African military, a white Afrikaner talking to a black officer from the African National Congress (ANC), whom had become one of his very best friends come to tears in their discussion. The white officer said, all of my life I never knew I should ask the black people around me what they felt. I was taught they were simply the background, and they were taught the same. The day I realized how much I had ignored you, was a very, very difficult day for me to reconcile. All I can say, that was my world, it was all I knew at the time. How could we not take the formation of his lens through his life stream into account when interpreting his leadership?

ADJUSTING THE LIFE MODEL

We must now try to understand the internal model's depth and breadth to fully develop it. I have referred to it generally as mutual development in the introduction to this book. Let us be clear what I am asking of you, as it is far more difficult than at first glance. I am asking you to reflect on your own theory of life and model, which represents the lens, processor, and repository for your interpretation of events, as a means of addressing your own leadership development. It can be thought of as the basic structure that you use to guide your attention, interpretation, and actions. The difficulty in all of this is that the model is part of who we are and what we can become. It is not something separate from us, but an integral part of us. It is working right now to understand what I am saying to you, and at the same time I am asking you to step back from it, to understand what its potential and limitations are for you.

When I asked you to complete the STAARR report, the act of completing that report involves your invoking your life model or construct. You chose what you considered was a positive and a negative incident, and for some, a negative may be a positive experience, based on the composition of your model. So one of our greatest challenges for leadership development is to take apart the lens or framework people use to interpret events, but unfortunately that framework is always activated. So it is working to interpret what we are interpreting.

Recently, I had the opportunity to hear Archbishop Desmond Tutu speak. The theme of his presentation was that people were essentially good, and all of us are unique and have something special to offer. He said that all people were VSP's or Very Special People. He told us a story of a white woman, who during the Apartheid years in South Africa was severely maimed by a bomb blast. After she had recovered and some years later in her life, she was asked to testify at South Africa's truth and reconciliation hearings. She said that being injured was one of the best things that had ever happened to her, as she came to realize who she really was and what really mattered in her life. She wanted forgiveness for the people who had harmed her, and she asked for their forgiveness as well. How do you take someone like this woman and simply ignore her life stream and launch into her leadership development? You just can't!

The reality we must face in leadership development is that some individuals have very significantly upgraded versions of their life models. Yet, we still must jump into their life stream, just as you do with the person sitting next to them, who may have come down a different life stream and is currently working with an earlier version of the life model ... one that might crash like old software does.

There are those individuals who seem to be able to provide profound insights and oftentimes are described as having wisdom. *Born to be wise,* or was it a strategy to continue developing a life model so it could be productively used over the person's entire life stream? I believe that leadership and wisdom are both made, even if both are built on the genetic abilities people are endowed with at birth like cognitive abilities, energy levels, and how attractive we are to others.

In terms of our own process here in this book, we are working to grow each other's models by incorporating information that will help each of us influence others more effectively. When we fail to augment our life model, we each fail to develop ... we fail to become and to evolve. Have you evolved lately? I say "we" because each time I sit down to write a book like this, I have found that my own life model has changed as I am trying to apply what I have learned and am learning to my own development. Writing a leadership development book itself involves self-reflection, going back and reviewing events and actions that I have been a participant in, and coming to some new realizations of what took place.

Although we are bounded or even blinded by our life models, we must use them to understand and develop the way we look at the world around us. Reflection is one of our most powerful tools to help us challenge the way we view the world around us. Reflection helps us go back to revisit the life model to examine how it has shaped our perceptions of an event. Feedback from others is also useful in understanding the boundaries of our model and its depth. When you say, "I just had an insight," or "That was insightful," you know you are operating at the boundaries of your own model. Debriefing is a third way of structuring what just happened, and it is a way to analyze how we use the life model in entering into and shaping events. Tragic life events are a fourth way, but I would prefer you work with the first three.

Let me try approaching our discussion of the internal model using a specific case of leadership development. One leader has in his personal model that the core to human motivation is self-interest and that to achieve the highest level of motivation, he must direct people to specific goals and rewards that satisfy personal interests. There is little room for anything else to consider as part of motivation. Motivation is interpreted based on self-interest and that is the lens the leader uses to interpret the behavior and motivation of others. "Sam did this or that, because it was in his own self-interest."

A second leader views human motivation in a much broader sense, trying to understand why some people willingly sacrifice the things they most desire for the good of others. His internal model considers how different generations engage leaders in different ways. He does not fully understand why, but perceives that the World War II, Baby Boomers, Generation X, and Generation Y have different sources of motivation that seem to guide how they respond to acts of leadership. He explores the why, to better understand how different groups of individuals are motivated. He does not lament that these new generation types are no longer motivated, which of course makes no sense. He tries to understand differences in motivation, to determine what the keys are to motivating each and every person within and between generations. One leader says, "I see that Generation Y'ers are much more comfortable with multitasking, and therefore presenting the tasks to be accomplished sequentially creates much less motivation for them."

The first leader contracts with others and rewards when contracts are completed. Here there is little if any concern for who the individual is or what he or she needs for further development. The second leader enlarges and tries to understand the source of his challenge and how to use it to understand the range of people they work with over time, as a first step. The Gen-X follower may reject authority if they were a latchkey kid from age 9 onward. Why would they accept close supervision now, when we told them at 9 to handle their own responsibilities absent any oversight? Who is this I am leading, and where is this particular person in his life stream? Keep this question in mind and reflect on it each and every time you meet someone new called a follower. Leadership with the second leader represents understanding the process, shaping the process, and moving toward some goal. For the first leader the goal is the goal, and the reward is the incentive that is the only option for motivating performance.

REFOCUSING ONE'S INTERNAL MODEL

Let us consider some other examples to see if we can bring our discussion into even clearer focus for you. Some people experience terrible forms of discrimination early on in life and it shapes their model of life to include certain groups and exclude others. Many people in my generation have become very accustomed and I believe comfortable working with women as supervisors. I believe the next generation now moving into key leadership roles will feel even more comfortable with women taking on leadership roles in the United States. In 2000, Madeline Albright was the U.S. Secretary of State, which perhaps 40 years ago would have seemed unimaginable. It now is not for the Generation Y group and it will not be for their children or their grandchildren. The context in which their life streams will emerge will be different than current older generations experienced, and this certainly affects people's mental models of leadership. The fact that HP, Xerox, and Lucent all have women CEOs has to have an effect on a generation of followers coming through our educational systems.

Yet, there are some women who grew up in a period of time where it was not acceptable to have a career in business, and some that unfortunately came to believe this would always be the case, limiting their state of becoming. Indeed, there are many countries around the world today that are still evolving through this period of development. Wired into their life model, there were certain roles for women that were proscribed and prescribed. These models now shape the events they choose to engage in terms of career and educational choices. These choices dictate the opportunities available to them throughout life.

About a month ago, there was an article in a local paper, with a photo showing a young woman sitting at a computer screen in Iran, and the authors discussed how the Internet was now presenting women in Muslim cultures with possibilities for life and career that seemed unimaginable even 5 years ago. How will the current generation of women in Iran engage their life streams?

In many cultures still today, the possible roles for women in business are to be the communications or public relations director at best, certainly not CEO. However, this is rapidly changing in each of these regions. For example, in a special issue of *Newsweek* (2000) entitled "The New Asia," the authors discussed how the new cohort of Asian women—and men, for that matter—are coming to work with a new attitude. They are going to secure their careers and they will make it happen, challenging the full range of Asian traditions. There is some good in all challenges, especially those that force us to challenge our models of life, or in terms of culture, the collective models shared by all members of the culture. I hasten to add, I am not saying that one culture is necessarily better than another by any means. I am simply arguing that cultures create the set of trigger events that shape what people come to believe in their life models as being feasible and possible.

Of course, we can say this is all changing, and it is both in terms of the demographics of leadership positions and the life models maintained by many women. There are many women who would not think twice about pursuing careers in what would have been traditionally a male-dominated career field, such as medicine, the military, politics, or engineering. Yet, since generations overlap to a great extent in terms of their collective life events, what impacts the models of people between generations are not totally unique from one generation to the next. That is why it typically takes multiple generations to witness a sea change in the collective models held by people. Although as Peter Drucker has said, there are points of discontinuity where transformative change occurs and of course there are points where there is little change at all. We are at a point in history, the time between times, where transformative change is the norm, not the exception. This is due in part to the easy accessibility of information that is challenging the assumptions that we have maintained in our models.

Since 1960, we have seen in many parts of the world a tremendous change in the range of opportunities now available to women. Yet, there are many women in the United States that still struggle in their minds with the conflicts between careers and family. Men also perceive conflicts, though not as vividly, because career has come first in the male world of work. If we look to other societies, we can clearly see that the life models that existed in women of past generations is very much present in many societies today where there are no CEOs, senior government, or military officials who are women. Across cultures one may see the model of an earlier generation, still in force in a current one where little change has occurred. It is quite helpful to keep this in mind as you attempt to develop your employees who come from diverse cultural backgrounds. Keep in mind the differences in various cultures in what constitutes acceptable roles for men and women.

TRIGGER EVENTS

The internal model can be described as being shaped on a very micro level by family experiences, school experiences, peer groups, and work experiences. Yet, on a more macro level, the internal model is also developed by certain trigger events that appear to have more of a collective impact on generations and societies. World War II and its Holocaust shaped a generation's thinking about the right to use instruments of war to avoid such enormous human tragedies. In the United States, the Vietnam War made a generation resistant to sending military forces into regions where our country had no clear agenda, mission, and exit strategy. Even today, as I am writing this book, a war just ended in Kosovo and still continues in Afghanistan and Iraq with people asking in the United States what has become a standard question, post-Vietnam: What is our objective, and what is our exit strategy? Also, we are now entering into a new era for U.S. foreign policy, having successfully prosecuted a war with Iraq, where the United States has caused a regime change, where the exit strategy becomes even more complicated, but not necessarily any less relevant. Almost every day someone asks, "How long will we be in Iraq?"

I met someone in Malaysia recently who brought the events that shaped my life model regarding Vietnam into very sharp focus. He was near my age, and had grown up in what was then South Vietnam. When his government fell, he recounted the day for me when he and his family had to leave their home, as his father and brothers had been in the South Vietnamese Army. Shortly after leaving home and while in hiding, they risked their lives to take a boat to Indonesia, and then on to Australia to start a new life. I was struck by our parallel lives, and how the same event called the Vietnam War had so profoundly affected our lives in very different ways. I also marveled at his level of optimism and positiveness given how difficult his early years had been for him and his family.

I do believe my life model is changing, but nevertheless I cannot help but interpret current events based on how my life model was built in terms of how my generation reacted and learned about specific world events. The same seems to be true for legislators in Congress who served in the Vietnam War, and will be true for similar trigger events for subsequent leaders, like those who have lived through the 9/11 attack on the United States.

What I find interesting in my own development is that I have come to understand my own life model by looking at it from another shore, through the eyes of others, and once in a while based on deep reflection. When I travel to other cultures, I seem to understand better how I view behavior in my own culture. I can see how women, minorities, older workers, or all of the aforementioned are treated and can contrast those observations with what I understand to be fair and just treatment in my own culture.

I am far from saying here in the United States that we have successfully resolved the fair treatment of people of color, or people with different sexual orientations, age, and so forth, but our collective life models have certainly changed on what constitutes fair treatment. Clearly for some, it is by the numbers in terms of those who are hired, while for others it is the full integration of a diverse array of cultures, values, and experiences that are seen as a fundamental benefit to bottom-line results versus being compliant with some regulations. There is no doubt that our collective life model has changed concerning the assimilation of minorities into leadership positions in our society, even though there are many in this country who still harbor deep prejudices and biases.

I just opened today's paper to see the Ku Klux Klan was marching in Cleveland, Ohio, a city led by one of the most successful mayors in its history. Mayor White is African American. Yes, we have changed, and yet many people's models are stuck in time.

INDIVIDUAL LIFE MODELS VERSUS COLLECTIVE

In our discussion, I have raised the level at which we were discussing the life model from the individual to the collective level. Let me explain the logic in raising it to the group or collective level in terms of your own leadership development. If each of our life models is indeed shaped by the trigger events we experience in our own lives, then when we collectively experience major events, there may be some collective model that emerges from the experience. My reference to how a generation thinks is one global reference to the collective internal model. When we say people who have lived through certain events see the world this way or that way, we are saying something about their collective life model. It does not mean they view the world in a uniform way at all, but rather there are parts of their life models, which are common and some parts that are uniquely shaping the way current and future events are interpreted. As I said, this is a very important issue to keep in mind when you are attempting to lead across cultures, cohorts, and generations.

Prior to the assassination of Prime Minister Rabin in Israel, it is probably fair to say that it was almost unthinkable that a Jew would be responsible for assassinating the Prime Minister of Israel, particularly as revered a leader as Prime Minister Rabin. However, there is an emerging generation of Israelis who will have as part of their collective life model a belief that will differ quite dramatically from those who founded Israel. It will not be uniform, but it will impact the way this generation, and the next, sees its roles and responsibilities. A Jew did take the life of another Jew and it may have fundamentally shaped the collective life model of a generation. The other day I read an article on Israel, and it concluded by saying the most traditional values of Israeli culture are now being challenged by the new generation entering its workforce. I wonder how much the collective life model has changed and what events in the life stream of this generation are shaping the directions that it is now choosing and will choose to pursue that will determine its future.

I also wondered what would happen with the election of Prime Minister Ariel Sharon, and how his tenure will shape the current generation of Israelis' thinking. With the Intifada in full force, how will the systematic killing on both sides shape a generation of Palestinians and Israelis? I saw on the front page of a newspaper recently, a young boy who was Palestinian, screaming at an Israeli soldier who was female, who just smiled back at him. Another generation of hatred is being reinforced among the youth on both sides and one wonders how these events will shape the collective life model of this next generation of leaders.

In my generation and older, we ask the question, "Where were you the moment President Kennedy was killed?" I realized the other day in a training workshop when one of the participants revealed his birth date this event was something he had only read about in history. I even wondered if he might be thinking of this former president's son, who died in a plane crash in 1999. We both train leaders, but I wondered at that moment how the events of 1963 had shaped my thinking about leadership, and what events had shaped his views of leadership development post-1963. I even thought that rather than war, assassinations, and other catastrophes, maybe he had some trigger events in life that had shaped his internal model that were of a significant and profoundly positive sort that I could learn from and incorporate into my model. I know this sounds quite radical to me as well, actually being able to learn about leadership outside of studying wars and disasters. Why not?

IN SUMMARY

Let me summarize some of the major points in this chapter for us to reflect on. The life model is the basic structure that contains our views of the world, and thus our views or lens used to lead others. The model is shaped by events in our life streams both individually and collectively. The collective events are common events we experience in our cohort or generation that shape how we interpret subsequent events. These events may make us more cautious about making certain decisions. They may make us more reflective on new events that somehow seem like the ones we have experienced earlier in our lives. Keep in mind that cohorts have accumulated similar life events, but as we previously indicated they may not interpret them in the same way through the lens of their life model.

I started with the life stream concept to help offer a broad understanding of how leadership emerges and is subsequently developed. I then introduced the life model so to speak, which provides the structure and process for the leadership model that one uses to guide how one chooses to influence others. We also learned the same events are interpreted and integrated in very different ways into different life models, which makes understanding the special effects of leadership all the more difficult, but not impossible.

One thing I hope you have taken away from this chapter is that leadership development is fundamentally and inextricably linked to one's life development. It is not a style you put on and take off. It is who you are as a full person when it is having the greatest impact on you and others.

MR. C

Let me end this chapter with a brief example that provides an application of the life model. There is a boss out there somewhere, who believes that being in control of all events is at the core of what people expect from leaders. He designs his relationships with others around this principle, which is a core element in his life model. At work, in social relationships, and with his family he must be in control to avoid the unexpected. His vacation trips with family have schedules, events, and activities that are all laid out neatly for his family to follow. Family members find it easier to comply than to spend time challenging his system. Their behavior seems to show compliance, but oftentimes their minds are elsewhere, free to roam without his official constraints.

For many years, Mr. C was able to move up in organizations by controlling events to achieve success. However, following a big promotion to head a relatively new facility that had already established a culture of inclusiveness for decision making, his approach began to falter. At first, most of his employees felt that he would adjust to the new culture, and that maybe some structure was required to be more efficient. However, over time they realized he was not able or willing to learn how their culture operated and their relationships with him became increasingly strained. It was not on his radar screen, as was often said by his colleagues, to be inclusive.

Increasingly, there were groups of employees spending too much time debating how to address Mr. C's problem. They went from a culture where conversations were typically based on a sharing of best practices, to one in which Mr. C was the center of conversation about how this did not work and that did not work because of his controls! So much time was wasted on conversation that it had little impact on how things worked or did not work.

Unfortunately, Mr. C almost always saw the reactions of his employees as a direct challenge to his authority. Indeed, as they expressed more concern about his controls, he became more control oriented. His beliefs about control were so much a part of his life model that he simply could not understand that for some groups a higher form of control was the ideal, where controls were internalized and tied to commitment versus compliance.

AN EXERCISE FOR YOU

Pick up a biography of someone you really respect as a leader. Generally all biographers try to explain a leader's leadership by what may have happened to that leader earlier on in their life stream. Jot down what significant life events shaped this leader's life model, and how you can use what you have learned to engage in events that can positively enhance your full potential as a leader.

For a second exercise, take a look at your supervisor's behavior, or any supervisor for that matter. Examine how they "construct" the world around them in terms of their perceptions and reactions. For example, does the leader see the world as quid pro quo, or an exchange, or are they able to "go outside themselves" to view what is significant about others? Do the same with someone close to you, whom you really respect. What conclusions can you draw from this analysis?

Take a significant "trigger event" that has recently occurred in your life. What I would like you to do is to debrief that event by doing what in the military is called an After Action Review or AAR. The AAR allows us to step back from events and to systematically debrief them, to understand more fully how they emerged and what was "ground truth." By conducting AARs one learns what could be done to change the course of events if they happen to emerge again in a similar way. The AAR is based on the idea that self-disclosure and discovery go hand in hand. It is a process that requires you to be honest with yourself about "what just happened." I would say that is being *authentic.* Also, by revisiting "what just happened" frequently what we thought happened is not exactly what took place. In the AAR it is called getting to "ground truth," as if on the first review, you may not achieve what is on the ground the truth. Since reality is based on the way we construct and perceive it, the concept of "ground truth" is very important to achieving objectivity in leadership perceptions. In the AAR one focuses on the following:

> "What good is experience if you do not reflect?"
>
> –Frederick the Great

STEPS IN AAR

-Performance Standards/Expectations That Were Set
-Discovery of What happened
-Identifying & Reinforcing What Worked
-Identifying & Addressing What Didn't Work
-Generates Lessons Learned

- *Review intent relative to standards achieved*
- *Debrief events – What happened? Why? How can you improve?*
- *Followers describe observations/feedback what they saw*
- *What you did … what you can do better*
- *Share reasons for success and failures*
- *Share leadership in getting to ground truth*

To create this process with others will require trust in you and also the process. You need to build an environment of trust to fully take advantage of the AAR. You can start by discussing why the AAR is important, how it will be used, and what are its boundaries in terms of things that should or need not be discussed. In other words, build an agreement and execute that agreement reliably—that builds trust.

3

The Selfs: Image, Reflection, and Discovery

Have you ever had the experience of someone saying to you, "At some point in my life, I finally discovered who I was and what I really wanted to become?" This has always struck me as somewhat odd or humorous, and my initial reaction in terms of my internal voice has been, "Well whom did you live with all of those years?" Apparently, this person was a stranger to himself until he discovered himself. Then we meet people who are described as being comfortable with themselves. Again, I have this image in my head of me liking Bruce because he's Bruce, and I am comfortable with Bruce. The interesting thought here is that our self is not a static quality, but rather an emerging quality that provides the foundation for reflection and further discovery and growth of ... you got it, the self. Taking this to extremes, if you think you have totally found yourself, you are probably really, really lost!

To develop leadership one must work at developing him*self* or her*self*. The transformation of the self is central to the leadership development process. The story about Mr. C in chapter 2 is a classic example of someone who has a rather narrow definition of his *self* or even his *possible self*. We also know that how one defines oneself in part is based on one's life stream and it is inextricably linked to the life model. We learned the stream takes different turns depending on the choices one makes in life, and choices can arise by what we stop and reflect on and reconsider. Even though streams are not always under our control, we also discussed that choices can be made to redirect one's life stream, enhance a person's life model, and ultimately his or her leadership potential. Since we are discussing leadership, by enhancing your life model, you invariably enhance another's life model as well, through your influence on that person.

MY RANGE OF POSSIBLE SELVES

The life model was at the core of our previous discussion, and it can be viewed as the repository for how we define ourselves as individuals, how our self is defined, and what we envision our self can become over time. The life model provides the framework in which we can remain in a state of becoming our entire lives. Ask a normal healthy child what they want to do when they grow up, and you often will get a very broad range of fantastic opportunities. Ask an abused child the same question, and the possible selves they will explore will likely be much more limited in scope and range. Ask an employee who marks the time at work by how many days left to retirement, and you often will get a rather narrow range of possible selves they believe are available to them at any point in time, and of course over time. Who taught them to limit their possible selves? If we were not born to lead, then were we born to be limited in what we considered as our potential possibilities?

How would you answer this question now? Who taught you what your range of possible selves was in life? Have they been at all limited? How do you now choose to contribute to each self? My point here is that many of us were taught restrictions on the range of possible selves that applied to us, and those restrictions directly limit our potential and unfortunately the potential of people who we influence. Once we are aware of these limitations, then the next big step is to work at redefining what is possible for our selves. Sounds a bit like a life AAR. Of course, we do not have to just focus on limitations at all. We can focus on what we are really good at and see how those strengths translate into the range of possible selves we can become in our lifetime. Why don't we ask what we are best at and leverage those strengths?

For me, I have seen my possible selves grow over time. During the first 18 years of my life, I would have answered the question previously posed quite differently than I would now, because of people in my life that encouraged me to challenge my limitations and to focus on my strengths. Oftentimes, those challenges were not, "Bruce you are completely limited in the way you view this opportunity, and ...." They were displayed to me by example or vicariously, of what others felt was possible and they became a model that challenged my own model of what was possible. It is why the role model in leadership models is so incredibly important to achieving one's full developmental potential. You never know whose future life you are shaping simply by pursuing your own aspirations and living up to your own core values.

If you have children then the followers watching you are your kids, each and every moment you are together. Recently, Warren Buffet came to his old alma mater and was talking about leadership with a group of junior and senior college students. One student asked him how he had learned about the importance of ethics and integrity. He responded simply by observing his father each and every day, and how he treated the people he worked with, and customers in his grocery business. His father was always scrupulously fair. Mr. Buffet also said that he could not recall a time when his father discussed or lectured him on ethics, integrity, or leadership.

You need to consider who taught you your range of possibilities and limitations. For me, I was afraid as a young man of many challenges and I would oftentimes use my well-crafted New York humor to avoid them. There was a moment in my life that my fears no longer mattered, as I chose to take a position and stand. Well, to be honest, I was forced to take a position, and I have never looked back from that moment. Sure, I am still afraid of things. I am afraid that I cannot protect my family from every bad experience. I am afraid that I will not be able to make an important difference in this world. However, now I am afraid just like everyone else and it has provided me with a base to explore all sorts of possible selves, and I still wonder which ones are not on my radar screen. However, the operative word here is *wonder,* and that is what we need to put back in those adults who have lost that capacity. There is a sense of wonder that comes along with evolving oneself to the next and next and next higher level of development. I can say based on personal experience, the view is far more interesting at the next and next level.

NURTURING THE SELF

The main theme of our discussion is what constitutes the self, and how you can develop it over time to the image you choose it to be. I said "choose" because I believe we have a lot of choices over who we become as people and leaders (I do not mean to make a distinction here between the two), and that making certain choices that positively guide our development can be essential to what it takes to lead others. For example, pick an area about yourself that you are most uncomfortable talking about with others. Your lack of comfort is part of your current self: "I feel very uncomfortable disclosing to people ...." To disclose aspects of yourself that you are uncomfortable with relates to making yourself vulnerable to others.

Mr. C was control oriented and demonstrated little interest or competence in making himself vulnerable to others. Yet, such leaders become the most vulnerable over time, in that followers never learn how to fully identify with them, nor do they internalize what is important to the leader. They comply, which is an external form of identification with the rules and procedures versus from a sense of deep commitment, which becomes internal and something a leader can leave behind without external guidelines or enforcement of rules to guide future behavior. The rules are hard wired into the individual that identifies with his leader. Also, in that way, she comes to define a part of her current self with the leader's self-concept. Let me briefly expand on this point.

I have a very good friend named Marty, who has told me many times that he tries to search for and bring out the very best in people. As Archbishop Desmond Tutu said: "People are good." I saw the same in Don Clifton, former Chairman of Gallup and now the grandfather of positive psychology. All of these people search for what is good in people, what are their strengths and talents. I have seen Marty in the most difficult times, searching for what he can do to bring out the best in people, even those people who are not his greatest supporters—indeed just the opposite. I have marveled at his ability to stick by his beliefs in the most difficult times. I must admit, his words now ring in my mind each time I am confronted by very difficult people, who are challenging me directly. It has caused me to search in my heart for the best in that person. I still fail at this many times, but I am asking the question of my self and it is affecting how I define my self relative to my relationships with others. He has gotten me to reflect on this view, and with interactions with others to conduct my AAR based on his principle and what I think is his talent. The AAR is the process we can use to review events or tasks that have transpired to see how they evolved, understand their development, and see where improvements could be made next time we pass through those events down stream.

In a similar vein, Don was always searching for the best in people. He built his life's work on focusing on the positive side, the strengths in people, and helping them to discover their talents. Imagine working with someone who only focuses on how to help you maximize your strengths.

It is a way of thinking that has significantly transformed the way I think about developing others and therefore it has changed part of my possible self. Every time people met Don, they came away saying almost the same exact thing to me: "He made me feel like I was the most important person on earth." When you were with Don, nothing else mattered and his attention was locked on you and your life stream.

EXPLORING THE COMPONENTS OF THE SELF

Let us begin a deeper discussion of the self by addressing the self-image first. Your self-image is part of the life model previously discussed. To improve leadership potential, you need to come to know yourself better. The selves I am referring to is your past self, your current self, and the range of possible or future selves that you may need or should be interested in exploring. To take two extremes, for some leaders the self is completely transparent as compared to others who have layer upon layer of impression management protecting who they are beneath the surface. The first individual has the confidence to know what they do not know and tell people so. Their style of interacting with people and influencing them likely does not vary much from one group to another. People describe them as authentic, and in touch with themselves. They likely know their strengths and do not care very much about their weaknesses because others can fill in where their strengths end.

I always like the phrase, "She is quite comfortable with herself." It is a very interesting observation to describe someone in this way. Such people are not only in contact with themselves, but are also usually very aware of others. They are not consumed by themselves, and therefore have the energy to explore others, their needs, and possibilities. The most authentic leaders have far greater energy to explore others, as they have a solid idea of themselves. It allows them to allocate a tremendous amount of energy to developing others. I think that is why Confucius said that you "develop yourself to develop others."

A person who is always protecting himself expends so much energy on maintaining the shields with others, that little energy remains to understand what others are looking for in their relationships with this individual. Perhaps one of the greatest ironies associated with this type of individual is that he spends so much time protecting an image, and yet he rarely fully understands who he is as an individual. Oftentimes, such individuals have created shields which do not even allow themselves access, and that puts a real damper on development, both their own and that of others. How much energy are you deflecting to the shields right now? If you are in the midst of a crisis, it is likely to be much more than when things are relatively calm in your life stream. However, in turbulent markets, organizations must open their boundaries, not close them down in order to survive. Since people are very complex organizational systems, they too must remain as open as possible especially when under extreme stress. This is no easy task, however, the next time you are watching a film where there is someone leading people through a very stressful situation, see how they are depicted. Acting cool and calm under fire, taking in information, and giving direction, which is what we expect leaders to do in times of crisis. This is exactly how Rudy Giuliani was described on the day of the terrorist attack and in the aftermath of what has come to be known simply as 9/11 for September 11th, 2001.

Alternatively, on the day that President Reagan was shot, then Secretary of State Alexander Haig was at the White House. When he got word of the attempted assassination, and in the midst of some degree of chaos, not knowing Reagan's condition, he ran up a series of steps and entered the White House briefing room, exclaiming "I am in charge." He was not technically in charge based on the U.S. Constitution, but he was trying to reassure a nervous nation that things were okay. That is what a former General would be expected to do in that it is part of his self concept. Yet, his sweaty and out-of-breath presentation did not reassure anyone, and indeed people were wondering why he thought he was in charge! There is an old axiom in leadership: If they wonder why you are in charge, likely you are not.

Regardless of how resilient people are, there are limitations to the energy one has to achieve whatever goals have been set. Expending energy to one's shields is a defensive strategy that will limit the range of possible selves explored. In a very extreme sense, neurotics are people who have developed so many protective layers between you and them that there is little energy to reach out and focus on your needs. How can such a person lead effectively never having the energy to understand your needs, aspirations, or what you desire, or all of the aforementioned? I do not think they are able to.

Are you a Star Trek fan? Remember when Captain Kirk would ask Scotty to deflect energy to the shields and away from the phasers? You cannot put all of your energy into the shields and expect to go on the offensive. It did not work in Star Trek and that was fantasy. It will not work in leadership development either, which at times can also appear like fantasy, especially when you go where others have not ventured before, especially into your self.

Most of us fall between the two extremes previously described. Those interested in developing leadership potential will need to work on exploring the roots of what constitutes the self-image or the personal model that we maintain in our heads, which describes for us how we want to be viewed by others. Building on the previous chapter, we each maintain a model of ourselves, and then we describe the model with either our internal or external voice to translate the image we eventually project to others. Part of what constitutes this self-image can be very temporary in nature due to life events that are impinging on us at any one point in time. For example, at mid-life a spouse decides to end a long-term relationship with her partner. Such an event leads her to question not only what went wrong with the relationship, but also what is wrong with her, and who she is now. When that relationship ceases to exist it affects how each partner defines himself or herself, and frequently how they choose to define relationships with others in the present time, and eventually over time. In other cultures, less individualistic than the United States for example, the definition of self is even more closely tied and defined by the relationships one has with others. For example, in African humanistic thinking, there is an expression that a person is not a person unless considered in relationship to someone else. We are who we are because of who we are with others. A similar form of self identification linked to the group's concept can be found in collectivist cultures throughout Asia.

Life can be a very messy training program indeed for our self-development. My suggestion is to work on redefining oneself each and every day in smaller increments rather than during or after major catastrophic moments. By doing so, you can develop a more flexible and resilient self-image that can be adjusted over time to changing circumstances and events. Self-reflection is the process that is being recommended here as a means to accomplish that end and it has important links to how resilient one becomes as a leader. Resiliency can be developed and you ought to work on developing it well in advance of it being needed.

WHEN WE NEED TO REDEFINE

In over 20 years of training, I have met many people in the unfortunate situation of having to redefine themselves, oftentimes at the worst possible moments in their lives. What is common to all of them in varying degrees is the search to define themselves in the absence of their partner, relationship to some group, linkages to a larger entity such as a previous organization, profession, or occupation, or all of the aforementioned. I should add that some of them would not even qualify for being at the beginning of the search as they are still suffering from the trauma of separation, as if it had not really occurred. They are not searching and in many instances they are simply lamenting what once was versus what now could be. If there is one thing I have learned from reading biographies of great world-class leaders, is that they almost always see something positive even in the worst situations. It is a very powerful lesson to learn: *Remain positive until otherwise notified!*

The type of self-exploration previously described for a married couple, has occurred countless times for those who were downsized from their organizations in the 1980s, 1990s, and now in the 21st century. For many of those individuals, they had built a self-image that was tied to their long-term relationship with a specific company. They were married to their companies in much the same way as the two individuals previously described. Indeed, a number of companies fostered such tight links between how employees defined themselves and the image the company wanted to portray to the public that when that relationship ended abruptly, it became a direct challenge to the individual's self-image. Keep this in mind as you develop your independently-minded followers. Tying their self-image to you is an important facet of leadership as long as it does not build long-term co-dependence. Leaders should develop followers to be resilient, with a sense of one's own hope, optimism, and independence. It is the vital force that keeps organizations alive, challenging, learning, and constantly moving forward. It is the vital force that keeps all of us moving forward, emerging, and continually redefining ourselves in our relationships with others and in relationship to changes in our environment.

Downsizing always forces most people into trauma mode and many, but not all, into discovery mode. The question is how to move from trauma to discovery, allowing time for some denial and grieving. Unfortunately, we have seen that for some people this forced discovery process is too overwhelming and it can lead to psychological breakdowns, physical breakdowns, and in some cases loss of life.

One of the greatest bonds ever invented, is the link between a person's self-concept and that of an institution, group, or another individual. People will give up their life for such bonds. Tell me, what are you most proud to be? Are you proud to be the director of the XYZ Corporation?

Are you proud to be a Jew, a Catholic, Protestant, or Muslim? Are you proud to be a police officer, firefighter, financial analyst, or pediatrician? Are you proud to be a mother, father, or partner? What makes you proud? It is the linkage between how you define yourself and whatever you are linking that definition to, which may be an institution, organization, religion, profession, or relationship.

Recently, I was in Singapore working with a large hi-tech firm that had recently merged and acquired a number of companies. One of the goals of the workshop was to integrate the diverse cultures of these respective organizations now combined under a new banner. The first day of the workshop, I noticed there were five different T-shirts with five different company logos in the room. I also noticed that at break time, the T-shirts that were in common tended to congregate together. When I pointed out my observation to the workshop group, one of the participants started to discuss how proud he had been to work for his former company, and that he was having difficulty making the adjustment to this new company, even its name bothered him. He said, "In my heart, I will always be an ABC employee." That is the type of self-image and identification that is so powerful when bringing people together, but a major obstacle once it is time to redefine who those people are and what they are supposed to represent. It may be one of the reasons why nearly 60% of the mergers of companies fail. A lack of cultural integration seems to be a major contributing factor to these failures.

In contrast, the CEO of Wells Fargo when it merged with Norwest said to both groups, we will not be one identity for at least several years, and you should not worry about it, because if we learn what our new values are, and practice them we will become an even stronger community together. I met one of the most senior managers from Wells Fargo 3 years after the merger, and she described it as one of the most successful in the financial services industry.

Okay, let us try another approach. What country are you from? Now pick another country and simply say to yourself, from now on this is my newly acquired country. I will live in and love this country and completely abandon my home country. We cannot simply discard who we are and redefine ourselves without a lot of discipline and also by creating a new sense of meaning and then identification. There must be some compelling meaning underlying the change, and that is essential to effective leadership. By providing meaning to the employees previously discussed about what the new entity means versus the old, there is a pull to move to redefine oneself. At the time of that workshop back in Singapore, there was no pull and most of it seemed like push to me. No one can be pushed to identify with an organization. Ultimately, they must be pulled toward identification by themselves.

There is a tragic irony in this whole discussion. Inspirational leaders develop in their followers a strong connection between the follower's self image and whatever image the leader is promoting via the vision or mission to be pursued. Such leaders work to get followers to identify with a vision and by identification we mean they begin to connect who they are to what the group is striving to accomplish. Without such identification, we are forced to all be like Mr. C, who felt people should just comply and do what they are told to do!

THE DOUBLE-EDGED SWORD OF INSPIRING LEADERSHIP

The irony is that inspirational leaders create something they must break when new and fundamentally different challenges arise. First, they build identification with some amazing goal, organizational mission, agenda, or all three. People become connected to the direction that has been set and then identify themselves with the leader and that agenda. Then a day comes when change must occur, perhaps even radical change and this involves a reengineering of the self-image and oftentimes the organization. Without a change to the self- and collective image, the group becomes stuck in a way of operating and wedged into an eddy of development in their collective life stream. This is particularly true of successful organizations. Success builds a near concrete identification with what made people in the organization successful and who they are as individuals. One knows an organization is in deep trouble when it has stopped, either by conscious choice or neglect, to question who they are and who they need to become after a long period of success.

Let me offer two extreme cases. The first case is that of the evangelist, who builds in his following a strong identification with his mission to serve God, based on a total dedication to the church. Over time, people fully if not blindly identify with him. Let us call him Jimmy Swaggart. Then one day, his followers discover he has violated one of the most sacred principles and rules of the church, "thou shall not commit adultry." At first, many of his followers refuse to accept the evidence. Of course, this is partly due to what Mr. Swaggart himself created, which is a self-image connected to him, the church, and God. This is a horribly difficult thing to untangle once built because for the congregation to say he violated the principles of the church, means the church has less meaning, and its members have less meaning, as each person's self image is tied to the church, and to him indirectly. Yet, it must be untangled if the followers are to develop to their full potential. This is the formidable challenge confronting those leading Martha Stewart's enterprise. A company so wrapped in the image of its founder will have extreme difficulty unwrapping their image when it has become tarnished. Ms. Stewart represented a very pure image of everything appropriate, and since convicted, the image and the organization will likely suffer.

For some of the scorned followers, development may come in the form of being more questioning of leaders if not downright critical or cynical. For others, it may simply mean they are able to forgive the leader, but would not be so naïve in the future to accept any leader's word unconditionally. While for still others, they may feel the need to redefine themselves by separating from the organization or church altogether. All of these examples represent at least at the outset a forced self-discovery process, and an approach to development we will all likely go through at some point in our lives. You can model self-discovery by being willing to question your most tried and true assumptions. It does not mean you change them at all over time, but that you are willing to simply question them to see if they are still appropriate.

The second example comes from some work I was involved with in a military college that was an all-male institution for 140 plus years. Talking to alumni of the school and current cadets, it was obvious that multiple generations of leadership in that school had built up a very deep collective image that was inextricably tied to being a male institution. The strong connection of its graduates in terms of their self-image exhibited the importance of protecting the institution from admitting women. When it became abundantly clear that women would be admitted, many alumni refused to adjust their image of the institution and were willing to spend whatever funds necessary to fight the good fight to keep it an all-male college. They were fighting for something they identified with, which was inspiring to me, even when I disagreed with the principles underlying the fight.

Year after year the leaders in this institution promoted the importance of single-gender education to developing the best leaders. When I asked them to identify what they specifically did that built the best leaders, their answer was nearly identical again and again from cadets, instructors, and senior officers. "Well, we are not sure what actually develops leadership, but we seem to have the best formula, so let's just allow it do its magic." It sounded like Coca Cola's formula. Or, perhaps you are reflecting back on my example of the special movie effects that I used earlier: too many camera angles to explain what happened, so just enjoy that it works. As a research scientist, it is hard for me to accept the conclusion, "If it ain't broke, leave it alone and don't try to explain it with your academic mumbo jumbo!" When it applies to human behavior or the soft sciences, you hear people say this often, but think how ridiculous it would sound in genetics research. Stop the Genome project; it is all common sense! Let us allow the genes to work their magic on their own. Actually we did allow them to do that since the beginning of humankind, but felt it was time to understand them.

Fortunately or unfortunately, the all-male institution previously described was forced to change and it had a profound impact on its members' collective self-image. I say "fortunately forced to change," because I felt the leaders who came from this institution were not well trained to lead both men and women in today's military. This organization like any close-knit group of individuals had its own collective life stream, a very deep one indeed. Over time, it was able to move along without significant alterations in some of its collective core beliefs, including single-gender education. And maybe single-gender education is a key factor in leadership development at that institution. However, the fact the institution was forced into self-discovery and reflection mode, in my opinion is generally never an optimal strategy. Why? Being forced into learning about oneself and challenging the protections in one's self-image should come from YOU. Indeed, I would go so far as to argue that is a critical ingredient to authentic and resilient leadership. Ideally and practically, your approach to development should be forward seeking versus passive, reactive, recovery mode, or all three. It is not surprising to me that when some people get 360-degree survey feedback, especially those who rate themselves higher than others, they tend to reject the data as inaccurate. When forced to discover, some people may reject the data as invalid. Being ready to discover seems like a much more effective strategy, and something I believe great organizations work on each day in preparing their workforce to confront their boundaries and to explore beyond them.

DRIVING TOWARD AND THROUGH LEARNING

I find it incredibly ironic that organizations will refer to themselves as learning organizations, but then fail to challenge and explore their own collective self-image. I should have said, "continuously challenge in varying degrees the image one has of oneself." Why let someone else challenge something you should and can do yourself? It is leadership at its very basic level to challenge one's own self-image. Again, call it self-defining leadership and here unlike Webster's dictionary, the definitions should change over time. I purposely did not use the word *self-defined*, but rather *self-defining* to infer continuous and dynamic change. You can fight to protect an image, or you can continuously fight to make sure the image you have is still relevant. It is your choice as always, and that too constitutes leadership.

The example previously given about the military institution offers some learning principles that can be applied to developing the self. First, an image should never become something that cannot be challenged. This is true for people, teams, and institutions. There are many self-images that are worth protecting, but none that should not be questioned over time. I worked with a company that prided itself in having an image of maintaining the highest levels of integrity in its work practices. This particular company had employees who exemplified a level of moral reasoning that tried to achieve the fairest solutions. It was able to do so because it developed integrity as part of each employee's self-concept.

We recently had one of Warren Buffet's CEOs attend a leadership class at the University of Nebraska. She started her presentation reading the yearly memo to all CEOs from Warren. In the memo, he indicated that Berkshire Hathaway is one of the top five companies in the world. He said it took them 37 years to get to that level, and it could all fall part in 37 seconds, if those CEOs choose to do what they think is not right. Buffet suggested if you think something is not right, then do not do it. Each year he challenges his CEOs to reflect on the importance of each and every decision that they make and to choose the one that is right.

By challenging the core self-image of a company, I am not saying integrity is passe or irrelevant. To the contrary, a company with a healthy and authentic self-image, which operates at the highest levels of integrity, would by definition willingly question itself to improve its performance. For this organization, integrity was not something that was marketed. It was a core part of how everyone saw themselves. Questions of ethics will change over time. Should we clone body parts? Should we use genetic testing for profiling job candidates? Should we dismantle Affirmative Action in favor of affirmative development? Should we attack a nation that has not attacked us? We must question who we are over time, to learn who we are over time, and more importantly who we might become. To be in a state of becoming requires a continuous state of self-reflection ... not self-absorption.

It is also important to keep in mind, that when people are putting up a fight for something they believe in, it is because the opposing party is saying, "call yourself something different now." Where there is a fight, there is oftentimes a self-image issue at stake. As previously noted, 60–70% of mergers and acquisitions fail! From the data collected thus far, I can conclude that a large share of the failure is due to people being unwilling, incapable, and frequently not reinforced to redefine themselves. In one case, in a large financial institution on Wall Street, the two merged companies had one department where people sat on opposite sides of the room and refused to work with people from that other company. They would not sit together, as they belonged to different tribes, one who buttered the bread on the up side, and the other on the downside, according to Dr. Seuss.

Second, the way we come to learn who we are comes in large part from this self-reflective process. The example previously given forced the military college and its leaders to self reflect. As I said, life has a messy way of getting us to change how we view ourselves, and what we choose to do about it in terms of our own development. Although this is one way to facilitate change, another perhaps smoother way is to build in a norm for continuous self-reflection. Of course, I do not mean about everything, as this would fully occupy every day of our lives 24/7. What I mean is to reflect on those events, actions, and behaviors that you deem important to success, however defined by you, by your team, by your organization, and even by your community. To do this requires some attention to conducting personal debriefings or AARs.

GETTING INTO SELF-REFLECTIVE MODE

Let me ask you some questions that pertain to this self-reflection process. When was the last time you debriefed a significant success versus failure at work? Each of these events has powerful learning potential, but the response I often get from people is sort of this strange look. Sometimes they will say, "Now why would I debrief a success?" Or, if they focus on the failure part, it is usually to get the thing straightened out and to move on! Quickly! I find the lack of attention to self-reflection fascinating particularly in those companies that have the plaque on the wall, exclaiming that one of their core values is continuous improvement. If you have as a core value continuous improvement, then wouldn't you continuously assess successful executions to see where even a marginal improvement could be made in the process? Minimally, wouldn't you want to learn how you were successful in replicating that success over time? Of course the same could apply for reducing the incidence of failure. By focusing on success, you can also highlight your strengths and take time to celebrate the win.

Part of the problem is that most people are not encouraged to reflect on what just happened. Of course they are encouraged to do so in training programs and by personal coaches, but once out of training there are very few inducements to go back and debrief an event. Indeed, just the opposite is likely to be true. One comes back from training to a backlog of e-mail and voice mail messages that leave little time for reflection. Also, workshops usually provide a safer island for reflection than the work environment. Yet, if there is a hallmark characteristic of authentic and exemplary leaders, it is that they continuously reflect back to move forward. They see the future in the confluence of events in which they are presently embedded. How? They step back from the present scenario of which they are a participant, and see what is happening, then they choose a direction they think is best to pursue. To do so requires a willingness to give control to others to review the entire process, including the leader's role in that process. Some leaders are unwilling to be that vulnerable. Unfortunately, they fail to see the future in advance and allow events to create what will be. As I said, the present is always emerging, it is not fixed, and therefore leadership is about shaping this emergent process toward a particular focus or direction that achieves certain aspirations set by leaders and followers. Even the most static, dull organization is emerging, frequently in a direction that will ultimately end up in its demise.

The debriefing process I have previously described can be done in stream as you come across certain experiences. Ask yourself how you entered the last conflict you had with someone at work? How did your verbal and nonverbal behavior affect that person's reactions to you in the beginning, middle, and end of that interaction? What happened right before and during the engagement? What might you have done to prepare the person for the conflict that resulted? Examine how the interaction ended, how you could have changed and how you behaved. Conflicts are emergent processes; while in the midst of conflict you can choose to change its direction and where it will end up next. Were you like Marty, searching to bring out the best in that person? And, if you do not make a choice, that is also a choice.

There are many events that occur in your life stream that provide you with invaluable real play versus role play exercises to help you improve upon how you influence others. Yet, most of us are not well trained to take advantage of these events to learn everything we can from them at the time they occur and afterward through self-reflection. They are also not seen as very productive in terms of an allocation of one's time in the short-term, bottom line, results-oriented cultures that characterize many organizations around the globe. How do we expense our self-reflection time? Or is it an investment? Why is it that over 40% of Americans recently reported coming back from vacation with some new ideas to improve what they did at their work? It may happen that one idea makes a difference for the whole year! We do not necessarily measure these sorts of intangible contributions, but fortunately we seem to be moving in that direction.

There is an accounting professor by the name of Baruch Lev, who has been moving the accounting field toward recognizing the importance of measuring such intangible assets as relationships among people in organizations, and how well ideas are generated throughout the organization. He and others refer to this as the human capital or assets in organizations, as well as social or structural capital. It stands to reason, the more money we pay for people the more valuable people are to what actually gets produced in organizations. Today, people assets and relationships are intangibles, yet over the next decade I suspect they will become our most tangible assets in the emerging knowledge-based global economy.

In my opinion, one of the cheapest ways to develop leadership is to learn how to reflect and debrief what happened. It takes no books, Power Point slides, nor role-play exercises. It is the cheapest and most profoundly productive form of development. By making debriefing a norm for your own behavior, you are saying to others as a leader: I want to look back to understand a better way of working with you to move forward. By looking back, I can reconstruct how events took place, to see whether we followed the way we had intended to follow. We can examine our roles in the process, what worked, where more time may have helped, and how even the initial set up may have improved our results. I can shape the future based on what I just learned from the debriefing process. Since learning typically comes after the life experience has taken place, we might as well take these experiences and derive as much meaning from them as we can. In doing so, we begin to move leadership development closer to the point where it is actually being executed.

I know what I have previously said, that deriving meaning from your experiences is so much easier said than done, particularly with the most traumatic life experiences. Yet, again and again as I meet leaders whom I have tremendous respect for, and those who I have read about in the same group of highly respected leaders, they consistently work at taking the worst events and search for meaning in those events to help improve their life models. This point has never been characterized more poignantly than in the book entitled, *Man's Search for Meaning* by Victor E. Frankl. The book is written about what a man set as his goals to survive and to learn from the Holocaust.

The U.S. military, following the Vietnam War, worked to reinvent itself using the process of collective self-reflection that I previously described, and called it as indicated, After Action Review (AAR). It was decided that to improve the Army's culture, morale, performance, and self-image after its loss in Vietnam, its leaders needed to take a very close look at its self-image. Elaborate training facilities were designed to put units through near-combat missions to provide a context in which the units could go back and conduct an AAR, debriefing, or both. According to all reports following the 1991 Gulf War, this process seems to have worked very well. Many soldiers felt that the simulated training they went through was more difficult and rigorous than what was actually confronted in the first Gulf War, except for the potential loss of life in the war.

SEEING AAR UP FRONT AND CLOSE

As part of a military grant project, I spent several days in the field at the Joint Readiness Training Center in Fort Polk, Louisiana observing a series of AARs conducted by professional Army facilitators. There were several observations that I took away from my field experience that I would like to share with you concerning leadership development. The first is to check the weather before leaving winter in the Northeast for the southern climate of Louisiana, as it hailed the first 2 days in the field and was below FREEZING at night!

The AAR's goal was to get to what has been called ground truth, or what actually happened to the unit during the course of a series of events. The facilitators never assessed blame or evaluated, but rather promoted self- and collective discovery in the AAR debriefings. It usually started with them revisiting what the mission had been, who owned parts of the mission, special conditions that arose that impeded the mission, for example, a bad thunderstorm, and the outcomes achieved. Then, the facilitators prompted members of the unit to discuss their perceptions of what they saw in their own behavior and that of others. For some leaders, this was extremely difficult, as they were neither accustomed to looking at themselves nor having soldiers subordinate to them in rank, challenging their perceptions of themselves. Indeed, some did not engage the process very well, and their self-discovery was meager, at best. They were affectionately called "cement heads" to characterize their resistance to any sort of self-discovery process. Cement heads populate many of our organizations and we know them by their fixed attitudes and resistance to any changes, someone at the Gallup organization told me that such people are affectionately called "Chronically *A*gainst *V*irtually *E*verything—*CAVE* people."

Yet, there were many others who embraced the AAR process, and appeared to find out things about themselves, which they had not realized. They became more attentive to how they affected others, what reactions people had to their behavior, and how to get their people to open up and discuss what just happened. Over time, they came to the AAR thinking in advance what should have happened, what did happen, and how they could have altered what happened.

For nearly 2 weeks, unit after unit went through the AAR process. The U.S. military has used the AAR as one mechanism for reinventing the Army culture to make it more open to continuous improvement and feedback from all sources, particularly from the bottom up. I have tried to think of organizations in private industry, education, the not-for-profit sector, or all three that spend this much time on debriefing, including my own university. As yet, I am hard pressed to find units including ones that you would expect to conduct an AAR debriefing, like critical care units in hospitals, negotiating teams, R&D units, or all three except of course when something goes wrong.

USING THE AAR PROCESS

I am suggesting that making the AAR or personal debrief part of your leadership routine is a very significant way of improving your leadership potential. The idea that you are willing to revisit a process to make it better, especially one where you are the central figure, is critical to developing a full and deeper relationship with your followers. It also builds a culture of transparency and greater openness to sharing over time with each other. Even without a professional facilitator, you can use some very straightforward processes to improve your leadership potential. Let me provide some questions for you to consider:

- How was the action or task set up in terms of mission, objectives, and ownership? Did everyone back brief what they heard to assure they understood what was said and expected of them?
- Can you chronicle how the events unfolded? How does that correspond with various interpretations of the events?
- What roles were you supposed to play, and what did you actually do and accomplish?
- How did your behavior impact on others? What behavior of others stands out in your mind regarding how things unfolded? (This is not an assessment of blame, but merely a reporting out of what you observed, which is very difficult to achieve in a unit where trust is low. To fully debrief any significant events you must build a basis of trust that you are searching to make things better, not assessing blame.)
- What could you have changed to alter the course of events? What could the others have changed?

By asking yourself these types of questions about events that are important to you, you can begin to enter into a self- and collective discovery process. By using self-reflection we can begin to identify patterns or areas that can be addressed and improved upon in our relationships with others. Minimally, it is a great model for helping the newest member understand what just happened. It is also a great model for the most experienced member, who has gotten to a point where they have forgotten to observe, question, and challenge their own self-image, as well as those of others around them.

COLLABORATIVE SELF-REFLECTION

We are quickly moving into a period of time, where the self-reflective process itself is being reinvented in organizations. To some extent, it is not so much based on the self. Specifically, there is a clear trend toward more collaborative or shared leadership in organizations. This is especially true in organizations that are more virtually designed, and geographically dispersed where sources of influence come from all directions. It is also true in organizations that are more team-based and self-directed in terms of their culture. The great advantage now is that you do not have to do it all alone. However, self-reflection has been by no means made obsolete, and in many ways is now becoming more a responsibility of the collective or group.

Although the U.S. Army has a very set and specific command structure, there are significant attempts to go beyond hierarchy to analyze in the AAR what just happened. There is no doubt that hierarchy can impede the collective self-discovery process and getting to ground truth. It suggests that in order to promote collective self-discovery, the leadership must set the culture for it to occur comfortably. Oftentimes, one must build the culture to be open enough for a full and honest debriefing to occur. It cannot be done in a culture of suspicion, hostility, and fear. Leaders help to shape the context and its readiness for such learning.

Today, we have the opportunity to connect people up in ways that were not feasible a decade ago. My colleagues and I have conducted research to develop strategies to optimize e-leadership and collaborative virtual teams, where we have used web-based technology to facilitate learning and development (refer to www.gli.unl.edu). Let me offer some examples of things you may try with your team.

E-LEADERSHIP

After an initial training program is completed, we form what we call virtual learning centers. In these centers, we have members from the same or different organizations contract with each other to offer feedback to one another, to promote collective self-reflection on events that arise after they return to work, obstacles confronted, pending opportunities and new challenges. In some instances, we have formed these groups anonymously to allow people to freely and openly discuss their observations on line. One way to overcome problems with hierarchy is to make interactions in a group anonymous. Our research shows that people are much more willing to discuss controversial issues, when their discussions are mediated by information technology and they are kept anonymous.

Another strategy we are exploring is to connect virtual coaches with people who are going through a long-term leadership development process. The virtual coaches meet with their people via the web to dialogue about any progress that is being made with their leadership development plan, how to work around obstacles, and debriefing significant events that have occurred. Using this virtual coaching format allows for repeated follow-up with trainees, which we have seen in our work helps to sustain, if not boost, the impact of leadership training over time. It is through such follow-up that we can deepen the self-reflection process, as well as deepen the understanding we have of ourselves. Then we can begin to make behavioral changes in leadership style followed by changes in the self.

We are currently building a leadership development Web site that will include options for virtual coaching, peer learning centers, a library repository of resource materials, links to feedback tools that can be used as part of the self-discovery process, and video-streamed short lectures. Yet, our overriding philosophy is to use technology to augment any face-to-face interactions versus to replace them. We continually apply a self-reflective rule to our own work, which is to question whether our developmental interventions should be done face-to-face versus virtually. Virtual is our fall-back option.

THE THREE SELVES

Let me end this chapter with a discussion of the three selves using another application. This is a story about Mr. P. Mr. P used to be a lot like Mr. C., but realized after getting feedback on his leadership style early on in his life stream, that most of his people were not very engaged nor inspired at work. They did not identify with his core beliefs. They were clearly challenged, but only by meeting hard standards if he continually pushed them, but rarely if ever exceeding those standards. Many of his followers felt their full capacity was not being tapped by Mr. P's style of leadership. They told him so through anonymous survey feedback.

Until he had received feedback on his leadership, he had not realized how little energy he was tapping into with his followers. At the time he received the feedback, the facilitator asked him what was the legacy he wanted to leave behind in his unit? He was shocked to realize that he had never given any thought to what he intended to leave behind in terms of processes, values, systems, culture, or all of the aforementioned. What part of himself he intended to leave behind was not on his radar screen. The facilitator asked if he would allocate a few minutes 5 days a week to reflect on what he wanted his legacy to become in the unit. Mr. P agreed to do so for the next 6 months, with the facilitator checking in from time to time to discuss what Mr. P had observed, reflected on, and initiated.

Mr. P realized through self-reflection supported by coaching, that he had not built any sort of embedded system that would sustain itself over time. The system that was currently in place would last as long as the next leader deemed it appropriate. There was nothing in the culture of the unit that had Mr. P's mark on it. Mr. P did not care that a system that he might have created would be made obsolete by a new leader, instead he cared that he had not given even a few minutes of reflective thought about the system he was ultimately responsible for creating, of course with contributions from other members in the unit. It is the act of thinking about a system of values, beliefs, and processes, that is the important objective here and not necessarily that some cultural or systemic monument to the leader be left behind. Indeed, the ultimate goal is to build a system that is naturally adaptive and will transform easily into some new system, which is even more adaptable. Understanding one's value system and applying it consistently through one's behavior are both very important elements of building leadership potential in all members of a unit.

A FOUNDER'S LEGACY

A very resilient system that was built in the United States over 200 years ago shows the type of legacy that can sustain an entire country through years of growth and dramatic change. It is of course, the U.S. Constitution. The Constitution has been able to adapt to huge transformations in society with very modest adjustments along the way. This has allowed the United States to remain at least until the current millennium, one of the most adaptive cultures on earth.

I am not using the U.S. Constitution simply to be patriotic for my own country or ethnocentric. Rather, I chose it based on being a researcher of organizations and communities that remain potent and viable over time based on developing a system of values that carries the organization, community, and society to higher levels of development. They are never perfect systems, but they are characterized as healthy to the extent they are adaptable. Thus far the U.S. Constitution would be considered healthy even when aspects of our society are not. Indeed, to say that a framework is perfect and does not require adaptations over time, in and of itself is a sign of being unhealthy.

The U.S. Constitution has provided one key ingredient that has separated us from many other world cultures. It has provided the basis to accelerate the assimilation and advancement of a diverse range of groups into our culture, sometimes within only a single generation. Some have gone from being boat people to valedictorians in their high school graduating class, to attending the best institutions of higher education.

In one case, there was a young Jew who barely escaped with his life from the Holocaust in Europe. He came to the United States with virtually nothing. By the time he was in his fifties, his company was transforming the way we relate to each other, work with each other, teach each other, shop, and deliver healthcare. His name is Andy Grove, and he still leads a company called Intel. We have a remarkably adaptive system, even with its shortfalls, biases, and problems with discrimination. However, as long as it is evolving, stimulating debate, and creating alternative ways of adapting, it remains relevant. Are you still relevant in your organization? Will you be 5 years hence? What will be your legacy? How resilient is the system of beliefs, assumptions, and values in your organization?

Mr. P decides that he will work on culture development as his legacy. Cultures are the bedrock upon which organizations are built and sustained. Mr. P realizes that to develop a culture will require enormous work, persistence, and exemplification of certain key behaviors on his part that reinforce the values in the culture. He must live the core aspects of the culture for the culture to have any chance of sustaining itself over time. Again, people must come to tie their self-concepts to the core values of the organization.

Each day, Mr. P reflects on the words people use to describe actions and events. He sees their words are often associated with being hesitant, cutting one's losses, costs of mistakes, and narrowing of options to be efficient. The culture is one where mistakes are not deadly, but they are certainly not seen as part of the learning process. Mr. P decides to use debriefings to work out mistakes that have occurred to achieve some positive resolution. He emphasizes the purpose of debriefing is to dig into the elements that led to a mistake. He also asks whether the mistake is of some benefit, something one can use, or should consider to use in the future. He provides countless examples of how mistake after mistake led to the best discoveries in science. He shows how mistakes can be translated into both learning opportunities and innovation. Mr. P works at building a model in people's heads of how quickly mistakes can be translated into learning experiences. Within a year, many new ideas are generated from mistakes that were previously totally avoided in the unit.

One more thing about Mr. P, he realized something about legacies that he had never considered before in his life stream. He realized that if he had never made a concerted effort to redefine mistakes, he would have still left a legacy behind for the next leader to address. The legacy would have been to have a culture that was not very oriented toward learning from its mistakes. If you are a laissez-faire leader, you still get to leave a legacy behind. However, it is usually one you have little control over in terms of what happens next.

Have you given any thoughts to your legacy lately? If you were to leave behind one core value in others, what would that core value be? Your legacy clock is now ticking and it can be emerging if you choose it to be so.

SELF-REFLECTIVE EXERCISE

I want you to think about writing your own autobiography. Chapter 1 is what you fear, chapter 2 is what you feel you ought to do, and chapter 3 is what you think is possible for your next level of development or your future possible self. You may need to go back in time to reflect on things you thought you wanted to be, and to see how they might fit together now in terms of your future development. Or, you can look to someone you really respect, and see what it would be like to develop yourself in their image, using them as a role model.

Once you have written it put it a way for a year and come back and see if your thinking about those three questions changed.

4

Building Perspective

I never traveled outside the United States until I was in my early twenties. The world as far as I knew it stopped at the shores of the United States, except for the occasional trip over the border into Canada. Today, 25 years later, I have traveled the world extensively, and see how our culture is only a microcosm of a mosaic of cultures that exist in our global sphere. I can see where our culture is shallow in certain respects versus others. I have come to the realization that sometimes the hardest cultures to fully understand are the ones that seem so similar to ours.

When I travel to Australia, I am lulled into a sense of complacency that our cultures are similar because we share a common language and heritage being a former colony of Great Britain. Yet, after my five or six trips, I have come to realize that Australians are quite different from us in terms of how they view the world and particularly leadership. We place charismatic leaders on a pedestal, revere them, and then find a way to bring them down. Australians are part of what they call a mates culture and simply knock down leaders as soon as a glimmer of charisma is apparent and they stand apart from their mates.

The worldview a person develops is linked to her or his life stream, life model, and self-concept. We have been discussing how life impacts on the development of leadership potential, particularly focusing on how the individual comes to view herself over time, in terms of some model or framework that guides development. The model contains what we view as our current selves, our possible selves, and those selves we avoid becoming. Thus our focus has been more on self-perspective than on our perspective as it applies to others. Leadership is not just about who we are, it is fundamentally about who we are with others and they with us. How you conduct yourself with others is determined to a very large extent by your perspective of yourself and then of others, in that order. Let me provide some examples of four different lenses that might be used to describe different people's perspectives. Think about which ones apply to leaders you have worked with in your past, or to your self, and the boundaries it implicitly set on your relationships.

THE FOUR LENSES

Control Lens

With the control lens one sees people as needing tight guidance and control. To lose control over others is to lose what is at the core of leadership. Other people's intentions are seen as being based on self-interest, a lower level of moral reasoning. Thus what you want as a leader comes from satisfying your own self-interests. Your responsibility to others is to direct them to the goals, which meet your objectives and your self-interests. It does not mean that you set out to disadvantage others, but rather to advantage yourself, which is your top priority.

Quid Pro Quo Lens

With this lens all interactions are seen as transactional. You get from others what you provide based on incentives. People are driven by rewards and to avoid punishment. Control the rewards and you can control the direction people are willing to pursue. Without the right incentives you do not see any way to lead effectively. Incentives are usually viewed as tangible ones that you can literally give or take away from people.

Stakeholder Lens

With this lens the leader now begins to see the benefit of making others stakeholders in the mission and vision of the unit. The leader is still compelled to drive motivation by tying what people do to tangible rewards. But, they also realize the need to provide the bigger picture, the longer-term incentives and the importance of the work to be provided for gaining people's allegiance to the unit. Of course, the allegiance is still based on offering what people want in terms of rewards, but now there is a greater level of inclusion in the direction set for the unit and in turn the beginnings of a deeper sense of commitment.

Transformational Lens

With this lens, the leader now begins to concentrate on the growth and development of others as being a functional responsibility of leadership. People are viewed as not only being driven by rewards, but also by ethical and altruistic means. They are seen as being driven to improve themselves and to remain in a state of becoming versus some end state. There is a focus on enhancing the developmental potential in people, to eventually lead themselves and to be ultimately self-directed. To transform means to transcend oneself to another self. Development occurs as you unleash the possible selves that lay dormant in your identity, and ultimately the identity of others. Trusting the work will get done is now based on inner controls linked to identification and commitments versus external controls linked to compliance or contingent rewards.

How is it possible that leaders can have such varying perspectives or lenses? It is possible based on the life model that each person develops the life stream experiences that he or she has accumulated and incorporated into development. Life training helps shape our perspectives of others and how we will eventually treat them as a leader. We have to learn to transcend our interests for the good of the group we are leading, and unfortunately many leaders still do not see the direct benefits in such behavior. That is the problem we need to confront at the core of leadership development, how to get people to understand that by investing in others, their intangible assets, they gain at the other end, in terms of achieving higher levels of commitment and performance. The empirical evidence exists in volumes to support this statement, yet we are still challenged by getting leaders to see the benefits of investing in others and reaping the benefits in the long term.

DIGGER DEEPER INTO TRANSFORMING LEADERSHIP

The transformational lens previously described has been associated with having parents who are seen as being the best role models for high ethical conduct. Those who are more transformational also tend to have a broader educational perspective, which can be developed through both formal, informal educational processes, or both. Yet, some evidence indicates that one of the most significant contributors to the shape of the lens or depth of perspective is whether someone has gone through some form of higher education. Why? People who have gone through college are typically exposed to a much broader range of cultures and diversity of opinions during a period in their life when their life model is undergoing significant transformation. The exposure early in their life streams to a broader range of views apparently shapes a broader and deeper perspective.

For individuals who have developed a deeper and broader perspective, it would be unreasonable to even think that everyone is driven simply by incentives. They see others in terms of a much richer profile of characteristics and differences, and apply this perspective to how they work with, relate to, and lead others. Certainly, some are driven by external rewards, but others are simply driven to achieve something of value to people, their groups, organizations, and communities. They are motivated to do what is right for others, even if it involves sacrificing their own gains for the gains of others. I personally have a bias toward working for people who have developed these perspectives.

Such people have seen through their own experience the benefits of being exposed to a broader range of views, and this exposure is likely to have a positive impact on their own views for developing others. Diversity in culture, values, and ideas is seen as an enriching and potentially a valuable resource for development. It is not seen as a threat, as would be the case for the leader who has a control-oriented lens or perspective. They might think, "Now, how can I control all of these differences?" Such development also occurs in other institutions such as the U.S. military, or in organizations that place value on bringing different lenses to work, and discovering each perspective's unique contribution. College is only one place lenses can be stretched.

HOW WOULD YOU DESCRIBE YOUR LENS?

The question I hope you are now considering is how well developed is your lens or perspective? This is a tricky question, in that I am asking you again to look at your own model of life and leadership through the lens that you use day in and day out to judge others. It is like saying, look through your glasses and try to have 20–20 vision now, when in fact your vision is less than perfect. Sticking with this analogy, I should perhaps ask if you are near-sighted like our control-minded leader? Or are you both near and far-sighted like the transformational leader? The near-sighted leader only sees that things work his or her way. They lead in the moment, oftentimes controlling one situation to the next. Their orientation is likely to be reflected in a more managing-by-exception leadership style where they target potential errors, deviations, or both and try to eradicate them on the spot. To some degree, this is a very useful style if the situation is risky and warrants such control-oriented leadership. However it is anathema to creativity and change, and certainly does not promote the exploration of one's possible selves. It can create great conformance, but usually the most profound developmental jump occurs where there is a lack of conformance or discrepancies.

On the other hand, the near-sighted and far-sighted leader understands the importance of what it means when we say create unity through diversity close in and at a distance over time. They understand that it is often through the convergence or integration of diverse ideas that great inventions are created. They understand that it is the diversity of competencies and perspectives that make up a high performing team, differentiating the good teams from truly great ones. They understand that to be optimally effective they will have to entertain divergent opinions and perspectives—including mistakes.

The essence of development is based on divergence. One does not develop from one uniform stage to another, but rather by diversifying and moving up to a higher level of understanding, which we can then label convergence. Throwing ourselves into a divergent state is what makes change and development uncomfortable, and noticeable, so we know we have to work at what is going on within ourselves to make it to the next level of development. If I do not fully understand what is going on, but also want to learn more about what could be going on, then I am motivated to develop to the next level of understanding.

Without such tension created on the outside or inside, or ideally both, there is no motivation to develop. Going back to an earlier comment, very successful firms who feel they have the right formula may not question the need to develop any further. There is no inherent tension that compels them to develop, and therefore they stay at the same developmental level. What is true for organizations, which in the end are people, is true for groups and individuals. Tension is what makes leaders, organizations, communities and societies vibrant and adaptable. We diverge to adapt to new contingencies and new emerging realities that we can help shape.

REAL DEVELOPMENT

The development of your perspective and capacity to understand other perspectives is one of the central facets in leadership development. That is the good news! The bad news is that no one in their right mind can say that we can fundamentally change someone's perspective or capacity to understand others' perspectives in a 2–3 day workshop on leadership training. If they do say this to you, simply do not believe it! We may be able to develop the technology to do so in the future, but right now it is analogous to transporting oneself from one physical location to another using only mental energy. We can understand what it is, and truly believe it is possible, but it is still very much special effects even for those scientists currently working on this challenge and making some progress moving energy from one location to another.

Please consider now the people in your life stream who were really significant to your development. I do mean *really* significant here. How would you describe them in terms of the four lenses that I have previously presented? We are all products of life's leadership training program. Perspective-taking capacity and its development are the more critical areas that can enhance your full leadership potential. I understand that you may be someone who was not developed by an individual that had a transformational lens. This was true in part for me as well. Let me explain briefly.

I was fortunate to have a mother who had a broader perspective about others and looked for the good in people all the time. My father was category 1 all the way! He felt he needed to control others, including his family to get done what needed to be done. Upon reflection, I now see how important college was to my own development in terms of broadening my perspective-taking capacity. It was really the place where I began to embrace diversity in the richest sense possible.

I also realized going through college and later on in graduate school, that one's life stream was continuous and that I had the opportunity to continue to advance through the experiences I chose. It was a realization that came through to me based on a lot of self-reflection, and observing others who had this enormous capacity to appreciate the full range of potential that people bring to a task. I am saying all of this to you, not to promote any quick fix, self-help strategy, or as a plug for a college education, as such development can occur in many, many other settings. I am saying where I believe my life stream turned for me. I too have to be vulnerable to allow you to understand that I am a product of the numerator or made leadership. I have expanded the possible selves available to me in my own work and relationships based on the experiences I have accumulated in my life stream. I still have a long way to go to get it right! Recall that writing books is one way I reflect on what I should be developing in myself, as well as in others.

When you started reading this book, you began with the life model that trailed into the room, airplane, classroom, library, or all of the aforementioned. As you look back on that moment and reflect did you ever have the opportunity to work for someone at the upper end of perspective-taking capacity that was transformational? He or she could have broadened your perspective in ways that you are only now able to appreciate, giving a broader range of perspectives in others that are stimulating to your own thinking as opposed to being threatening. If so, it is likely that people throughout your life stream looked to you to take the lead. We trust people with this type of perspective, other capabilities and competencies notwithstanding.

A GREAT EXAMPLE OF PERSPECTIVE-TAKING SHIFT UP

President Mandela accomplished what I would call a fundamental perspective shift in South Africa. It is a place I have visited many times, and I can say that President Mandela is at the very upper boundaries of perspective-taking capacity. He is walking altruism! He sees the good in all people. He is color-blind in a country that, for most of his adult life, used color as a way of segmenting people into the groups they were supposed to belong to, groupings that marginalized nearly 80% of the population. He changed all of that with the force of his belief in the African Dream. He believed in the Ubuntu philosophy of unity through diversity, and brought special effects to South Africa's transformation that have wowed the world. What an incredible legacy he has left thus far in terms of a fundamental shift in perspective.

Color should not matter, correct? It is the essence and spirit of people that should matter. As the United Nations discussed setting up cantons in Kosovo to separate ethnic minorities for their own protection, it is quite incredible to witness how a nation such as South Africa has so far peacefully transitioned to a nation where everyone has a better chance of achieving equal rights. Today President Thambo Mbeiki is leading the next phase in Africa's development called the African Renaissance. He and other African leaders are calling for Africa to solve its own problems now, with help from neighbors around the world, as opposed to direction and manipulation. This is a fundamental shift in perspective for many people in a continent who were trained by colonization that everything African was primitive and not useful. Well, the times are changing, and it appears that a new leadership perspective is finally taking hold in Africa, which represents, from an economic point of view, the biggest and last remaining emerging market on earth.

Unfortunately, what President Mandela accomplished in South Africa is not possible for leaders who see the world through the first two lenses previously described. Such people see almost any diversity as a threat to their position and status, if not status quo. From this basis, they are guided in their leadership style to control either through rules and regulations or rewards–incentives. The worst authoritarian leaders and dictators are quite a bit left of the control-oriented type. They not only believe that control is the preferred style of leadership, they have no sense of what constitutes human dignity, frequently leaving behind again and again legacies of destruction that we have to rebuild. If we can keep just one of these perspective-challenged leaders from ascending to power, we may save countless lives and communities. I would be happy to knock out more, but I will start with one for now.

LOOKING BACK AT LENSES THAT HAVE SHAPED YOUR DEVELOPMENT

Ask yourself which type of leaders have you mostly worked for in terms of the four types previously described? If you worked for the two extremes how would you describe each of these leader's concerns for your development and future? Were there any substantial differences in their approaches to working with you and others? What did you admire in each of these leaders? What would you have changed? Have you adopted any aspect of their leadership perspectives and styles in terms of your own leadership? What have you adopted? What have you chosen not to do as a leader? What have you gone beyond? How engaged were you in your work, when working for such a leader?

The life training that you receive from leaders can profoundly affect how you choose to lead others. For example, if the leader was successful, you might be more likely to adopt her style. There are many control-oriented leaders who are successful, and this may have been or indeed is appealing to you. A question I would ask you now is how do you define success? How did they define success? Does it just comprise bottom-line performance? Or, do you have a more diverse definition of success? How does it include your followers and their followers?

What did they consider an unrecoverable mistake? What was recoverable? Was their range of unrecoverable mistakes broader than yours or was it narrower?

I believe those leaders who find ways to create broader amounts of freedom rooted in trust have more sustainable success over time. Of course, to provide freedom, people must be willing and able to accept it and to use that freedom for the right means and ends. Having freedom goes along with taking full responsibility for one's actions—there is no free lunch, so to speak. At the control end of the lenses previously described, I as the leader am responsible and you are just told what to do. At the transformational end, we are each responsible, and both of us have our areas that we must take accountability for in our relationship. By the way, I do not mean equally responsible. We may differ dramatically in our level of responsibilities, but nevertheless each of us has our responsibilities that we need to attend to and address. Development is, in its simplest form, the incremental accumulation of greater levels of responsibility, which frequently begins with oneself and then transcends to others. Such leaders can create a culture of engagement and willingness to take responsibility for one's actions versus the finger-pointing type of culture.

CREATING A LOOSE-TIGHT FIT

Development is critical to building and maintaining the transformational lens because we cannot hold people accountable for areas they have not been developed to handle. Thus we should not give people freedoms they are not yet able to handle unless it is part of our developmental plan to stretch them to the next level. For example, providing freedom to fail is a perfectly legitimate way of developing others. Of course, we provide people with freedoms that are way beyond their capacities all of the time, but frequently the results are less than optimal. Aligning freedom with capability, strengths, and stretching people in their development is a very sound basis for developing others that takes a lot of time, effort, and follow-up.

Let me provide one example of what I previously meant about balancing freedom with development. A few years back, I interviewed a number of teams that came from a Martin Marietta plant in New York. The plant had been structurally and culturally designed by General Electric to be totally team-based before General Electric sold it off to Martin Marietta. Early on in terms of workforce development, the plant management team told employees they would be responsible for monitoring their sick leave and vacation policies. Unfortunately, within several months, the plant teams were running into some significant problems. Some employees viewed sick time as an extension to their vacation, or number of days they could take off each year. While other employees lived up to the highest standards of conduct, never using sick time for anything else but for when they were really sick.

It is easy to see in this example, that developing the perspective to take personal responsibility for one's own conduct is a prerequisite to offering such freedoms. So, providing a little control up front until people are ready for a loose system is very helpful. Another way of stating this is that continually balancing a *loose-tight* fit in terms of development and controls is probably the best way to advance people's competencies in one's organization. It also provides the basis for cooperation at all levels. Given the changing nature of organizations and markets they operate in today, this is an essential direction that must now be pursued. People at lower and lower levels are making more and more important decisions. The information revolution has brought all organizational levels into the decision-making process, and in so doing, requires that leaders develop people as quickly as possible to their full potential. Thus by necessity and because it is the right thing to do, leaders must work to create loose-tight fits at all levels to optimize motivation and performance.

This loose-tight fit is occurring across the board, including in organizations traditionally run by command and control systems such as the U.S. Army. A few years back, the Army began placing emphasis in its training on understanding what constituted commander's intent. This was a significant shift in the Army's decision-making process, as they were saying, "understand the officer's intent, even if you have to go about your tasks differently than what he or she intended." In other words, things change so rapidly, that once a decision is made, you should minimally adhere to the commander's intent, but the commander understands that your actions may not always be in line with the initial directive.

I have to be honest and say that some organizations I work with around the globe that are nonmilitary still do not get it. Many managers still think they can run a command and control system that guarantees that both intent and the actions deemed appropriate by the leader are followed to the letter. Unfortunately, this approach not only stifles innovative thinking and development, it also positions people to take actions that may not be appropriate given changes in the context. What do I mean? First, by using such a tight system of control, we signal people they are not trusted to make the decision, either because of a competency issue or because of motivation. Moreover, if conditions change on the ground, so to speak, we are telling followers to simply execute what you have been asked to execute. The truth is that any dumb organization and follower can do just that for the leader. However, smarter organizations are clearly moving in the direction of executing intent, and providing flexibility in terms of what actions get taken in the end.

I know there are some hard-nosed managers out there, who are seeing chaos on the horizon right now. They may also fear that in an environment where risks are high, this is about as dumb a strategy as one can imagine. Let me reassure them, I am not advocating that employees exercise degrees of freedom in terms of choice across the board. Indeed, smart organizations will develop their employees to realize where discretion is warranted and where flexibility is required. No one wants people to be creative defusing a bomb, operating a nuclear facility, flying in formation at Mach speed, or clearing millions of transactions on Wall Street. However, even in these situations there is room for discretion, especially when things go awry, and innovative action is needed. Almost all the time, a pilot will follow doctrine and discipline. However when something occurs that is unusual we expect them to take action that is outside the chapters of the manual. In less extreme situations, we want people at all levels thinking about what is the best option, why did we choose that last option, and what should we be considering next. We want the brains to come into work, and not to hang outside the door. One of the hardest things for your competitor to replicate is a smart, highly motivated, and fully engaged employee.

In the leadership development process, we should be continually striving to provide greater amounts of freedom coupled with the appropriate levels of accountability. Imagine an organization filled with people who know the mission, who hold themselves accountable to owning parts of the mission, and who willingly offer others assistance and help with their development. In this organization, people realize the merits of working toward a common goal and providing each other the support to achieve it. They do not enter into interactions with the expectation of being rewarded for every unit of output or personal production. Their perspective is much broader than that and they realize that oftentimes one must sacrifice short-term gain for doing the right thing with each other and ultimately for themselves over time. A collective sense of trust has been built upon higher-level transactions that are able to take place over time.

A PROGRAM FOR DEVELOPING PERSPECTIVE-TAKING CAPACITY

It is not yet possible to send everyone to college to enhance their perspective-taking capacity. Lacking a scholarship for you to attend the university of your choice, perhaps building on the development that you may have already experienced in college, or both, let me offer some suggestions in terms of this thing called perspective capacity and how to develop it in yourself and others.

First, what happens when one goes to a university? Here are 10 areas that I believe affect people's perspectives or lenses during their college years. For each area, you can think of a substitute for the experience that has nothing to do with going to college:

1. In most colleges and universities you are quickly exposed to a very broad range of groups, values, beliefs, religions, ways of thinking, etc. The differences that you confront generally lead to a testing of your own assumptions and beliefs. You are quickly pushed to go outside your comfort zone after entering college in terms of prior perspectives. Think about the social group or sphere you interact with and how you might expand that sphere to broaden your understanding about cultures, values, religion, etc.
2. Similar to point one, colleges are set up to expose you to different disciplines of thought and ideas. Such diversity comes in courses on Western philosophies, African Humanistic Thinking, Sex Roles, Management, Marxist Sociology, and so forth. The exposure to diverse perspectives provides the opportunity to test your own perspectives, their assumptions, and base. The web now provides an enormous array of opportunities to explore a broad range of interest areas. Why not set a goal over the next 6 months to explore three completely unrelated areas to your work that can broaden your philosophy about science, sociology, history, psychology, anthropology, etc. It almost does not matter what you choose as long as you choose to diversify.

3. There is a certain culture that has emerged over centuries in colleges and universities that reinforces intellectual exploration and engagement. You receive unofficial permission that it is okay to be different, think differently, and act in different ways. You are in college and it is a time for you to experiment. You have the freedom to be different and in fact are encouraged to explore a range of possible selves. The type of culture previously described, is what you can institute for yourself, if you simply provide yourself permission to do so. Or, if you are in charge of a unit, why not explore with your members how to offer each member the opportunity to bring something unique to work each week, something that people do not know about each other's background, or something new you are currently exploring as part of the goal previously specified.

4. For many teenagers, going to college is the first time they are away from the epicenter of thought, which included their high school peer group and family. With distance there is a greater range of freedom to define one's day, schedule, the people you choose to live with, and to have relationships with over time. The freedom to explore can enhance one's perspective into domains not included at home. Why not take one day every several months to allow yourself time for complete self-reflection. You might choose to go somewhere that you feel completely free to think, and to explore. Again, you are offering yourself permission to explore, which is the very essence of helping you to build a more diverse and deeper perspective.

5. You are given time to reflect, to think the big thoughts. It can happen in the college quad, in your dorm room late one night, at the coffeehouse, on a trail somewhere, or in a study group. You are expected be reflective, or at least look like you are doing so! Now go out and think about the universe, peace, and love, or ways to measure intellectual capital if you are in accounting in a B-school. Similar to this point, target a day where you retreat to explore areas that you have not given deep thought to before. Perhaps you can have everyone in your unit, if you are currently leading a group, read a particular book that you can all discuss from your own perspectives. By picking and choosing a common book, it provides you all with a common experience from which to start the discussion. You can even rotate responsibility for selecting what to read, so you enhance the diversity of material. By the way,

you can start with an article if a book seems too overwhelming for some people.

6. In college and university campuses there are a broad range of causes that are being continuously discussed, including many ongoing ethical dilemmas, which are more openly addressed than in most organizations. Oftentimes, outside speakers are brought in by opposing groups to stimulate controversy. It gets some people to think differently. On my previous campus a few years ago, a member of the Ku Klux Klan was invited to address a class in political science during black history month. The professor felt that he should expose groups like the Ku Klux Klan to his class, so they could witness up front their lack of depth and prejudices. Why not try to explore some controversial dilemmas, but agree up front to the rules. For example, you could have coworkers simply take the opposing side to identify and clarify the important issues. Agree there is no solution, and that you want to simply identify as many different views of the issue as is possible. This is something very challenging to do, particularly if people are emotionally invested in the issue. Thus, I would recommend you select an issue that is a dilemma, but not something that would polarize the group in its first discussion. (By the way, when I say group, it could be just one other individual that you work with or like to interact with, whom you feel would be interested in such exercises). The important point here is to set the ground rules for discussion up front, so the discussion can lead to an expansion of thinking versus solutions. The first rule is that there need be no solutions and that you will work together to achieve the greatest number of alternative ways of looking at the issue.

7. Unlike any other point in your life stream, college is defined by a finite set of time in which you are to make your mark. This is generally not true at all once you leave college. Perhaps with a finite set of time, it is easier to think about yourself 4 years down the road and the type of experiences you would want to accumulate in your life stream. There are also countless examples of role models just ahead of you that you can choose from, a group typically much more diverse than one might find in most organizations. It is much harder to find these defining moments in life later to do whatever you want to do with life. This comes from personal experience and reflection, as well as observations of others who are

tracking through their life streams in parallel with me. Yet, at any point in our life, we can define a period of time in which we will choose to accomplish something that can have an impact on our perspective. It is harder later on, but not at all impossible. So by the time you are 25, or 30 or 32 or 45, you will do what?

8. For many students, college is a time to step away from their early upbringing, and to compare it to others. How open were your parents to different points of view? How did they challenge your perspective and that of others? Were they ethical in their behavior? Do you admire them for how they developed you into an adult? Are you an adult? You may examine how different groups you meet now look at the world, when you are traveling, establishing new business associates, taking a new job, moving to a new community, starting a new hobby, or simply starting a new relationship.

9. During college the freedom to choose comes with the responsibility to set your own direction. As you advance through college, you are treated more as an adult. For many the change in how one is treated comes when they return home. It is oftentimes hard to fit back into the model you left, even if it still exists in the form that you left it in. It is a form of reverse culture shock. This is part of reflecting on where one was and how far you have come in your own development with regard to an emerging perspective. It is harder to see standing still. To do this as an adult, probably requires that you write down your reflections using the STAARR format presented earlier. Then you can put those observations aside and come back to them in 6 months when conditions have changed to see if they are still relevant, or if they are seen the same way as you first saw them initially.

10. There is a great pygmalion effect that occurs in college. The pygmalion effect is a self-fulfilling prophecy, which can be stated as follows: "I am expected to grow intellectually, and therefore I do!" Taking the premise of the first chapter, we are all positioned to grow up, if we choose to look at our own development in the life stream as an emerging process. For some reason, there appear to be forces out there that signal us, that at some point in the life stream one is not growing up anymore, but rather maintaining what you have acquired. I believe that this too becomes a self-fulfilling prophecy for many contributing to organizational stupidity versus growth. There is no point in the healthy life span that

people are not continuing to grow up, unless they have made the choice not to do so.

WORKING ON THE HOLY GRAIL OF LEADERSHIP DEVELOPMENT

We have been discussing for some time now a very abstract and nebulous construct called perspective-taking capacity. It comes in many forms, but we have been discussing four general categories for ease of reference. Other authors have talked about it in terms of moral and ethical development. It is clear that most people writing and training leaders today see that enhancing perspective-taking capacity is probably one of the most important things we can do to build authentic leadership. I personally believe it is the holy grail of authentic leadership development and at its very core in terms of development.

So what can you do right now to begin developing your perspective-taking capacity, regardless of where you are in your life stream? First, think about a curriculum for your own personal development. What can you read that would enhance your philosophy about other cultures, values, and beliefs? Take an area that you have very strong beliefs about and find ways to explore the opposition's point of view. Take the other side in the argument and see if you can find ways to defend the position. I am not asking you to change your beliefs, but rather to merely understand them from another shore so to speak.

Second, try to seek out people who have a different view of the world from your views. What is different about their views and beliefs? Explore how they have come to establish their beliefs without coming to premature closure on your judgments. Suspend judgment for as long as you can to analyze the why underlying their belief system.

Third, there are several writers who have written eloquently on the issues of ethical leadership. These books are not how-to books, but rather stimulating theses on how ethical leadership evolves and takes root in people, groups, organizations, and communities. My recommendations for readings are listed at the end of this book.

Fourth, year after year there are listings of the best companies to work for in terms of their strategy for developing their employees, their fair and ethical practices, as well as successful performance. Look into those companies to gain a better understanding of their philosophies and beliefs. Go to their web sites to see how they portray themselves to the global community. Study the best ones that appear to sustain and reinvent themselves over time. Do not worry, the list is not that long!

Fifth, history has a way of providing great examples of ethical leadership. Reading biographies of authentic leaders will provide you with immense insights into the character-building process of the leader. One of the best books I have read on leadership development was Nelson Mandela's *Long Road to Freedom*. It is a masterful example of how some African leaders use reflective learning and collective values to build ethical cultures. It speaks volumes on how a community can help bring up a great child, and a great leader.

Sixth, I oftentimes look for examples in newspapers, magazines, and journals of exemplary leaders in terms of their perspective-taking capacity. Last year, I came across a man who owned a large construction company in Michigan. Over several decades he built the company, along with a very loyal workforce, into a successful, large organization of 500 employees. This past year, he decided to retire and sold his company for 400 million dollars. After he retired he decided to distribute proceeds from the sale of the business to his employees. He gave away over 125 million dollars to his employees to bolster their retirement plans. During an interview on national public radio, he was asked why he gave away over half of his wealth after taxes, to employees who already had great retirement plans. He kept saying, because he believed it was the right thing to do. His family and he had plenty of money to live on. The people that worked for him day in and day out made his company successful. He said they oftentimes had the same exact equipment as a competitor bidding on large contracts, but his company frequently won the contract because of the reputation of his people and company. Find more examples like him. Find out why people like this contractor, do the things they do for others based on it being the right thing to do. In 2001, when Jack Welch was preparing to retire from General Electric he was asked in an interview, what was the most important thing he had done at General Electric? He said that "he focused on people."

To reiterate, Warren Buffet said in his annual letter to his CEOs that Berkshire Hathaway was ranked number 5 in the world in terms of being the best company, and that it had taken them 37 years to get to that level of accomplishment. He then when on to say that in 37 seconds a bad decision by one of his executives could bring down this venerable company. He implored them to come to him with bad news early and as often as needed. Why would this CEO place emphasis on integrity as being paramount to business success?

Seventh, you just died! Sorry. I do appreciate your buying my book and am sorry for the inconvenience that sudden death brings. Okay, let us simulate death or role-play it for just a few moments, if that makes you more comfortable. How would you like people to describe your greatest accomplishments in your life stream now that you hit the big waterfall? Please hurry up because you are being lowered into the casket, or the top is off the urn and you are on your last sunset cruise! Any thoughts about what you would like to be remembered for by others, let us say for eternity as a starting point?

Eighth, to build perspective you need to expose yourself to differences, which you have done if you followed the first seven points. Yet you will learn nothing from those differences if you do not take the time to reflect on their importance to your own development. Write down your initial interpretation of some dilemma that you are currently dealing with at work, in your community, or at home. Over the next week, collect more data to broaden your understanding of the very core issue. Explore different perspectives and ideas that relate to the issue. Talk to people who may have very different views on the topic. Come back in a week and look at your initial interpretation, judgment, decision, or all three. How does it differ now in just one week's time?

Ninth, I want you to select who you believe is the best leader in your organization, community, or both. Now spend some time observing how that leader interacts with others. How does he or she work with people at the same level or position versus those below? What does this leader emphasize? What seems to be important to the leader? How does he or she deal with conflicts? How does he or she secure agreements from others? What stands out in terms of this leader's development of others? How does the leader view his constituency? Who is this leader's constituency? What do you see the leader willing to sacrifice? If you can sit down and talk with this leader, simply ask him or her to describe the philosophy of leadership and life that guides resolving the most difficult decisions.

Tenth, the next time you are dealing with a very difficult dilemma, ask yourself whether you have all of the data you need to make a fair judgment. What is it about the situation that makes it a dilemma for you or the other party? Is there any way to resolve the dilemma while maintaining the dignity of all parties involved? How do you solicit opinions from others that may shape your opinion of the dilemma? Should this dilemma be handled by consensus? Are you bringing out the very best in others? Once you have made a decision, track its impact over time. A few weeks out, do you feel it was still the right decision? Are you willing to debrief the decision and the process you used to achieve it, to make the next dilemma easier to handle?

What I have been trying to do here with these suggestions is to offer you as many ways to develop your perspective-taking capacity as possible. Those leaders who are most vibrant and adaptable are constantly shifting perspective up, even in small increments. This is what I have called CPI or continuous people improvement. They are continually searching on the inside in order to improve on the outside. It is a journey that should only end on your last sunset cruise!

MAKING PERSPECTIVE SHIFT

When I started writing my first sole-authored book on leadership, I wanted to entitle it, *Perspective Shift*. The publisher was less thrilled about the title, so it only went so far as the editing room floor. I wanted to use that title to emphasize the central importance of perspective-taking capacity to achieving exemplary leadership. Leadership development is fundamentally a shift in perspective. The shift occurs when you realize the importance and value of developing followers to lead themselves over time and not just follow when you are present—more loose than tight. The shift occurs when you entertain the benefits of coleadership or shared leadership. The shift occurs when you provide for the needs of others first versus your own needs. The shift occurs when you stop to reflect on an opponent's view to fully understand how he or she can believe the position he or she has taken and then refuses to move from that position. The shift occurs whenever you develop, plain and simple. Or it occurs when a very special friend of yours is hurt at work by his boss, really hurt. He calls you and tells you that he is trying to get the best out of this person. He sees the goodness in even the most difficult people and will work to bring out their best in spite of their extreme shortcomings. He is what Archbishop Desmond Tutu described as being a VSP.

What You Might Do to Further Your Development

Think about adding to the autobiography you have started. In each 5-year-period, write down what you felt were the highlights in terms of your development, the impact you had on the development of others, or both. What accomplishments were you most proud of, and what opportunities do you feel you took the best advantage of at the time? Do you see any trends emerging?

Now look out over the next 3 to 5 years, and write down specific accomplishments you would like to achieve in terms of your development or the development of those around you. You can integrate your reflections from time to time around the goals you have set to accomplish to see if you are on the right path. So the latter part of this autobiographical experience is your future autobiography waiting to be written, or the course your life stream will take once you decide upon its direction. You can either write the script, or wait for life to write it for you.

5

Feedback to Inch and Leap Forward

I recall working for this one company, where every couple of months I would do a 2-day training session on leadership development. During my first several programs, everyone seemed to be very pleased with what we did, and engaged in the learning process. Yet, when I would return to my office, I would frequently have an e-mail from my colleague who worked for this company laying out all of the things people had problems with in terms of the workshop. I thought this was rather strange, until I began to reflect on the culture of this organization. Over a period of 90 years, this very successful financial institution had grown a culture based on a business that dealt with very high-end clients. Image was incredibly important to them, as well as what you said. People were hired only if they graduated from a select number of prestigious universities. There was a company speak that people used that to the uninitiated never quite told you exactly what people meant to say. There was a certain linguistic skill that one had to develop to get to the root meaning of what people were saying, and it was through that feedback and discovery where I believe we began to have a significant impact on leadership development in this organization.

FEEDBACK ON FEEDBACK

Implied in much of our discussion up to this point about leadership development is the importance of feedback. I have used it indirectly in our discussion of debriefings and AARs. Both processes are representative of different forms of analyzing situations and providing feedback. I have also used it in our discussions of self-reflective learning. If you step back to reflect you are beginning to use feedback from the situation to better understand what just happened. Feedback starts with your own reflections, and eventually expands to other's observations and their reflections about an incident, your behavior or some interaction.

Whether feedback comes from others or from you it provides a mechanism for self- and other regulation. Recall the case of Mr. P, who was the overly controlling manager who even planned his family vacations with total control orientation. He received feedback for the first time about the lack of inspiration in his people. Upon receiving and interpreting this feedback, Mr. P chose to make a difference. This would represent an early stage with regard to a shift in his perspective. External feedback challenged the regulations that he had maintained in his behavior and created new boundaries or regulations for interacting with others. Feedback, if used constructively for development, can help to expand the boundaries in which you are working with others, or at the very least to make appropriate adjustments.

Feedback directs your attention to something that you should focus on. I can ask you to present your best vision to me. Then, I say, "Let me comment on your nonverbal messages that went along with your articulation of that vision." Immediately, most people realize that what they had thought about in terms of a visionary message was the verbal presentation and its content. Now, their attention is directed to the nonverbal part of their presentation. Feedback directs attention to areas for reflection and for making minor adjustments on up through to fundamental changes.

We can potentially regulate our behavior based on the feedback we receive and consider important and relevant. Obviously, we seek feedback on areas that we consider important, or at least someone in our organization has deemed important. The process of regulation associated with human feedback parallels the type of regulation processes that advocates of Total Quality Management (TQM) discussed for many years. How? The quality gurus asked us to consider looking at feedback based on the process versus the end product. By looking at the process, we would get feedback on how things were developing or emerging, which allows us to make adjustments when the process is out of range or beyond tolerance levels. Dr. Edward Deming discussed reducing the variance in processes as the Rosetta stone of total quality management. It applies equally well to leadership development. If viewed as an emergent process, it follows the same pattern of development where we refine and focus it over time.

FEEDBACK AS A REDUCTION IN VARIANCE

Feedback in the form of charting processes shows where unwanted deviations occur in a process. We can then intervene to change by making adjustments to our behavior. Take a walk through most manufacturing plants today, and you will see charts delineating process deviations on the walls. The charts provide feedback on deviations and where adjustments were or should have been made to correct the process. Imagine if as a leader, you could chart the clarity of your communication to others day-by-day, examining deviations from what you consider acceptable performance. Keeping a diary of your activities and seeking feedback from others are ways that you can obtain such data on how you are doing with others in terms of effective communication.

Now imagine yourself as a CEO, and your task is to communicate the strategic intent of your organization to all units at all levels. If we could imagine the organization as a map of each unit, then we could color some units red, who do not get the intent or are against it; gray for those units who show confusion around strategic intent, and green for those units that are completely aligned around the intent and direction set for the organization. The point I am trying to make here is the same type of variance that affects the quality of a manufacturing process, will affect the quality of the human interaction process. In both cases, we can measure the quality and provide feedback to make the appropriate adjustments needed to bring processes (thinking or otherwise) into alignment.

For example, we can measure what the social networks look like in organizations to see whether some groups are excluded versus others. Who do you go to for advice? How wide is your social network in terms of advice seeking and advice giving? How knowledge is transmitted within and between units within an organization is very much a function of the social networks that have been created. In an open environment, the networks will be much more highly integrated and diverse. In an autocratic environment, the networks will be highly regulated, not highly integrated and certainly not diverse.

Dr. Deming was vehemently against performance appraisal systems because these feedback systems generally occurred too far downstream in the process, when the feedback was no longer relevant or helpful. The product was already messed up by the time the feedback was provided. Providing feedback in stream allows for more modest and continuous adjustments in terms of both processes and behavior. If you play sports, you will know immediately what I mean. Make a slight change in your grip in tennis, golf, racketball and you can see the results almost immediately. I have asked you repeatedly to consider adjustments in your grip, so to speak, in terms of how you work with others. What to adjust takes reflection and keen observation of your own behavior and oftentimes feedback from others to help you make the appropriate adjustments.

SENSING THE ORGANIZATION'S PULSE

Some companies are using what are called e-pulse surveys or indicators. These indicators can be one or two questions that tap into how employees feel and are reacting to some event. How do you feel about the upcoming merger or acquisition? What is your greatest reservation in terms of decisions made in your company? How much do you trust top management? What is your opinion of management's decision not to invest in X, Y, or Z?

These e-pulse indicators are providing immediate and constant feedback to managers to help them judge the direction they want to pursue. It is in many ways an extension of the type of political polling that candidates use to judge reactions to positions that have been taken in a campaign. An example occurred in the presidential campaigning that took place in 2000. George W. Bush, the front-runner representing the Republicans was asked by a reporter whether he had done hard drugs. He decided that he would not feed on the media frenzy and chose not to answer the question. The polls day after day showed that people did not care what Bush had done years ago, but they did care how he responded to such queries. Over a week's period of time, he kept updating his response, saying he could pass a federal background check going back 7 years, and even 25 years back, prior to his father being President. But he never answered the fundamental question asked of him, "Had he done cocaine?" He did not answer the question and judged the public's response well based on polls. The public kept indicating in poll after poll, that going back in a candidate's life to uncover what he or she has done is NOT relevant to how they will vote. At this writing Bush appears to have judged the public's view on this issue quite well, as he was elected President of the United States.

What we have covered on feedback thus far can be summarized as follows. Feedback can come from other sources, from yourself, from the task you are doing, or all three. Feedback provides an opportunity for self-awareness and self-regulation once it is apparent what is being fed back to you. Feedback can be corrective depending on one's perspective. If you do not value the feedback you receive from others, then it will have little impact on your development. If you have the controlling type of perspective, you will get very limited feedback that is out of range. People will tell you what you want to hear, and probably things you already know or should know. In fact, if you are frequently told things you already know, then that may be very useful feedback to consider. For example, when is the last time someone took a position that was directly against your position in public? How comfortable did the person appear to you in taking such a position? Are people around you hesitant to discuss their mistakes? Unfortunately, the failure to do so may very likely place you in an uncomfortable and potentially highly vulnerable position, as you will not know what you do not know because no one will tell you. If what you do not know is critical, you are highly vulnerable right now.

I have worked with three organizations that went through very significant ethical and legal dilemmas. In each case, many people knew about the ethical problem as it was unfolding, but no one was willing to provide feedback to someone who could have made a difference in what eventually took place. The conditions for providing useful and in these cases critical feedback had not been well developed in the leadership culture. When employees asked themselves, " What's in it for me" to tell the leaders something was wrong, they oftentimes concluded trouble and therefore said nothing. You are always perched on a cliff waiting to take that fatal step, when your followers have not developed a sense of why they should provide feedback to you on such critical events. I must say, I tend to agree with them if the leaders have trained them that feedback is not well received, especially when it is bad news. Now reflect on what Warren Buffet said: Tell me bad news early and often. Consider the value of his authenticity in the markets where his opinion seems to count. It is an awesome brand indeed.

If you are thinking that you have not heard much critical feedback lately, then I suggest you go to your most trusted peer and discuss with him or her, whether your colleagues are hesitant to challenge you on your most sacred assumptions, project, ideas, or all three. To lead others most effectively you will need to seek feedback constantly and from all levels. You will also need to learn how to derive feedback from your work context–culture. There are oftentimes things going on around you, that if you take the time to really observe them, you will have a much better sense of people's reactions and therefore will be able to anticipate them the next time around. For instance, take the next week and try to identify what are the top three topics typically discussed in your work group, unit, organization, or all three. Are those topics current issues, past issues, or future issues? What does much of the conversation in your unit, organization, or both focus on? Does it focus on prevention issues, or on future-oriented promotion issues? Perhaps most important, who comes to talk to you about anything of substance or meaning? Look back over the last month and reflect on who has come to talk with you, and what they have come to talk with you about. Perhaps, you can spend the next month simply jotting down in your reflective notes the main topics of discussion. Do not change anything in your behavior, except to record your observations and see what your baseline assessment comes up with. You might think of this as a passive polling of the people who work with you. Some CEOs now even observe the content of chat rooms of their clients, suppliers, or employees to see what they focus on, in the same way I am asking you to do your own passive polling process.

I was recently in a meeting with some close colleagues and we were discussing the development of a Web site called www.eleading.com. One of my colleagues was showing me feedback data on a new Web site he had worked on. The feedback consisted of things like which web pages were most frequently opened and in what order? From which countries did the most hits occur and on what days or even hours was the site most active? The type of feedback that he received from this simple program is so far beyond what many people in leadership positions take the time to collect and deeply examine and reflect on. What he was showing me was a way of reconstructing patterns of interaction within a Web site that would help him to improve the delivery of information through that Web site. If only people were so diligent about the patterns of interactions that occurred around them, we would probably be better able to resolve many misunderstandings and conflicts that typically arise in organizations, which I frequently hear in the form—"We have communication problems here."

Using the Web site as an analogy, would you consider identifying particular behaviors or interactions that you have exhibited, let us say over the last month, to determine how you could improve your leadership Web site? Let us say you collected some baseline data on how people reacted both verbally and nonverbally to you when you gave them directions or feedback. Then after collecting some baseline data for the month, you could decide how to make some adjustments in your behavior based on the feedback that you have received. Some managers would say they do not have time for such data collection, which I find curious when I see that one of their core values is continuous improvement. (I know I keep coming back to this one, since I feel it is the one most often violated in practice.) I also find it interesting that we want precision feedback built into our technical systems, but when it comes to human behavior, we are pretty comfortable making decisions based on very unreliably collected data sets. This is especially problematic for me, as most technical systems are not nearly as complex as any one human system, let alone the human systems we call teams and organizations. Clearly we need to build some discipline around collecting targeted feedback data.

Let me give you another example, which I came across in a book entitled *The Tipping Point* by Malcolm Gladwell (2000). In this book, the author discussed how certain events occur that tip the scales into a major trend. He gave examples of how some trends evolved, and why they became what web designers and he called sticky. By sticky, he meant that people kept coming back to it again and again, because there is something inherently satisfying with this activity or trend.

In one part of the book, he described how *Sesame Street* began, and how the designers of that show would calculate a distraction index to see during which segments of the show the kids watching it were most engaged. These researchers would examine short segments of the show calculating distraction scores to see what worked with kids, what was too complicated, what bored them during the show, and so forth. If we were only that systematic in our analysis of leader and follower interactions we would likely have a much better idea of what works and does not work in leadership. Again, I am asking for your discipline to be a more systematic observer of the people you set out to influence over time. In doing so, I am confident that you can markedly improve the quality of your interactions and collectively your performance. Minimally, we should be able to lower their distraction index score.

HOW ORGANIZATIONS USE FEEDBACK AND COULD USE IT TO ACCELERATE LEADERSHIP DEVELOPMENT

Today, one of the most popular forms of leadership feedback comes in the form of what is called 360-feedback systems. What this simply means is that feedback comes from all around you in terms of followers, peers, supervisors, clients, suppliers, etc. There is not just one 360-feedback survey instrument. To the contrary, any survey that takes a 360-degree view of your impact on others can be considered a 360 survey of leadership or management style.

One of the reasons for moving to 360-feedback systems was to provide people with feedback from all the relevant sources around them. However, some still do not believe in the value of feedback from, let us say, their followers. Let me explain why it is important to get their feedback using the following scenario. I want you to imagine that you have just been told not to have any more interactions with your customers. You are no longer allowed to ask them to fill out any surveys on the service they have just received. You are not allowed to call them up and ask them for feedback on any product. You are to have no contact whatsoever with them. Sound reasonable? I would venture to say that most people out there would say the approach I am suggesting is ridiculous, in fact ludicrous in the age of the enabled customer where everything must be customized on demand. Customers are the most important end users, and we must constantly dialogue with them to understand their needs. We can make adjustments in our products to meet current and future needs if we just listen carefully to our customers.

To apply some TQM terminology again, what about your internal customers are like your followers? Why would you not want to know how they view your leadership, top management's strategic intent, the culture of innovation or handling of mistakes, etc.? Of course, I hope you realize now, that you close such channels of information at your own peril. Also, how dumb do you want to be as a leader? I say "dumb" because I believe that leadership is a collateral, interactive process, or both. There is a give-and-take between leaders and followers that over time can be represented by collective or shared leadership and shared intelligence. One way to build a mature collateral relationship is to be open to feedback and to learn from followers, peers, and supervisors. If you are not open to feedback from others, it would be difficult if not impossible to build one of the most important facets of human interaction in organizations called *cooperation.*

Most times when I do feedback sessions with leaders, they are amazed at how different their own ratings of leadership styles are versus other sources, especially their followers. Evidence indicates that the overraters feel the data is less accurate, because it perhaps does not agree with the leader's inflated estimates. A common response is feeling out of touch with followers. Evidence indicates that overraters tend to have poorer performance, reduced likelihood of promotion, and career derailment versus underraters.

Survey feedback is one way to stay in touch, and probably an artificial way at that! We use 180- or 360-survey feedback to do what managers should be doing every day, and that is getting feedback from their followers on how they and the leader are doing. I say "artificial realizing" that I myself use a survey that we have developed and validated over a 20-year period of time. We use anonymous survey feedback because that is where we are in terms of the development of open and trusting organizational cultures. Many followers need the protection of anonymity to be honest with their feedback to leaders. How unfortunate given the importance of feedback to improving the quality of all of our interactions in organizations, especially between leaders and followers.

I see the ideal feedback environment being one in which the most relevant feedback is provided at the direct point of contact where it is needed. With advanced technology available to us, there is no reason why we cannot provide leaders with much more continuous feedback on key target behaviors. For example, why not track a particular behavior a leader is attempting to change by polling that leaders' constituency base every month with one or two items? Leaders should not have to wait 6 months to receive the survey report or profile. It should be provided in stream near to the time the action or series of behaviors occurred.

I also believe that for organizations that are developmentally ready, such feedback will occur closer and closer to the point of contact between leaders and their followers. What I mean is that people will receive feedback in stream, rather than after long periods of delay, along the lines of the AARs mentioned earlier. Of course, the survey can help to summarize trends and provide some time for the rater to reflect on how he or she is being led. In this way, it can be a very useful instrument. However, without building trust, it will always remain an artificial means for getting the best feedback you can possibly get from those around you. Of course, the less feedback you receive the more vulnerable you become as a leader, and ultimately as an organization. No feedback and you are high on the vulnerability meter and certainly not as smart as you could be as a leader. Indeed, many organizations have collective IQs that are much lower than their average IQ. They are dumber than their intellectual potential because they do not share knowledge and information in a way that would at least make them as smart as their average IQ.

There are several points that I would like to highlight in this chapter for your reflection:

1. How can you as a leader develop a feedback environment where the most central and important information is passed along about you or any critically important issue?
2. Can we make sure before survey feedback is ever introduced that the source of feedback is viewed as being credible?
3. How should feedback be spaced over time when it is of the more formal 360 type?
4. How can we ensure that feedback is interpreted as it was intended?
5. Are there ways to know what feedback is relevant and what feedback is out of bounds?
6. If you were to examine the culture of your organization, how would you describe the nature of feedback in terms of how it is given and received? What is the balance between effective and constructive feedback versus critical and negative? Do you have a ratio in mind? How honest is the feedback given and received in your opinion?

Many of these questions regarding feedback have been addressed in the leadership literature. Some of the questions deal with the importance of developing an authentic culture in which feedback will be thoughtfully provided, received, and utilized. In one case, an individual was describing to me her boss, and how he was the anti-role-model for her in terms of leadership. Thus, any feedback on her leadership style coming from him was simply seen as irrelevant and hypocritical. She discounted any of the data he provided whether valid or not.

Similarly, I have worked for organizations where the management team is lacking in credibility, so that any feedback given is usually seen as having some agenda behind it. One manager said to me, "Everything I say has an intended purpose … everything." He, like Mr. C described to you earlier, was quite control oriented and limited himself as a leader in terms of growing people to their full potential. After 3 years in a leadership role, he derailed and was fired. He was fired in large part because everything he said had some intended purpose behind it, which fueled suspicion, mistrust, and a lack of commitment to his agenda.

There is also recent research on how the feedback context can affect the interpretation of 360-feedback processes. For example, the more cynical the culture in an organization the less useful feedback is seen for development. What people are saying is that all the change in the world will not change this organization, so why even bother to put in the effort to provide legitimate feedback. If the organization is that cynical, probably investing in an expensive 360-feedback system would not be worth the money spent. Like people, organizations need to be developmentally ready to receive and fully utilize feedback. Leaders can help make that developmental readiness happen, or they can work to retard development, as would be the case for Mr. C.

GETTING FEEDBACK IN STREAM AT THE POINT OF READINESS

Based on work that I have done with colleagues over the last 5 years, I am convinced that feedback provided in stream and over time is far more effective. Specifically, providing people with feedback at the point of contact with an issue or problem seems more effective to me, than waiting for the next workshop or appraisal session. However, I should add that you also must assess whether the person is ready for that feedback at that point in time. Such just-in-time feedback is now even more feasible and cost effective, given the developments in web-based feedback and coaching systems.

Developmental readiness can be critical to how feedback is used and evaluated. For example, recent research indicates that only feedback-standard gaps that receive attention have an impact on active regulation of one's behavior. That is why it is so important to get leaders to really focus on keenly observing the environment around them to assure they are paying attention to relevant standards (even those that apply to behavior) and the gaps between the as is and the ideal.

Based on an extensive analysis of the literature on feedback, Kluger and DeNisi (1996) concluded that feedback actually decreased performance in a third of the cases. This may be due to a number of factors. First, the context in which feedback was given may not be all that friendly to feedback, and therefore even positive feedback can be misconstrued. The impact of feedback may also be due to how people regulate their own behavior. For example, if a person is geared toward always minimizing failure, then positive feedback may be of little interest or consequence. They may only react when the feedback is negative to avoid falling below standards.

Someone who is geared toward positive improvement may see either negative or positive feedback as closing the gap between where he is and where he would like to be in terms of higher standards of performance. These authors suggested that people self-regulate either to prevent something from happening or to promote something to happen. People who have a prevention focus will monitor their work environment for errors to minimize them, and will try to prevent them from occurring. Conversely, people who are promotion oriented will seek out the positive value of feedback. Thus, in prevention mode, such people view any critical feedback as a threat, and will not benefit from such feedback in terms of advancing development; whereas in promotion mode, feedback that is positive will likely be used to enhance development and performance, while negative feedback will get them to reduce doing one thing and likely substituting that behavior with something else.

One of the central points to take away from this discussion is that the impact of feedback very much depends on the orientation the individual uses to self-regulate her behavior. The type and level of self-regulation is linked to the individual's developmental readiness and in part to the culture of the organization. To the degree the individual is developmentally ready to make adjustments to either positive or negative feedback it is likely that feedback will have a more positive influence on motivation and performance. Generally speaking, feedback has been examined too simplistically and without consideration for the needs and capabilities of the individual. Clearly, we need to take a much closer look at how the type of feedback, the timing of feedback and the developmental readiness of the individual and organization all interact with each other to influence the positive contribution of feedback to development.

FEEDBACK AND TRAINING BOOSTERS

What we have also found is that feedback in general can boost training effects over time. So, spacing feedback out over time to enhance training effects is a useful, productive strategy. Indeed, we are now using feedback mechanisms delivered through the web to offer virtual coaching to follow people into their interactions as leaders helping them through difficult transitions. Part of the strategy we are using is to provide feedback at the point of contact where it can have the greatest positive impact on an individual's development and performance as a leader. In attempting to do so, we are aligning the feedback with the specific developmental needs and challenges at that point in time in that individual's life stream.

I would like for you to consider that you are attempting to replicate the services we are providing via the web to your followers. Do you think it is realistic to try and determine how your followers are prepared to receive positive, or critical feedback, or both? Do you think it is feasible to make adjustments to feedback so that it can be provided in line with the developmental readiness of the individual? Have you ever worked with a leader that was able to say just the right thing at the right time, even if it was not what you wanted to hear at the time? If yes, then what I am describing here is eminently feasible.

PRACTICE WITH FEEDBACK

Let me summarize some of the learning points in this chapter with an example and an exercise for you to consider doing. Imagine that you are a project leader and you have asked your team to assemble to discuss its performance. During the meeting, you discuss areas where you feel they are achieving excellent performance and also point to areas that need development. Subsequent to meeting with your team, you hear that several of your colleagues are rather angry about the session. Have any ideas why?

- Do they consider you a credible source for feedback?
- Was the timing correct for the feedback session?
- Do the people in the group translate feedback in very different ways based on their own perceptions of themselves and developmental readiness?
- Are you sure they even heard what you intended them to hear in the feedback session?
- How well prepared in advance were they for the feedback session?
- What is the culture for feedback in your unit? In the organization?
- How cynical are your followers about the intent of your organization?

I would suggest that if you have such reactions from your group of followers, any and all of the previously mentioned are distinct possibilities, and you need to collect more data on the individuals, the group and the context before coming to any firm conclusions. I am even wondering now how you might have received the feedback I just provided to you! One never knows exactly, but at the very least it is worth asking the question.

When giving feedback you need to consider its content, timing, source, the receiver, and what has been given as feedback in the past and by whom. The content includes how specific the feedback is and what you are focusing on in terms of incidents, actions, behaviors, or all three. The range can be behavioral through your personality to conjecture. I would prefer you focus more on behavior in your feedback to others because people can change behavior. The timing as previously suggested is critical in terms of the developmental readiness of the individual to receive it. Also, by timing the feedback to be presented, you likely will catch more people being ready to receive it. It also gives you more opportunity to prepare them for feedback and to remind them of what they did. The source is you, and as I previously said, if you are not trusted the feedback will not be trusted or even heard. The receiver is your follower perhaps, peer or even leader, and you must judge how prepared they are for receiving the feedback. Have you done what you should have done to prepare them for the feedback you are about to provide to them? Finally, how does the current feedback that you are planning to provide fit with feedback they have already received? How consistent or inconsistent is your feedback with prior messages? How does your organization support change after people receive feedback both in tangible and intangible ways?

6

Reflection

Recall that we discussed how important the reflective process is in one's development as a leader. Taking time to debrief life's events and how they effect your life model, is a critically important aspect of reflective learning from experiences.

While in Malaysia on a recent trip, I was riding up a river on a ferry to a seaside resort called Desaru. Halfway up the river, we slowed down to pass some fishing farms in the middle of the river. The sun was setting, and the shadows of the fisherman were cast across the water. For some reason, the whole scene reminded me of watching night after night events that were going on in Vietnam back in the late 1960s as a teenager, wondering if I would be in the news over there in a few years. There was this moment of tranquility embedded in this very beautiful spot that could turn dangerous in seconds. Images one has of Vietnam having grown up in the 1960s. Although I was draft eligible and ready to be called up for service in 1972, President Nixon ended the draft, fundamentally affecting my life stream.

On the way back from Desaru, I was traveling with a group of people who had participated in our leadership development workshop. About halfway down the river, the man sitting next to me started up a conversation. I asked him where he was from, and he replied Vietnam. He and his family had lived in the former capital of South Vietnam called Saigon. He described the days leading up to the evacuation of the American forces, watching from his home the American troops coming through the streets to the embassy where they were air lifted by helicopters. Since his father and brothers had served in the military, they realized that staying in Vietnam after its fall was probably not feasible, so they like thousands of others who survived (and many did not) set out in boats leaving their homeland behind. This is the same man I mentioned earlier, who was about my age.

I reflected a great deal on how fortunate I was to not be a year or two older. I wondered whether I might have been part of the scene that he described if my life stream had taken a different path. I also marveled at his optimism given all that he had to sacrifice so early on in his life. How had this event shaped his leadership of others? How can our leadership development workshops compare to such tension in life events, in shaping who we are and who we become? Is leadership forged through the handling of such difficult events?

To be an effective leader means to reflect, deeply reflect, on events that surround oneself that have relevance to how you see your own behavior and actions influencing others. Let us take the daily interactions of a leader and view them either as a picture or a film. Both have single frames, so to speak, but pictures are seen as the total reality of the moment when that picture was taken. The film is a sequence or stream of reality moments that is difficult to separate out frame by frame. Some leaders look at the context they are in as if it were a series of pictures that are independent events that are not connected. Other leaders examine their context as if it is unfolding into the next context and then the next. The act of viewing the context as unfolding provides a deeper basis for reflection, which is far more forward thinking in my opinion. By viewing events as if they are the precursors for something that is coming versus the way things have been, you can begin to focus yourself as a leader on being more forward thinking and reflective.

I came across an interesting example of the importance of this distinction in a book I mentioned earlier called *The Tipping Point*, where Gladwell (2000) discussed what is called cultural microrhythms. Apparently, one of the pioneers of this field back in the 1960s by the name of William Condon spent a year and a half analyzing a segment of film that lasted 4.5 seconds. He split the film into 1/45-of-a-second segments, and coded it over and over again. What he observed in this conversation between a husband and wife, is these micromovements, that he called interactional synchrony. As Gladwell (2000) noted:

> Their conversation had a rhythmic physical dimension. Each person would, within the space of one or two or three 1/45 of a second frames, move a shoulder or cheek or an eyebrow or a hand, sustain that movement, stop it, change direction, and start again. And what's more, those movements were

> perfectly in time to each person's own words—emphasizing and underlining and elaborating on the process of articulation—so that the speaker was, in effect, dancing to his or her own speech. (p. 82)

The author goes on to note that people around the table involved in the interaction were also dancing along as well, with the moves all being in harmony with each other.

The linkage to leadership is clear, in that leaders who have strong charismatic qualities are oftentimes described in terms of the rhythm of their speech, nonverbal behaviors, and mannerisms. The rhythm is seen in the choice of words, phrases, metaphors, alliteration, and story telling that goes on in their presentations. Some have even joked that Italians never listened to what Benito Mussolini had said, but instead followed the opera in his voice and knew the rhythm, but not the words.

LEADER'S ADJUSTMENTS TO FOLLOWERS' BEHAVIORS

Your reflections depend on what you observe, take the time to think about and to incorporate into your way of leading others. How perceptive you are affects how able you are to adjust your behavior to the behavior they see coming from others. This is called self-monitoring ability, and it provides leaders who are high self-monitors with the cues to adjust their behavior as they watch the impact it is having on followers. During a stream of interactions, high self-monitoring leaders will adjust their behavior based on the feedback cues they are receiving from their audience and by doing so they can manipulate the behavior of others to be in line with the reactions they desire. By manipulation, I do not mean the leader's behaviors are necessarily negative, simply that they are controlling the reactions of followers as they adjust their behavior based on feedback cues from followers.

Step 1

Target collecting data that you consider to be relevant concerning what is going on around you. On a micro level, you could focus on how followers react to your directions. Simply focus on what they say each time you provide them with instructions both verbally and nonverbally. Are their verbal and nonverbal reactions in alignment, or is there some disharmony?

At a more macro level, you might spend time looking at what is the single most important advance in disciplines that support the work you do day in and day out. Or you might focus on social, technical, and cultural trends each year to see how they may impact on your organization. You could put together the top three in each area and look for interconnections across disciplines. This is also something you could do with your peers or followers as part of expanding your thought processes about leadership and its development.

For example, approximately 8 years ago, the Internet crossed over the chasm from the science community into the broader public domain of use. Looking back on this intervention or reflecting, what type of impact could this technological change have had on social, organizational, and cultural differences? What type of impact will it have on privacy issues over time? How can it be used for continuous on-site development? What are its implications for empowering people to do work anytime and anyplace? What will happen to the notion of supervision, as we move to this new conduit for interactions? What type of leadership will work best teams who only interact virtually across time zones, cultures, and geographical regions?

Just before writing this section, I read an article on "The New Asia." In the article, the author discussed how the Internet was changing how the younger generation embraced Confucian values and respect for authority in traditional Asian cultures. The author hypothesized the Internet would change the social relation patterns in Asian society to be more democratic and challenging of authority. In a related article about Israel, the author discussed how the Moussad, the highly secretive intelligence agency in Israel, was now openly advertising for applicants in the public press because the number of young people applying for careers in this field had dropped significantly. Indeed, the younger generation of Israelis saw that it was much cooler to work for hi-tech companies focusing on the Internet versus being a secret agent! Many Israelis were seeking careers in the dot com industry foregoing careers in more traditional fields including the military. Could we have envisioned these emerging effects? Today, with the intifada at full bore, and the Palestinians and Israelis at war with each other, I wonder how those views may have changed in just one year.

Since the future emerges in the present, and the present can be as finely sliced as 1/45th of a second, being able to reflect on what is going on in the present and what may evolve in the future is a critical leadership skill that must be developed over time. How can one do this? Let me lay out some basic steps for you to consider practicing or making part of your ongoing leadership development plan.

In both previous examples, one can view the situations presented as snapshots of the way things are and will be, or one can take the data to indicate a new situation or context is emerging that will affect future patterns of relationships. Yes, it would have been very nice to anticipate these changes, but the fact of the matter is, we are still in the first few days of the Internet having an impact on the global culture. So, if you were to reflect on where the Internet would be headed over the next 25 years in terms of technology, social, and cultural changes, where would your predictions now focus? In some countries, a 25-year projection will put you right where the United States and other nations are today.

Step 2

In addition to collecting data, we must also test again and again whether it is reliable and valid. In the example I have previously given, one could test changes going on now in Asia, with changes that already have occurred in the United States that affect leaders and followers. If one were to examine the impact of the Internet on social, technical, and cultural change in the United States, would there be some reasonable hypotheses that could be generated concerning what is next for leadership? Which trends would generalize and which trends would end at the shores of the United States?

Step 3

Now let us create some scenarios of what you might do given the information that you have just collected. Test out the validity of your scenarios and present them to other people in your work group, to see if they can add any data to those scenarios. Give them a week to reflect on them and come back with any tangential information that may expand the ideas first presented. What scenarios do you believe are more or less feasible? Why do you think they are more or less feasible? What related scenarios lead you to those conclusions? What have you learned from their reflections? Is the snapshot you started out with the same, or has it now changed in line with the contributions made by others?

Step 4

Create a common reference point or framework with the people you work with. The framework can be totally futuristic and unrealistic. The goal here is to simply create a common understanding, or in fact, a number of common understandings surrounding different scenarios.

By creating a common frame of reference it is possible to develop opportunities to hear each other's self-reflections about the context as you have constructed it in your mind with each other. What should be emphasized in what I just said in the previous sentence is the word *common*. An entire organization can reflect on events that have happened, or that are expected to happen in the near and distance future. Yet, at some point there is a need for a common point of reference for different people to reflect on and to come to some judgment. To some degree, the common base is linked to the assumptions that underlie the scenario that you are attempting to create and understand.

LEADERSHIP VIEWED AS A PROCESS

Grundstein-Amado (1999) argued that we should focus on bilateral transformational leadership, which is comprised of both self-discovery and reflection and is represented as an interaction between leaders and followers. The starting point in this bilateral relationship is to first learn something about ourselves, and then use what we have learned to think about and understand others. I spent the first five chapters focusing on how your life model and perspective are formed and the impact they have on how you view others. For example, we judge people's intent and behavior based on the lens we have developed in our life stream, which is formed within our life model, and builds perspective-taking capacity. However, at the end of the day, we cannot simply focus on who the leader judges herself to be, as an individual. Rather, we must also examine how leaders and followers judge their collective being versus simply themselves as human beings. It is at this juncture that leadership described as a process really gets interesting, complex, and from time to time, frustrating. It is frustrating because as a scientist, I want to systematically test how *A* affects *B*, but with leadership there is always at least *A*, *B*, and *C* with *C* being the context in which leadership is observed, and as we previously noted, the context is dynamic, it is not a snapshot and is always emerging. Indeed, unlike a movie, it does not just go forward, it can also go back in time before the events you are currently observing. For instance, a leader and follower are observed interacting and arguing with each other. This goes on for 30 minutes almost to the point of physical confrontation. Then the argument suddenly ends, and they both go away ready to implement what they have just discussed and resolved.

Let us say that this unit deals with highly explosive materials and their agreement is that they must argue hard to make sure they come up with the right decision. Personalities aside, and feelings as well, they argue as hard as they can to resolve whatever dilemma they are confronting. Of course without that history for the current incident we have observed, it just looks like marriage! I am kidding to some degree.

Complicating matters further, when we judge the leadership of a person, we can do so by evaluating attributes such as his honesty, trustworthiness, intelligence, and energy. Yet, in isolation and without reference to others, these concepts have little meaning except to describe that individual. Once we introduce leadership, which represents some form of bilateral relationship, then we need to consider and reflect on how these concepts represent the relationship that exists between leaders and followers. As we continue this discussion, I would like you to consider what I am about to say keeping in mind the term *jointly*, and what might happen when things are not jointly defined.

Let me bring back for the moment two concepts that we have discussed earlier, which were the AAR, and the main concept for this chapter on reflection. When we discussed the AAR, we identified its central purpose as creating a common or joint perception of what happened based on debriefing the sequence of events that preceded the AAR. The AAR is a methodology that provides for just-in-time learning, or learning as near as possible to your experiencing particular events. Oftentimes failure in performance or not achieving full success can be attributed to different individuals viewing the same situation differently. Indeed, based on what we have already discussed, you can assume that people who you work with will almost always see situations differently than your perceptions. Now we have a better idea why if we look to the life model as the lens through which people interpret events around them. The AAR is a way of highlighting those differences so you are able to reflect on their importance to your work group's alignment and development. It also helps us remember that we all approach situations with different lenses and perspectives, and that coming to alignment and a shared understanding is one of the most important goals of leadership. This is by no means a trivial goal. Time and again I see managers assuming they have alignment, and they start moving forward one step and then back three. Frequently, people will typically just nod their heads as if they understand what constitutes the new direction to be pursued. Yet, they either do not want you to know they do not understand, or they think they understand but in fact they do not. Many of the communication problems in organizations stem from how different people perceive things differently depending on their lenses and life streams. These communication problems are exacerbated in cultures where there is a great deal of psychological distance between leaders and followers.

The differences that I previously mentioned originate in how we were all developed, the cultures in which we function, the technical training we received, and how these all interact to affect the way we interpret the world around us. One of the reasons why mergers are so difficult to lead is that each organization's culture shapes the way people see things. For example, at Intel, long-term planning is probably not more than 2–3 years, whereas at NASA, a long-term plan may involve 10-to 20-year planning horizons. The organizational culture will certainly shape how we perceive the same events, and will make it more likely that we will disagree about those events to the extent that the cultures we come from are different.

In another form of culture, we can also look at the impact of national cultures on differences in people's points of view. I observed with a Korean professor, that when students came in the room they would bow in his presence. If a student did that in my office, I would call the ambulance thinking that they may have ruptured an appendix, were having a heart attack, or were going into some convulsions.

DEMONSTRATING THE IMPORTANCE OF SELF-REFLECTION

Let us go inside the leader's head for a moment to examine how this process works. The task the group is working on is to develop new processes for assuring that each member of the work unit has a 360-degree view of its customers. First, the leader articulates what she means by creating a 360-view by describing that every aspect of the client's history of interactions and needs is known to every individual who will have contact with the customer. The leader has spent a lot of time describing what a 360-contact view means to followers, and has also emphasized its importance to future business success. (By the way, when you pick a concept like this, make the assumption that you will need to demonstrate it at least 100 different ways, to assure that everyone fully understands exactly what it means to them. I have spent an entire chapter on a concept, trying to model with you the importance of strategic redundancy around assuring the important concepts are fully understood.)

It is now time to roll out the program, and within a few weeks, things are not going so well. One customer remarked, "and now it appears that everyone in this company can work together to slow down service as opposed to it being the responsibility of any one individual!" They are all tripping over each other to service the customer, and the customer just disconnected his phone.

The leader asked her management group to come together to do an AAR on the interactions that occurred in the past month with one of the organization's largest clients. As the leader listens to her followers' depiction of the last interaction, several points are raised for reflection. First, some individuals perceive a 360-degree view as being threatening to their success. They believe that some members of their workgroup are not using information about interactions with the customer to enhance the service delivered, but rather to enhance their own positions in the organization. They are uncomfortable providing everything they know about the customer to other members of the workgroup, as they consider their relationship with the customer to be unique, and important to their own position, rewards, and future career success. It seems we have some mistrust rising above the noise and effecting perceptions of this workgroup.

Second, it is clear from the discussion there are many gaps in knowledge about the customer due to the lack of information sharing, and that the customer has now become the point of integration as opposed to the workgroup. The customer has become responsible for trying to piece together the various bits of information he is receiving, oftentimes having to resolve conflicting data coming from the different sources.

Third, there appears to be some misunderstanding as to what constitutes a 360-degree view of a customer. For example, some members of the workgroup have a very close relationship with the client, and are not sure the information they have is appropriate to share with others. It is not clear what information is proprietary and what information is in the public domain. Indeed, one might even question whether there is such a thing as proprietary information anymore with 360-degree service.

Finally, to share information with others takes time, and there appear to be no signals coming from the organization's leadership that an investment in the time it takes to educate your peers about customer needs is being rewarded. Indeed, there are no tangible rewards provided for cooperation, which to use the language we used earlier is a very important and critical intangible asset. Imagine how costly it is to get things done in a complex organization where no one cooperates, and you can see how important this intangible asset can become, especially where an organization is trying to achieve a 360-degree view of their customers.

Reflecting on these points, the leader sees there are several issues that require further discussion and reflection. First, her followers must be crystal clear on what constitutes a 360-degree view of customers. This represents a clear misstep at the start of the intervention, as there was no common or shared understanding of the concept exhibited. Second, to achieve a 360-view of customers will require that members have a certain threshold level of trust in each other to fully share relevant information. Third, the leader and the organization must signal followers that this is an important initiative that will produce tangible benefits and results.

By using an AAR, one hopes to stimulate reflection on aspects of workgroup processes and performance that can be improved by learning what happened as the process emerged or unfolded as opposed to waiting until things are broken. To accomplish this objective the AAR must, like leadership, be focused on a few key factors. In the case we previously described, the focus was on the delivery of 360-degree service, which led to an examination of how it was understood by group members and what impact the relationships of group members had on achieving such high service levels. Indeed, with some reflection, it is almost impossible to discuss 360-views of customers without discussing some specific levels of cooperation required among the work group members.

So we start the reflective process with what we tried to do, and compare that to what we perceived happened. Describing what happened is not always that easily achieved, as we all have different cuts on what happened in complex interactions. This point has been demonstrated so many times throughout this book, that I hope we are at the point of being totally strategically redundant. Yet, I will never know whether we are or not, without conducting an AAR. However, if you can assume we can come to some agreement or ground truth on what happened, the next and even more difficult step is to discuss why it happened. What are the causes for the gaps between what occurred and what was expected or desired? What have we learned, and what can or should we do differently? Life is an experiment that we have some controls over, and when we make a decision, we are redirecting the experiment in a new direction.

The AAR represents taking a step back to leap forward. Although it focuses on getting the past right, it is largely designed to recreate the future, to do things differently and more effectively. During the process of reflection, one can examine what the impact would be of altering some of the actions that were taken in the short, intermediate, or long term. Here, like the scientist, you are hypothesizing what might happen if you tried this or that. This goes back to examining various scenarios that may arise based on the sequence of actions you have chosen to pursue in order to achieve first, second, and even third-order effects. What do I mean? The first-order effect might be described as, "Every customer will say that no matter whom they talked to in this organization, that person understood his or her needs." A second-order effect is that the sharing of information has led to a much higher frequency of cross-selling with customers. Indeed, it has created a community of customers who have begun to share information with each other, solving their own problems. The third-order effect is that by continuously sharing client information with each other, the culture of the organization itself has become more open, transparent, and cooperative. Not only do you observe more effective customer interactions, you are seeing cooperative behavior manifest itself in many other ways, which has provided a foundation for greater horizontal integration within and between work groups.

THE AAR ON AAR

I would like to apply the AAR to the discussion of our own actions here. I know it may sound a bit ridiculous, but let us do an AAR on AARs! After Action means that something of significance occurred that you want to revisit and reflect on for further consideration. In this case, I used a major initiative by a leader to kick off the AAR process. The process begins with observing what happened and coming to a shared understanding of ground truth, which does not necessarily mean perfect understanding. Then we explored reasons to explain why things happened in the way they did, and discussed alternative actions that may have been taken. Of course, if we pursued those actions we could start the process all over again, and again, and again. This process is something that I would like to etch in your mind as a quick review that you can go through when you come across important actions that were or will be taken.

We have focused on actions that were taken and now we move to actions that will be taken. Now, we are not discussing *After* Action Reviews, but rather *Advanced* Action Reviews. Using the previous example, I asked you to consider the first, second, and third-order effects of your actions. I believe the best leadership occurs when people think beyond first-order effects to what might occur at the second and third-order level. I would liken this to the strategic use of speculation. Simply thinking about what the third-order effects will be from your actions will help you to develop a broader perspective on leadership. Also, as you move up in organizations, having the ability to examine the reverberations of your actions is not simply nice to do, but rather a must-have in terms of developing strategic leadership effectiveness. As you move up to higher-level positions, including in organizations that are flattened hierarchies, you lead people both directly and indirectly who are not your immediate followers or peers. To lead effectively requires that you consider first, second, and third-order effects of your actions and behavior. For instance, by taking a firm stand on not downsizing with your followers, what second and third-order impact will that have on people who are not in immediate contact with you? Or by taking a position based on a moral or ethical standard, how will others perceive you who do not have direct contact with you, in terms of their level of trust in you? My position here is that your leadership impact is probably most clearly shown in terms of second and third-level order effects. If you are clearly trusted and your actions are seen as being in line with your intentions, than at the second and third-order level, we would see your intent reflected in the behavior and actions of others. When someone describes you to others based on either direct or indirect exposure to you, they may say things like he is honest, sincere, highly moral, and authentic. The second and third-order effect of your actions in this case is to create the identity that people associate with you. By the way, once these second and third-order effects occur, they are not simply changed. Indeed, over time they become embedded and part of the organization's climate and culture. Of course, the reverse is true, if you are unethical, immoral, and unauthentic they too become part of the culture.

HOW LEADERSHIP CREATES THE DNA OF AN ORGANIZATION

How do the behaviors repeatedly exhibited by a leader become part of the organization's climate, culture, and DNA? If the leader continuously reinforces the importance of openness with all members of the organization, and his behavior is in line with what he says, the value of openness should be created in the climate and eventually at a deeper level in the culture. Initial evidence of its creation might be observed in the interaction I described earlier where two members of a team are arguing with each other to come up with the best solution. It may be evident to the leader that there never appears to be any surprises when things go wrong, because people are honest about admitting mistakes in this culture. Or, it may be evident in the orientation interview for a new candidate where you observe the interviewer presenting what is good about the organization and what needs to be fixed.

I previously mentioned flattened organizations, which provide an even greater challenge for leadership today with respect to the use of AARs, as well as the diffusion of leadership actions and intent, which may become a sticky part of the organization's culture. Within a steep hierarchy, information can be rapidly disseminated downward through control systems and via coordination built in by design. Of course, we know that even with a steep hierarchy in which the transmission of important information downward is suppose to occur rapidly, there is typically a shadow hierarchy that will mediate the diffusion and interpretation of information, representing a hierarchy within a hierarchy. I have found that in some flattened organizations, the hierarchies are just as steep, and do not go away, but are informal and as inhibiting if not more so than the worst organizational bureaucracies. In these supposed horizontal organizations, leadership is far more embedded or diffused throughout the organizational system making it even more difficult for leaders to speculate on the second and third-order effects. What route these effects follow is not as clear-cut in flattened hierarchies, since the channels of communication and command are much less clear-cut.

Applying an AAR as previously described, I would suspect that what would come out of the discussion if the organization was more horizontally challenged, is the idea that internal relationships really matter to achieving the best possible 360-degree customer service. Without cooperative relationships, the information that is widely disseminated will be less and less accurate. At the very start, we will have compromised the 360-degree view of the customer, limiting degree by degree what we know about that customer's needs. We are heading down toward 180 or worse!

USING GTE AS AN EXAMPLE

At GTE managers have been trained in the use of AARs to develop their workgroups. Going beyond the immediate first-order benefits of the AAR, GTE takes knowledge gained from the AAR and includes it in a knowledge repository. Using this approach, it allows others to use and reuse that information as new problems arise that are similar to those confronted in the past. AARs are structured discussions that take groups through to an immediate end point to address the situation being confronted, with the goal of helping others to work through similar situations as well. Such second-order effects require a level of cooperation and coordination, as well as sharing of information for the AAR system to work well. What we have described here is the escalation of the AAR as a microsystem used by leaders to clarify the links between intent, actions, lessons learned, and secondary action to a macrosystem that becomes part of what constitutes the total learning system of an organization.

The use of AARs at GTE was to facilitate the breakdown of hierarchical barriers by including multiple perspectives on what just happened. It also signaled people that their input was *valued.* One of the truisms that I find in organizations is that in the worst cultures people will invariably say that their input does not matter or is not valued, which causes them to become disengaged. If I could ask one question of people in an organization that I feel would tell me the most about that organization's culture, it would be, "How valued is your input in this organization?" or "Do your opinions seem to matter?" I would ask the newest to oldest member, and I am confident that I would have a very good idea based on the answers of how open the culture is, how much cooperation exists, and how much trust there is in fellow organizational members. Their responses would relate directly to how engaged they are at work, which has been shown by the Gallup Organization's research to be a very important predictor of performance, productivity, turnover, absenteeism, and ultimately commitment to an organization.

The AAR in use at GTE, as in any other organization, is also used to develop a mindset of possibilities. Recall back to our earlier discussion of possible selves. At GTE, they were using the AAR as a way of redefining the possible selves of employees. How? Your input is valued. You are responsible for observing our actions and improving upon them. You are enabled to not only observe and react to the process, but to be a stakeholder in its improvement. You are a part of the leadership system and your scope of responsibilities and how you define yourself has been expanded. You *should not* be a dependent follower dutifully waiting for orders. This is not the possible self we are trying to create in our organizations.

In the GTE AAR, as in any other, reflection occurs close to the ACTION. The reflective process is a key part of coming to understand what we have done and what the impacts are on others at the first, second and at least the third-order level, respectively. Understanding put into action can lead to continuous improvement.

The gap between action taken and understanding is bridged effectively by reflection. Shortening the bridge between action and understanding by introducing the AAR as a structured process of reflection is a very direct way to improve learning and performance. As we enter into this knowledge-based organization era, learning and performance will become increasingly closer in time.

Another important piece in the GTE AAR is the actions taken to record what just happened. Oftentimes, great leaders keep a diary or log of events that help them to look back on their own actions to reflect and determine a different course in the future. There are some leaders that do so simply to make sure they get to write their own history, which represents a very different form of perspective-taking capacity typically associated with being self-serving versus servicing the community one leads.

At GTE, they view the act of writing down these AARs as serving several important purposes. First, by writing down what happened, you are able to clarify your own thinking by clarifying what you want to convey to others. Second, recording lessons learned serves to make them more official and less likely to be forgotten and repeated in the same way in the future. In more dysfunctional cultures, I hear again and again how we repeatedly do the same old dumb things the same old dumb way. It is not an art, it is a science of dumbness we are observing here! Third, recorded lessons are much easier to share with others, long after the actual players in the AAR are gone. Sharing what was learned is a way to continuously improve what all members knew and know.

Let us think downstream now to examine what might be the third-order impact on the culture of an organization by using the GTE AAR system. First, it appears to me that the inclusion of experiences in a knowledge repository will make an organization's culture a much more open culture for future interactions. Second, if each and every member views the value of including experiences in the knowledge repository that reflect both positively and negatively on them, the culture will no doubt become more transparent over time. Third, the initial actions taken by leaders to open the system for greater coordination and cooperation will set a higher standard for inclusion in the organization. Obviously, leaders will need to be more open to challenges provided by followers. Fourth, if more transparent, then leaders must also be more authentic, meaning their values, actions, and words had better be in alignment; otherwise employees will become quickly disenchanted with the system and not disclose important information. Fifth, the type of future leaders this organization looks for and will no doubt be different than if the organization had maintained a closed culture. There are many leaders out there who are not comfortable with high levels of openness and challenge. They would not be the leaders sought after for this organization, if the AARs became as deep a part of the culture as I have previously depicted. Moreover, many leaders would self-select themselves out from becoming involved in such a challenging organizational culture, which is money in the bank as far as I am concerned.

Maybe you are saying, I thought this chapter was on reflection, meaning self-reflection on the part of the leader? It is. Yet, when I ask a leader to self-reflect it is almost always focused on the leader and someone or something else. That is the very fundamental nature of leadership, as it is about you leading someone else and is represented by some form of bilateral relationship. Self-reflection is likely oxymoronic in that it rarely occurs alone nor is it just about yourself!

SUMMARY POINTS ON SELF-REFLECTION PROCESS

Let me try to summarize the critical points that we have discussed in this chapter and how they may be applied to your development.

- At the core, reflection after action is a way of conducting learning in parallel with performing. It causes short delays, but likely the improvements in performance would counter the disadvantages associated with stopping to think for a moment about what you have just done. For your own development, identify the type of actions you want to focus on over the next month and discuss with your workgroup why you would like to use AARs to understand those actions better.
- AARs provide a process for developing and affirming what is a shared understanding of events. As processes in organizations become more complex and delivery times demanded by customers accelerate, we must be able to rapidly identify what is our shared understanding in order to execute more quickly and effectively. To use an extreme position, when everyone is in disagreement, there is no way that a unit can execute quickly, let alone accurately. So choose a particular area where you would like to improve the quality and time associated with your execution. First identify how quality will be assessed, and gather base-

line data to see where you are presently. Once you have the baseline data in hand you can use the AARs to work toward improving delivery time and the quality of execution.

- The use of reflective learning strategies is a more inclusive style of leadership; it teaches people what everyone was thinking when they were in the process of doing. It signals to people that their thinking and input is valued by the leader and organization. Start out by keeping a brief diary of events concerning what you have learned about people's thinking. Are there any patterns or trends in terms of what you have learned that would suggest to you what people were withholding prior to the introductions of the AARs?
- By consistently executing the process of reflection and highlighting its importance to the unit's development, one is able to change over time the culture associated with sharing and cooperation. Using your diary, what now gets shared that did not in the past? Or, perhaps you would like to target an area for sharing information that you can observe to see whether or not it increases over time.
- As has been true throughout our discussion of leadership, without some modest level of trust, people will not share information, nor will they record it for others to hold them accountable. A certain level of trust either contracted from the outside, or held internally in terms of beliefs must be in place for reflective learning processes to work. What is the level of trust in your unit prior to the intervention of AARs? If you do not know, collect some more baseline data.
- We also learned that the organization's leaders must clearly say that it is important to engage in such learning processes. They must visibly reward people for participating in such activities. You need to at the very least recognize the importance of participation with your words, if not the rewards you have available to distribute. Such rewards not only reinforce different behavior, they also signal to others the importance that you associate with these new behaviors and actions.
- Finally, when taking a significant action there is rarely less than a second-order impact on others or even systems. I have encouraged you to at the very least think third-order impact and to try and speculate what it might be prior to, during and after the actions are taken. By doing so, you can begin to go beyond mere speculation of how your actions will affect those people who have both direct and indirect interactions with you as a leader.

LEADERSHIP AND WISDOM

Let me reflect here on some of my own personal observations and then I will close off. When I attribute wisdom to a leader, I find that one of the facets such leaders display is their ability to derive more meaning from events that have just occurred and that most people have not observed as deeply. They appear to have insights into situations that we all lived through, but failed to observe ourselves. The insights are not only in terms of what happened but what will likely happen based on their keen observations. In my judgment such leaders build up their own knowledge repository, by reflecting on events that have occurred in their life streams. Over time, they are able to build a deeper and more expansive knowledge base that we later come to observe and label wisdom in action. Yet, if you follow the logic of this chapter on reflective learning, it is not something that is simply born into these leaders at all. It is made each and every day they take the time to understand and record just what happened. Indeed, my discussion in this chapter was all about the numerator and how to grow the numerator to be a more effective leader up close, as well as at a distance in terms of second-and third-order impact on others. Going through what I have said in this chapter, I am even more convinced that leadership is made in large part based on what you take the time to go back and learn, and then apply forward. So this is my own reflection on reflective learning processes.

Again, if you are willing to participate in a system that we have referred to here as AARs, you are being paid for what can also benefit your own development as a leader. Let us think about if you religiously used this process to continuously learn how you are doing with followers. Assume that these sessions helped shape your views of yourself and your effects on close and distant followers. If you kept track of what worked for you and others, and what did not work, and what you have to improve in terms of leadership, then leadership development has become seamless with what you had done anyhow as a leader to perform more effectively, build a more open culture, enhance cooperation, and enhance yourself. Well, it takes some energy, time, and persistence, which all happen to be associated with effective leaders. It takes the discipline to say, "I am going to start this process on Monday, and try it out for 3 months and then I'll assess my progress."

To use some literary license with a Fleetwood Mac song, "Don't stop thinking about yesterday, it will soon be here today, and reflected in tomorrow before we know it." Unless we see it and understand it the first time, it will repeat itself. When it is a success, well that is probably okay for us not to fully understand what happened. We all have a higher tolerance for not understanding success versus failure. When it is failure, it is seen as a bigger problem to address. Yet, most organizations fail at success as opposed to failure. You may now want to spend some time reflecting on what I just said.

AN EXERCISE TO GET YOU GOING ON SELF-REFLECTION

Over the next week, try to write down significant positive interactions you observe in your organization, family life, in some other social setting, or all three. Take those observations and try to group them into categories such as supportive, openness, cooperation, helping, and so forth. Out of all of the events that occurred and you observed, how many of them were the ones you coded as positive? What is your positive percentage in your organization? If you work in an organizational climate or culture that is cynical, I suspect the ratio is going to be rather low. Leadership is about increasing that ratio, and a starting point is to simply find out how much is present, where it occurs, who does it, under what circumstances, what its effects are, and so forth. By the way, you might pick how many times someone says something strange, or something funny, something sarcastic or something endearing. In essence, it does not much matter what you pick, it only matters that you are interested in spending the time observing it, and that it has some relationship to your development as a full person and leader.

USING THE AAR PROCESS

If you choose to conduct an AAR process, here are some useful guidelines to pursue: focus on a few critical performance issues at a time; conduct it either during the action or right afterward; the approach must be structured so as to identify ground truth; an important facet is to make sure multiple facets of a problem are recognized, as well as perspectives about the problem; and take learning quickly to action.

Steps

1. Review the intent before the action began.
2. What happened?

3. What exactly occurred? Why? How?
4. What were the results?
5. What have we learned?
6. Based on what we tried, and what actually happened, what did we learn?
7. What do we do now? Short-term; mid-term; and long-term?
8. Take action by applying lessons learned.
9. Tell others what you learned or teach them.

FACILITATOR'S ROLE IN THE AAR—A STRUCTURED AND PURPOSEFUL DIALOGUE

- Promote a focused, open, provocative, safe, reality-oriented exchange among team members for genuine learning to take place.
- Use the rule of objectivity in trying to uncover the facts of what occurred and in what sequence.
- AARs are a method to search for cause and effect.
- Participants must learn to listen hard to each other to make sure they get all of the facts and eventually the why.
- Climb the ladder of inference. First rung: direct observation like a videotape recording; second rung: interpretation of what happened; and third rung: shared understanding.

The overall purpose of the AAR is to develop a shared understanding of not only what happened in a given situation, but also why it happened and what could have been done differently to change the course of events. We must get people to go from what we observed to what we did, to where we will make changes to taking action again. To do that, we need to go across hierarchical levels demonstrating that input from all levels is valued. The skill of using reflection close to action may be one of the key components of the AAR. Through such reflection we promote a better understanding of ourselves, as well as others around us. We stop to realize there may be more than one layer to the behavior and intent we just observed. Experience and action provide an opportunity for continuous teaching events. By recording lessons learned, one can share experiences more widely and accelerate a learning and developmental environment on an organizational level.

7

Mistakes and Trust

This is a reflection on my part, but I often wonder about the strategic placement of articles in newspapers for effect. For example, this morning, there was one story in the paper citing how a nationwide survey of employees indicated that nearly 50% of the employees surveyed would leave their organization in a heartbeat, if a better opportunity came along. Next to that story was an article about how Cisco was paying one third of employee salaries for a year to work in a not-for-profit agency instead of laying them off outright. During the year, they could retain their benefits and be vested in Cisco stock. After that year, they would be considered again as a potential new hire. The national survey showed that compared to 1999, at the peak of the economy's long-term growth and now, the loyalty people have to their organization, was the same. Yet, the second article showed that, with some slight adaptations in your thinking, you cannot only do some good for the community, you may also signal employees that even when things are bad, you try to employ them as best you can. There is no data on how this will all work, just merely an observation and reflection.

One of the most interesting questions to ask people in an organization, which also offers you a pretty good insight into that organization's culture, is "What is a recoverable versus an unrecoverable mistake around here?" Generally, you can see in people's eyes, particularly in a low trust culture, that they have not made a clear distinction in their mind between the two. Mistakes are, well, just mistakes and should be avoided, and if they occur, you simply find out who did it. Some are pretty big, and most should simply be avoided. Considering anything as being a recoverable mistake in many organizations is simply treated as being oxymoronic. This is the no-mistakes culture type of organization.

When I ask this same question with a group of employees with a wide range of work experience, the response is almost universally the same. One person usually describes a mistake she made recently in her organization. She is typically a younger and more inexperienced employee, who describes something she avoided, as being the type of action that one could not recover from in this organization. Are you wondering what her possible self is? Good! For her, such actions would be seen as a career-defining or limiting event. Then a more experienced employee typically chimes in, indicating that the unrecoverable mistake was exactly what he had done earlier in his career. Then he describes how he has been promoted three times over the last 2 years, proving in his mind it was not an unrecoverable mistake at all. That is probably true, or maybe the standards have changed since he was a less experienced employee. One important point for these people to consider is that they should develop a shared understanding of what constitutes a recoverable and an unrecoverable mistake. It is not only important that they do so for their own development, but also for the development of the next new employee.

Another interesting context in which to have this discussion is when there is extremely high risk in terms of injury, financial, or reputation loss to an individual, group, or organization, or all of the aforementioned. The threshold for what is considered a recoverable and an unrecoverable mistake bounces around depending on the nature of the context in which one is embedded or working. Indeed, the willingness to use mistakes as part of the learning process will vary dramatically depending on the nature of the context or culture. How did what constitutes mistakes get embedded in the culture? My guess is leadership, or at least a certain form of leadership that trained people what to be afraid of, what not to do, what to avoid, and how to correct the mistake before noticed. This embedded part of the culture can be one of the most significant leadership challenges you will face in any organization. Getting people to realize that not all mistakes are to be religiously avoided is a mental mindset that will take a lot of effort to understand the root cause and how to work through it to open people up to exploration again. You cannot explore without making some mistakes. There is no map clear enough or detailed enough that will provide you with clear milestones and directions, especially when we are charting through unexplored waters. Getting people to be willing to experience mistakes is something that you must do if you are going to create an innovative, adaptive, and resilient culture.

MISTAKES AND LEARNING POTENTIAL

So why should we focus on mistakes now? As I stated earlier, to not debrief a mistake or failure is to compound it, and to create a second failure in terms of hampering future learning. Having read many biographies of world class leaders, one thing I have observed is that these people simply do not get it right the first time or oftentimes the second, third, or fourth time. They make terrible mistakes and suffer the consequences of their decisions. Yet, they also always talk about how they took their failures and translated them into the successes we associate with world-class leaders. What we read about is the leader contemplating her worst loss, and in those moments a thought or idea emerges that marks the new course and direction to be pursued. Indeed, in those dark periods of failure there is oftentimes instability and a readiness for change both in the leader and followers. It is not a bad time to make a difference and to transform and transcend the failure of the present to achieve the potential for the future. When these life-defining moments come along, will you be ready to make the choice to move forward in a new direction?

Many world-class leaders are described as being extremely persistent and resilient, planning their next great adventure in the midst of either success or failure. They simply never give up, and to be successful as a leader one must build such efficacy, or belief in one's ability to take on the challenge and to get through the most difficult ones. At the end of the day, those that continue to persist and believe in what they are doing, are generally the most successful. History supports this position again and again, particularly in the domain of leadership. Yet what is important is that you accept the failure as being on route to your ultimate success. For these outstanding leaders failure reinforces the self-concept over time. Failure does not diminish or destroy the self-concept. Indeed, failures likely develop a stronger sense of resiliency in both leaders and followers. If you can separate yourself from the failure, you will be able to address the emotional downfall of a failure from what can be learned and used in your development. This is by no means an easy challenge. You only need to think back to your last great challenge and how much of yourself you invested in that challenge to realize what I am saying here. However, what you invested in that challenge was your current self at that time; if you allow your performance to inhibit the growth of your possible selves then you are limiting your leadership potential.

Apart from failure, when you believe you are at the height of success you probably are and will go no further. My suggestion is to think that you are succeeding, regardless of how slow the pace is, and you will continue to be more successful. This goes back to viewing leadership as an evolving and emerging process.

In the early 1930s, Thomas Watson senior, who was the founder of IBM, suggested that IBM should never characterize itself as successful, but rather succeeding and of course continuously adapting to change over time. When John Akers quit IBM in its worst performance period in the history of the company, he lamented that IBM had become complacent in its *success*, which represented to Watson an end point versus an emergent process of continuously succeeding.

I was in South Africa, and attended a presentation by someone billed as a motivational speaker. His name was David, and even though I am oftentimes quite skeptical of such speakers, I did enjoy his presentation. At the beginning he discussed the topic of the day, which was transformational leadership. He said that *transformational* meant to transcend where one was to where one wanted to be. I said earlier that I referred to this as a deep perspective shift in a book title I never used! He described how as a young man he was a part-time employee of the South African correctional services, better known as an inmate. While growing up, he had challenged the system of Apartheid and all other South African systems at that time, which landed him in jail more than once. However, he told the audience that at one moment during his incarceration when he was really down, he made a decision that he was going to transcend the situation that he was in to achieve a dream, which was to become a PhD some day. He was speaking to us that day as a Dr. and was living the dream he had predicted he could transcend to at some future point in his life stream. He had decided to change the course of his life stream under those most difficult of circumstances. I still wonder why leadership development has to be so difficult.

He was inspirational and motivating because he turned his mistakes into life opportunities, or as he said, he transcended those mistakes to transform himself. Okay, imagine for the moment that he was a child born to an aristocratic family. He had gone to the best private schools in South Africa and over time he had gotten his PhD. The same achievement embedded within a different context lacks the depth of meaning as does turning failures or mistakes into a life opportunity. For the French Army fighting the British, it was Joan of Arc's ability to turn an impending failure into a great victory that created her legend and transcended her peasant status to sainthood.

CREATING THE GLOW OF LEADERSHIP

Turning mistakes into opportunities is what oftentimes builds what we later associate as the charisma of a leader. Recall that we do not find who we really are until we have really been challenged. It is the against-all-odds notion that the person emerges as being successful at what he sets out to do. In Western cultures such as the United States, this scenario is played out again and again, and builds the legends or leadership heroes we come to revere. It is an archetype in our culture. It is represented in Abe Lincoln, who came from poverty to attain the most powerful position in the United States, or J. K. Rowling, who wrote the books about Harry Potter and changed the reading habits of a whole generation, including my son. Here is this single mother who each and every day goes to a coffee house to sit somewhere with her baby to write a book that will ignite a generation's interest in reading again. We also see this scenario played out in inner city schools where the principal takes the worst crime-ridden neighborhood and turns the school into the best schoolhouse in the region.

The same scenario is rooted also in the process of invention. Companies such as 3M have built their legendary capacity for innovation on the foundation of mistakes. Johnson and Johnson took the Tylenol event, which was a mistake that was not caused by their own actions, and translated that tragic event into reaffirming the moral center of the company. Southwest Airlines' business strategy was fundamentally based on a mistake. Starting out in business Southwest Airlines only had enough capital to purchase three planes and they needed four to be profitable. Herb Kelleher and his employees could have simply crunched the numbers and said that it was not feasible to launch this airline. Instead, they decided that three planes could be as effective as four at the end of the day, if you could reduce the turnaround time on the ground significantly enough to create "a fourth plane." They did so, and went on to become the most admired and most profitable airline in history, in large part based on their ability to efficiently turn planes around at the gate.

Firestone and, indirectly, Ford Motor Company began recalling over 6 million tires that were linked to the tragic deaths of customers due to serious defects in those tires. The CEO of Ford, an Australian, was on T.V. in two separate spots explaining what Ford was doing to assure the safety of its customers and at the same time was taking the opportunity to articulate Ford's core values regarding protecting the safety of its customers. A year after the story broke both companies were locked in a court battle challenging each other over cause, as the customers still waited on the sidelines. How admired will these companies be after all of the blaming is over?

In two studies we completed 10 years ago, we found a very common pattern among the more effective transformational leaders. Transformational leaders are those types of leaders who are highly trusted, inspiring, intellectually stimulating, and oriented toward developing followers to their full potential. In one study, we interviewed highly rated transformational leaders and they described their parents as consistently challenging them to the extreme boundaries of performance where they then failed. When asked what happened after the failure, they said their parents worked with them to figure out where the mistake was rooted and what needed to be done to be successful. Then, they were told to do it again and again until they were successful. We do not know what we can do until asked to do it again. Effective parents do AARs just like effective leaders. Effective parents also become highly trusted for doing what is best for their children. The same is true of effective leaders.

In a similar study, we asked people to fill out surveys about the life stream events that had contributed to their leadership styles. For those leaders who were rated by others as highly effective, they typically described their high school years as going from one leadership experience to another, oftentimes not in formal leadership roles where they typically made a lot of mistakes. Yet, one of the patterns that clearly emerged was that the mistakes became a route for being more effective leaders because they spent time trying to understand why they made a mistake, so it could be corrected. Again, it sounded like an AAR and debrief in vivo.

Mistakes are one of the most powerful learning events for leadership development. We typically take mistakes more seriously than successes, so why not leverage them for learning and improvement? However, in many organizations and cultures, it is not easy to make a mistake that you can learn from and then develop yourself. The culture in many organizations is typically hard wired to avoid mistakes, and to emphasize success through its reward systems. In trips to Singapore, I have found this to be reflective of the overall national culture and in some ways Confucian cultures in general. Let me explain this observation, as anytime one makes a comment on an entire culture they are at grave risk of making a mistake.

WHEN IT IS TIME TO MAKE A MISTAKE

I know the popular and simplistic image of Singapore is that if you make a mistake like spitting out gum on the street you will be caned. The popular image of Singapore underestimates the enormous complexity of the social system that has been created and its success since 1950. As someone said to me on a recent trip to Singapore, this is a country that did the industrial revolution in 15 versus 100 years. Now that is improved cycle time! Yet, during a trip to Singapore in July 2000, there was a concerted effort underway from the Prime Minister's office on down in government, to encourage Singaporeans to make more mistakes! Well, they called it being more entrepreneurial, and also being more of a learning culture, but in many references there was attention to being more flexible about making and learning from mistakes. In the past, challenging the system was an unrecoverable mistake in Singapore. Now the country's leaders were realizing that only by challenging the system, which they had a large hand in creating, could it be reinvented and ultimately transformed. Only by challenging the system would young leaders emerge who would help create the new economy for Singapore, even though the old economy was at this writing still incredibly successful. With 3 million people on a little island with no resources, simply complying with the way things ought to be done was now seen as a recipe for failure.

A critical question for Singapore is how do you mandate that mistakes are now okay, when my possible self does not include that code or program? Which mistakes are okay and which are not? How can you get Singaporeans to realistically make the distinction between recoverable and unrecoverable mistakes when they have been taught since 1950 to err in the direction of no mistakes? They have been taught to be quiet, be precise, obedient, and at all costs to be successful. I am back to the challenge I posed to you personally as a leader, if you ever take over a unit that has been led by someone who taught your new followers to avoid making mistakes.

If you are from a culture that confronts authority, consider the following notion: In Singapore, if there is not a sign indicating you cannot make a U-turn, then you cannot. Read that again. The absence of a sign means do not make a U-turn. You have to be told exactly what to do. In many cultures, the absence of a sign means do it, and in some other cultures even the presence of a sign, for some, still means do it!

People in societies like Singapore have reservations about making a difference in terms of opinions, decisions, and actions, which comes from being afraid to make mistakes. You are very unlikely to make a difference without making mistakes. Very! Every great scientist out there knows that to make the greatest discoveries in their respective fields required many, many systematic mistakes, which we call experimentation. Benjamin

Franklin noted this by saying that the truth is out there, but it may take us many failures to come across it.

In Singapore and indeed in many organizations that I have worked in, people have been repeatedly reinforced for staying in line with what the leadership expects you to do. Then one day, the leadership changes direction dramatically, and it is likely to take at least a generation to fully make the turn in attitude stick. Fortunately for Singapore the need to transform what they believe is possible coincides with a generation already coming into the work world, which like their Western counterparts, is now challenging the leadership of all organizations and institutions. Also, having an authoritarian type government has its advantages, in that you can get people aligned around the message pretty efficiently, but not necessarily deeply in terms of a shift in perspective. You can get their attention, which is no trivial matter, but can you get their trust to make a fundamental change in perspective about learning and mistakes?

The time between times that we are in represents a quiet revolution where many of the younger generation are again questioning the institutions in which their parents worked as not being in line with their needs, expectations, and aspirations. Although this is true of each generation trying to define its own niche position, there are additional dynamics that make the transitions in this time period and generation a bit more revolutionary.

Part of the revolution has been fueled by the inversion of authority in many families, as younger people engage the new information technology that is advancing our economy and changing the dynamics in literally every aspect of our lives. Up until the present generation, the older generation mentored the younger generation and frequently made it possible for them to be successful. Now, it is quite common for the youngest to be teaching the oldest how to stay connected with today's technologies and be successful. For example, Jack Welch when at GE, as well as former President Clinton, each had a younger mentor teaching them how to use new technologies. Welch mandated that his senior managers be mentored one day a week by a younger GE employee with strong technology skills, in a reverse mentoring program. The goal was to make sure the senior GE managers understood how technology will change business processes and products. He also in one fell swoop eliminated the common problem of the older employee being embarrassed to ask the younger employee for help. He did this by inverting the leadership hierarchy in a way that is naturally occurring in societies around the world whether mandated by the CEO or not.

In a recent economic summit of nations in North and South America, one of the main items on the agenda was how to push the Internet into every home and business to empower people at all levels to engage in this new economy and, I might add, distribution of power. Uganda's leaders have committed to putting a PC and Internet line in every home to eliminate the digital divide in their country. The city of Houston recently set as its challenge to provide access to the Internet for its entire population. The insertion of these communication conduits will fundamentally change the distribution of leadership in these locations, as we will discuss later on under the heading of e-leadership.

A TIME BETWEEN TIMES

The Y generation, like the economy, probably needed this correction that occurred with the dot bombs to put things in perspective. I wonder how this will effect that generation's view of making and learning from mistakes. Success that is sustainable usually takes time to build and maintain. Sure, there are always opportunities for quick successes, especially when one century is ending and another beginning. The world was perhaps compelled toward a goal of getting something done before the last century ended. Now we have another 100 years ahead of us, so it may be time to pace ourselves again. Moreover, in periods of rapid innovation and transformation we create capacities that far exceed our ability to use them in a general population sense. Some reports indicate that companies like Cisco and Nortel are hurting financially because fiberoptic networks were built with capacities that far exceeded our current ability to use them. In one recent report, it was indicated that we are using about 2% of the capacity in these networks, so why would companies want to build more of them?

There were so many unique factors coming together in the last 10 years, that for all of them to fit together and to sustain success would truly have been a remarkable event. Most futurists in the early 1990s did not even consider the Internet in their predictions, globalization was still way off, the intrusion of technology in our lives was just emerging, and the next huge wave to hit us in biotechnology and engineering is still but a ripple in a vast ocean of potential. The world's economy took a break, it made some readjustments, and the real smart companies are now building capacity for the next run. The dumb ones are lopping out intellectual capital to meet the bottomline estimates for the next quarter. Dumb downsizing in 1994 was shown to be ineffective in an extensive study completed by

Cascio at the University of Denver, and it will no doubt be shown to be ineffective again.

Cascio demonstrated that companies who simply cut head count never recovered to their predownsizing performance levels when tracked over a 5-year period. Companies that used layoffs to strategically restructure operations recovered more quickly and significantly exceeded their predownsizing period of performance. Whether they have regained the trust of their workforce, or whether they lost a brilliant idea to another company as it walked out the door is a completely different issue not yet addressed. Loyalty goes out the door with those who stay and those who are asked to leave. There is no clear line that management can draw for retaining loyalty or when, say, 10,000 people are asked to leave. Also, to be off by 10,000 people in terms of the workforce required to complete what needs to be done, seems in my opinion to be an unrecoverable mistake that the senior leaders should fall on their swords over.

Teaching people to lead in this interesting and critical period of transition now must take into consideration the fact that one cohort of employees will respond without question, but also without the same level of trust, while the other will question almost anything because this has become part of that generation's collective possible selves and human code. In my own classes at the university, I have oftentimes cited a particular recent study's findings, only to be challenged by a student in my class with a more recent study that she pulled off the Internet that morning. This has made teaching so much more interesting and dynamic to have followers who are alive!

I spent a weekend with 50 medical school deans in Puerto Rico a year ago. One of the challenges the medical profession is facing is how to teach new and old medical doctors to handle being challenged by younger doctors, nurses, patients, consumer groups, insurance companies, lawyers, and legislators. With access to the latest research findings, and Web sites such as WebMD, more and more people are questioning these authority figures who may have never been questioned in the past. The web is an empowering mechanism that is linking peer to peer, leader to follower, community to community, and country to country, in ways that will fundamentally change the way we teach, work, and lead. The professions that were least questioned are at the front end of this change process and are being severely and in many cases appropriately challenged about mistakes that were avoidable. The same is true for the despot dictators who no longer have a lock on the press. Information builds power, and access to the Internet is changing how power is distributed in economic, social, and political arenas. The beneficiaries are those people who have not been part of the right networks, caste, social groups, or all three. Although the Internet is not accessible to a 90% of the world population, once it is in place it does not discriminate. It can uplift an entire community with information in ways thought unimaginable even 5 years ago. In so doing, it will challenge the very foundation upon which many societies have built their leadership systems.

This pattern of challenging people in leadership positions now runs across all sectors of our society in the United States, and has been growing overseas in countries around the world. Why? It has to do in part with an increasing level of vulnerability among all leaders and it has to do in part with the title of this chapter: "Mistakes and Trust."

THE PENDULUM OF TRUST

If we could look back quickly over the last 250 years and scan newspaper articles of leaders, would there be a trend toward leaders being less trustworthy? I think the answer would be yes, but I do not think that leaders necessarily are becoming more morally challenged. It may seem fair to say their mistakes are more obvious and more transparent to the public. What appears to be happening throughout the western world at least, and certainly in many eastern cultures, is a deeper awareness of what leaders do right and what they do wrong. Part of this exposure is occurring due to the mass media exposure that leaders must now function in to lead.

In my life stream, President Nixon's resignation was a very significant leadership event. I attribute a lot of the decline in how leaders are viewed in our society as being associated with his presidency's mistakes, some more unrecoverable than others, such as his racial epithets. I also believe it was significant that it was such a low level crime. Supporting a common thief simply denigrated the charisma that goes along with the office of the presidency. It was not even an elegant or a sophisticated crime, like the one attributed to President Reagan's arms-for-contras scandal. In some ways, that event enhanced Reagan's charisma over time. Similarly, when President Clinton admitted having an affair with Monica Lewinsky, he brought to the foreground his human frailty and subtracted from the high standards we still expect our Presidents to live up to both in their professional and personal lives. The same has become increasingly true for President Kennedy as more information is revealed about his affairs while president.

On the one hand, after the Watergate break in was uncovered, the press was much more enabled to go after the most powerful leader in our country. Also, Nixon had taped his oval office conversations, which provided an even darker glimpse into the inner workings of the White House. He was not the first to tape conversations in the oval office, by any means. And presidents have lied to us before, but now the president was caught on tape lying or at least presumed to be lying when key portions of the tapes were missing. Once President Nixon was exposed, I believe we began to question much more earnestly the actions of all of our political leaders, and it bled over to other areas as well. Early in my life stream, I was taught not to question people in authority, but after President Nixon, and the lies the Vietnam War promulgated, I felt like a fool not to question leaders. So the balance changed from being foolish to question to simply being fooled by those in authority if we did not question their intentions, actions, and words. Some will say today that we have set an unreasonable standard for leaders to live up to in both public and private life. I am yet to be convinced that the standard is too high for the leader, although I do admit that the standards applied to their families is simply overdone.

I am still left wondering what effects President Clinton's statements on national television denying that he had a relationship with Monica Lewinsky have had on the trust we place in our presidents. He lied directly to an entire nation, and I wonder how that will affect my children's life streams and views of leadership over the next 10 years.

While taking a tour of the Franklin D. Roosevelt monument in Washington, DC, our family came to the end of a beautiful walk through history with many great quotes from FDR. The guide asked us to notice where FDR was sitting along with his dog next to him. Where was Eleanor? She was around the corner standing alone and facing the White House. Why? FDR died with his mistress in Georgia, and not only did Eleanor have to deal with his affair throughout her marriage, she also had to deal with it in his death. Yet, FDR's personal life did not affect his ability to lead in his time, and most Americans probably had no clue that one of the greatest presidents in history, or at least in the 20th century, had committed adultery.

There is no doubt that the bar has shifted upward in terms of what is required of leaders to build trust, as well as the impact their mistakes have on our trust in them. It is also important to keep in mind that the height of the bar varies across different cultures. For your development as a leader, you need to be aware the bar has been moved up. And to be fair, it is not only President Nixon's fault; much of the trust that employees had in their leaders prior to the great downsizing decisions of the 1980s and 1990s has been collectively deteriorating. I must say to those leaders who lament the lack of commitment in today's younger workforce, what did you expect when you role-modeled for them that commitment and loyalty had nothing to do with whether you were axed or not from your company? It simply became irrelevant because of employer's reactions to short-term corrections that did not pay off in the long run anyhow. Until recently, many of these same employers were in the war for talent and spent millions on signing bonuses to figure out how to meet hiring quotas. We will pay billions more to restore the trust that was lost, and we are still at least one generation away from being successful in this endeavor.

The downsizing across the hi-tech industry sector is still continuing. The Dell corporation recently fired a number of employees for the first time in the company's history. Michael Dell commented that he was very distraught over this decision. He should be! All of the evidence accumulated throughout the early 1990s indicated that downsizing is dumbsizing. It corrects the balance sheet in terms of numbers, and it completely throws the workforce out of balance and erodes whatever trust has been built. I would love to see a downsizing that started from the top-down! I think such action might even have a positive impact on trust. It may surprise you to know that Toyota has never had a layoff.

A GROWING NEED FOR TRANSPARENCY AND MORE INFORMATION

Part of the transformation occurring on a global basis that I have previously noted is also certainly attributable to the rapid growth of the Internet, which has provided people in even the worst totalitarian regimes with contradictory data. The era of the traditional totalitarian regime is coming to a close as information that is more widely available challenges their informational grip on their countries. This is also occurring within organizations that have been led from the top, limiting access to information. Such organizations like the totalitarian regime are losing the battle in trying to control information. It can no longer be controlled in the traditional sense in terms of limiting what information people receive. Certainly, information can still be controlled by the use of manipulation and impression management, but even here access to alternative sources of information makes the amount of effort to control information far more expensive then in the past. Indeed, it has never been cheaper to simply be transparent and honest with people in your organization, which are the basic foundations for building deep trust. My colleagues and I would call this authentic leadership.

Hence, part of the reason for the rapid democratization of the world is the greater availability of information to people to make informed choices. It is also partly due to the fact that the Internet is marketing a culture, which is more appealing to a generation of new and emerging employees who want to participate in the global gold rush that occurred since 1994. I am not suggesting this is either good or bad, but merely observing a trend that offers a huge opportunity to influence the next generation coming into positions of leadership in organizations. As the nature of followers changes so must leadership.

One of the reasons why China's leadership initially did not allow its citizens to get on the World Wide Web was a very realistic fear that the information they as a government provided to its people would be inconsistent with what people would find on the web, which is not uncommon at all in more democratic societies. They even went so far as to create an internal World Wide Web, which was restricted to use within China, which grew to 5 million users and then collapsed on its own hypocrisy once people realized its artificial boundaries.

Today, the Chinese are coming on to the Internet at a very rapid pace, and the government is concerned that people are turning to rogue Web sites for the news versus the official news agencies. They do so because such sites have become more credible to a population weary of being told what the government wants them to know. The same pattern is occurring around the globe as well as in the United States, where the main and traditional news agencies are struggling to keep an audience. Not all of our news is veridical either, if you sense some jingoism in my remarks. The big difference between a democratic society and a totalitarian regime is its tolerance for discrepancies, inconsistencies, and multiple sources of information.

On the upside, almost everything is more open to challenge and inquiry today, which raises the bar for leaders to be more transparent with their intentions and actions. Leaders today have to be more vulnerable in their openness with followers to sustain trust. Being closed to outside inquiry presumably means guilty until proven innocent given the recent history of cover-ups. So here is the challenge as I see it today for leaders wanting to lead others. First, you must be completely open to outside inquiry and comfortable with making your positions open to challenge by others. This is true in part because the base rate for disclosure of sensitive information has been lowered. It has also occurred because people feel more enabled with the additional information they have available to challenge leaders, as the students in my class do more often today than 10 years ago. I should say North American students as many other students still do not challenge me openly in class, but they are making progress by using e-mail after class to politely challenge me when I have my facts wrong. This appears to be a small step in the right direction, which will no doubt spread over time to face-to-face interactions across different cultures on a global basis.

A more suspicious and informed follower is changing the balance in the leadership equation throughout the world. In our time between times, we are adjusting to this change in a variety of different ways. At one end, the dinosaurs try to keep people from getting information that would contradict their official positions, and we know from history that simply will not work. Since Guttenberg's printing press, this has been a losing strategy and will be even more so with the digital printing press.

At the other end of the spectrum are companies like Whole Foods that put every aspect of their company on the net. They disclose budgets, salaries, all decisions, etc. I continually ask leaders to be more vulnerable to seek out challenges and constructive conflict and to earn trust incrementally by demonstrating through complete transparency that there is a one-to-one relationship between your actions and intentions. This is the essence of being viewed as an authentic leader. Yet, even with totally great intentions it is unfortunately not simple. Let me explain.

President Clinton was asked prior to the 2000 Democratic National Convention how he has used polls in terms of leading others. He responded by saying that he used them to determine if the American public was accepting the truth as he presented it to them. I took this as a much more sophisticated position than he has been accused of taking with polling, where his critics say that he has used polls to decide on a course of action or when not to take action. It is more sophisticated because it clearly shows that today we are moving into an age of sophisticated forms of impression management. This age has been with us forever of course, and even Machiavelli discussed its use by leaders in *The Prince*. Yet, it has become much more sophisticated and more exacting, and I am afraid this will make some leaders far more dangerous than we have seen in the past. How? Today, we have much more sensitive indicators of what people think and feel. For the last 90 years in psychology, we have worked to develop such measures and we are getting better at it as we learn over time from our mistakes. Moreover, we have available to us many, many secondary sources of data that we can now quickly cull through with sophisticated programs to examine what was said, when it was said, and what patterns of interactions occurred based on what was said. Grocery stores now scan their data bases to see which products are purchased when and by whom, so they know when to promote a particular product, to a particular client, and at a particular point in the week.

Let me go back to a simple example I mentioned earlier. I was reviewing the usage of a Web site and examined who chose which page to review first, how many times that was chosen first, by whom, etc. As we become more interconnected in the digital age, it is relatively easy to track patterns in our behavior on a grand scale. Let me give you a local example. In my academic work, I have used various groupware systems to set up virtual team interactions on cases, projects, etc. Some faculty track the usage of each team or student on whatever basis they choose to use it, such as by session, or even based on minute-to-minute online interactions. When a team complains that one member is not contributing to the project, it is easy to see whether that person has been logging into and contributing to the virtual discussions. Of course, there are clear issues of privacy and confidentiality dilemmas embedded in this discussion; however, our political leaders are now more than ever vulnerable to questioning and oversight because information is more available. And if information is more available, people will use it to formulate their opinions and decisions.

Now the concern should not be whether data will be collected, as that is a foregone conclusion. The concern is how such data will be used to influence others. This issue will be one of the major issues confronting leaders over the next 25 years. It includes data on the genetic composition of an employee, how much time they are logged into a system, what they review on the web, who they interact with at work, and where they like to visit on vacations.

Recently, a case was brought to court by a group of nurses, who worked at hospital that required them to wear electronic badges that could track their every movement in the organization. The hospital was using this information to see if the nurses were where they were supposed to be throughout the day, and the nurses were claiming that this technology and its use violated their right to privacy under the U.S. Constitution.

Hence, what has been true for exposing our leaders to greater public scrutiny is true for all of us to a large extent today. So what should we do? It is simple, just do what is the right thing in your judgment, and be completely transparent about why you are doing it. The right thing throughout history, if you are unsure, is doing what you can do for the good of the group you are working with at that time and the next, on into the future. I know this is much easier said than done in a complex world where even the best intentions can be misinterpreted by others who simply do not trust leaders anymore!

Then my second suggestion is to wear them down and be persistent in linking your intentions to your actions. Being more inclusive and involving more of those questioning followers in how you think and decide, will help them to believe that what you said and what you did were in line with your intentions. It is like releasing to the press in advance through anonymous sources what you intend to do anyhow. However, I am suggesting that you drop the anonymous source of the leak and be transparent. The data will make you transparent whether you like it or not, so the choice as I see it is how best to be transparent using face-to-face and e-based strategies for interacting with others. This is one way of building conditional trust, in which people know the basis of your actions. Over time such trust can morph into deeper relational trust, which is a much more resilient form of trust.

Conditional trust is formed based on the reliable connection between your words and actions. You build conditional trust based on your consistency in executing agreements. Relational trust is built on conditional, but at a much deeper level. It is where your followers, peers, or leader come to trust you, not the conditions that guide your work and execute agreements. You have become the source of trust, because you have demonstrated over time your character that people identify with, and hopefully emulate breeding a trusting culture. With conditional trust, the source of trust is the contract and fulfilling its expectations.

To manage the impression of transparency versus to simply do it is more complicated and the risk of failure is way too high today with the broad availability of information. You have a choice, you can be a very sophisticated liar or you can get to ground truth. There is little if any residual trust associated with sophisticated liars, and even when they are telling the truth, one is still cautious about believing them. Conversely, with someone who works at being consistently honest and open with others, there is oftentimes the residual trust that helps them to execute decisions and actions more efficiently. Where would you estimate your residual trust index is at this point in time with your followers, peers, clients, supervisors, or all of the aforementioned?

Since this is a book about developing leadership, I cannot leave this discussion without some suggestions for actions that you can take. Yet, I also want to emphasize that what we are talking about here does not occur overnight. It is not a style you dress up and put on when needed. It represents the accumulation of people's perceptions and impressions of you as an individual, as being credible and trustworthy, which starts by building a conditional basis for trust.

Here are the top 10 ways to build and maintain trust, which are in many cases based on research in this area.

1. Deliver on all of your agreements or explain why you could not meet the agreement, and how you will take care of the situation. Do not miss one agreement, not one, especially when you are first building relationships. Overtime, you will mess up on some, but the residual trust you build up will be there to keep the relationship you have with others positive. Ed Hollander many years ago called these a leader's idiosyncratic credits, which in difficult times are credits a leader can bank on, and I mean literally.
2. Be absolutely clear about your expectations with others, to the point where they joke with you that they have heard you say what is expected enough. Be absolutely clear and transparent with what you expect of yourself.
3. Take responsibility for all of your mistakes, and err in the direction of taking responsibility for other's mistakes. You are in a leadership role, or will be, so if you are successful you will get more of the credit than you probably deserve. This is called the romance of leadership. If you fail, then take more responsibility for that too.
4. Realize that what you say to your inner circle or in-group (and most leaders have an in-group and out-group) will eventually be translated to the out-group. Make sure the message you wanted to communicate is the message that actually got to your most distant follower. Repeat everything that is really important for you to convey to others in your words, writings, and especially in your behavior. Then go around and check what was heard by others who report directly and indirectly to you, especially those people who are at a distance from you.
5. When a problem arises get to the source and talk to the person about it. Encourage others to get to the source, or to get help to get

to the source. Nothing builds mistrust faster than having spin doctors conveying messages that should be done directly by you.

6. Spend time working toward ground truth using some form of AAR and feedback system. The act of discussing and coming to agreement on what constitutes ground truth is a step forward toward building trust in others. To do AARs, you must also work on the value of maintaining openness with each other.

7. You should discuss what represents a recoverable and unrecoverable mistake with followers, peers, and your leader. This should be an ongoing dialogue especially with new employees, who are the most vulnerable in that they do not know what ground truth is in your organization.

8. Identify one core value that is central to what you believe in most strongly, and tell people this is your most important core value. Live every single day reinforcing that value in the eyes of others. Pick only one to start with and be sure you are successful demonstrating that core value! The greater the number the less chance you have of being seen as consistent.

9. Spend time getting to know the hopes and desires of people who work with you and for you. Show concern for their basic higher order needs, particularly when they are most vulnerable. People come to trust each other based on the observations they have of you during their most difficult times. Be there when people need you; it is well worth your time and investment of energy. These are moments where trust is built in an accelerated way, or lost. Be ready to sacrifice time for the newest employees, who are still forming their possible selves in your organization.

10. When you do violate someone's trust either through your actions or at least in their eyes, then work it out directly and quickly. Bring it out into the open with them so they know that you know what the violation was about. Move on with your actions, NOT words. Forget words here except to say, "I am sorry" and "I will fix it." That is all you should say, and then get on with the actions you need to deliver. Frankly, it may not work, but it is the right thing to do. I was watching a tape of the Blue Angels pilots, and during a debriefing session one pilot who had made a minor mistake, described it, and said, "I'll fix it." Everyone else nodded as though they trusted he would fix it. "Fix it, and move on."

The message I wanted to leave you with is that it is easier to do the right thing first versus to recover after the fact. The energy on the upside is always less than the energy it takes to recover, and when you are recovering you are not moving forward as quickly. To practice what I am preaching here, I have been at number 10. The actions I took were unrecoverable. However, I can only build the future versus change what I did in the past. Making the past perfect is not a strategy. The people who are reading this, whose trust I violated, know what I mean, and if not, they should know I am still working on being cast whole and trying always to fix it.

CHANGING PEOPLE CHANGING LEADERSHIP

Let me add another challenge for you to consider in your leadership development portfolio. Given the rapid globalization of this world, and the interconnectedness afforded to many of us via technology, the groups that we work with, teach, live next door to, and socialize with have become increasingly more diverse. The challenges for building trust and being more transparent are much more difficult today as we work with more diverse groups, over time, over distance, and across vastly different cultures. As Gardner (personal communication) said when asked in an interview shortly before his death about leading today, "It's a tougher game."

I am a white male, and when I walk into a group in some other cultures and discuss leadership, I am certain that some of my words are interpreted based on the source—me. If I believe that this is true, it is likely going to have an effect on some of the things I say, or how I say them to various groups. Let me offer several examples.

I was in Washington, DC meeting with a group of leadership scholars and practitioners to plan a project. During our introductions, one woman went into her past, explaining that as a Hispanic woman she had overcome very great odds to be successful in her career. Later on in our discussion, I made a comment about how leadership development is a strategic process and to develop leadership you had to change the context in which leadership was developed. The woman I mentioned reacted to me, saying that if she had waited for the context to be ready, she would never have had the career successes she enjoys. I believe her comment was motivated in part by the fact that I had said what I said being a white male.

In fact, I fully agreed with her point of view about the present and the past. Women of color have had to act heroically to achieve success in their careers. No doubt. However, I told her that in terms of the future, I would like to have fewer heroes like her, not more! I added that I want the context in business and elsewhere to be a place where your performance, not heroism makes the difference. That would be a world where all people are judged on merit versus heroic acts, and to accomplish this world we must strategically change the leadership in our organizations to support developing each and every individual to his or her full potential. Over this past year, I have stayed in continuous contact with her, sharing my ideas, experiences, and most importantly my dreams. She is getting to know me in terms of what I value and what I consider important in life. I hope I am not just a white male anymore.

In another setting, I had an Asian student who for nearly a year never corrected my mispronunciation of his name. In his words, who was he to correct me, because I was his superior. In many instances, I have had female managers and researchers question my understanding of the leadership issues confronted by women. This occurs even though I have published studies and written extensively on this topic.

Recently, in a meeting with two educational faculty members, one faculty member said to me, people in management look at leadership that way, like on General Motor's assembly line, but in educational institutions leadership is different. I have never been on a GM assembly line, and I have probably worked in more school districts than the typical educational professor; yet, she had an image of me and that was what guided her response, which in my opinion was totally wrong, but in her opinion it was who I was to her at that time. I cannot ignore the frame of reference she was using. I can get angry, I can attack it, or I can understand how it is affecting her perceptions of ground truth, move ahead, and fix it.

I have done a lot of work in Italy, and simply because my last name is Avolio, there is frequently a positive halo that I will understand more deeply the culture I am working in. This may be true, but my father was from Palermo, in the Southern part of Italy, and the North and South are culturally very different. I was also brought up by a Jewish mother, who knew as much as I did about Italian culture! Thus, my cultural background is not so deeply rooted in Italian culture, as someone perhaps who was brought up by two first-generation Italian Americans. Nevertheless, the assumptions that people make about me, and how they impact on me, certainly affect my behavior and theirs too based on their perceptions of ground truth!

We carry into the room how we look, what group we belong to, what color our skin is, and what accent we have in our voice. It is what we walk out of the room with in terms of other people's perceptions of us that is what this book is all about. It is where all of the hard work lies and what building trust is all about in terms of leadership development. Again, this all gets hard when one goes from description to emotion. However, it is at the extremes of emotion where profoundly influential leadership has always been tested throughout history.

We have the most incredible opportunity in the United States, to take what is quickly becoming the most diversified culture on earth and show through our leadership how best it can be integrated—fully. We are perhaps best enabled to accomplish this level of integration because we have a single and very important core value called liberty, which means that everyone has the right to express themselves, and to be different. Of course there is a gap between theory and practice. However, I think we are incredibly lucky here in the United States that the founders chose this as a core value, as it positions this country to accomplish something incredible, which I have referred to before and comes from what African humanistic thinkers call unity through diversity. This is the core challenge for all organizations and societies. The challenge is to have enough requisite diversity to keep the organization, community, and society vibrant, interesting, challenging, and developing. Like a genetic pool, total unity leads to stupidity. Diversity is what underlies the great changes we make when an entrepreneur comes along with a totally different way of thinking to challenge the way we have done business. In the more traditional sense, it also occurs when we bring together the best aspects of different cultures to create a culture that is far greater than the sum of its parts. However, please realize that in doing so, trust is a hard thing to obtain and there will be tons of mistakes and misunderstandings along the way.

Today, I live in an empire called the United States. Certainly throughout history we have learned that no empire has been successfully led. Could the leaders of the British Empire have imagined what would have occurred from the late 1800s to the late 1900s in terms of their position in the world? I suspect not. I suspect the same is true for the United States. However, there may be one key difference with the United States versus earlier empires, which may help transform the world and the United States itself.

The history of the United States was that you came from somewhere else to the United States, because there were supposedly greater opportunities here to be pursued. Although there is also a caste system in the United States, people do move to the top of its society not necessarily based just on family membership, although that can be a tremendous asset. There is in practice in the United States a form of equal finality with regard to the courses of action one can take to be successful. Some make it to the top based on achievements in education. Some make it to the top based on luck and being in the right location. Some make it to the top by working hard and making a success of their business. Some make it to the top by taking a great idea, getting someone else to believe in it, and invest in it over time. Some make it to the top based on physical determination and athletic capabilities. There are more routes to the top in this increasingly diversified culture, and therefore what you see at the top has greater diversity, although it is still not enough, if one just looks at how many women CEOs there are of the Fortune 500 companies. I think it is still three, one is the CEO of Hewlett Packard and the others were recently appointed at Xerox and Lucent. I suspect that 10 years from now, the number of women at the top at least in terms of industry, is going to change dramatically given the different routes to success and it will no doubt change the challenges for leadership and followership forever.

The United States currently transforms more people from a broader range of cultures into successes, which should be the goal for any organization that is interested in sustaining long-term growth and success. This capacity may also sustain the success of the United States itself over time, and perhaps to a point where it is no longer needed. What do I mean? The United States has a great opportunity to be the global experiment for the world, which demonstrates that by accelerating the assimilation of the broadest range of cultures, a community remains smart, vibrant, adaptive, and successful. The empire fades from the screen and a great federation of cultures emerges.

Understanding how people differ from each other will become a core competency required of every leader in every top organization. It will not be a program on diversity. It will be a hard-wired capability that will be a prerequisite for success in every organization, in every market, in every educational institution, and in every family.

We have a window of opportunity today to demonstrate what will constitute the global leader of tomorrow. There is still some trust that what we have begun here is exportable to other nations, who also want to build more open democratic societies. The question I have is how can we manage this position of great influence that we have as a society? It is a question that I am afraid that other empires did not ask or asked themselves too late. For my children's sake and my future grandchildren, I am trying to ask that question today. Once the empire loses the trust of its people, it is at point where it can no longer sustain itself. I am using the word *empire* to get your attention.

What I am exploring at the national level also applies quite directly to global corporations. They too have a unique opportunity to be a positive and trusted player in the communities in which they operate. For an organization to be sustainable it too must understand its core value, and it too must have actions that are in line with words. Never before has trust been so relevant to maintaining a strategic competitive advantage. In some ways, never has it been more fragile given the transparency and authenticity required of leadership.

You may be asking, and legitimately so, "Why is he getting into all of this stuff?" The truth is that it affects my thinking on leadership every day. We are all in a very important period of time in terms of how we lead others. It is when you are at the top that you are best positioned and probably best resourced to make fundamental changes, but it is likely the thing that most successful people, organizations, and societies fail to do. Let me give you an example of an individual who decided differently about what to question about his success.

At age 24, Tiger Woods has become, in the minds of most golfers and certainly the general public, one of the greatest golfers in history. Passing through an airport one evening, I caught a glimpse of a magazine that said, "the best of all times?" Perhaps there is now only one ahead of him and he still is out there hitting away on the links, by the name of Jack Nicklaus. In fact, in a recent tournament Tiger Woods got to play with his childhood hero and since he was a kid he has been targeting his game to be even better than Jack's game.

At the height of his short career, Tiger Woods called his training coach and said he had to completely redo his swing. He was doing great, but to be the best of all time, he had to completely transform his swing. His coach agreed to work with him, but also told him that the probability of completely changing his swing and being even as good as he had been was quite low. Many bodies lie along the path that Tiger Woods was now entering upon. Well, I am sure you are thinking that I am not going to pick a fractured fairy tale. After a year of one loss after another, Tiger Woods won four majors in one year, and is well on his way to being the best golfer of all time. I wish we could use this young man's example to redefine ourselves as a nation. Hopefully there will be a time when you are so widely successful that you wonder who in their right mind would consider changing their swing? Who?

In the world of unity through diversity, what type of leader will you need to be like?

- Someone who does not necessarily know all about the different cultures, but has the desire to learn about them.
- Someone who thinks from the outside in, in terms of how our community is affecting other communities.
- Someone who is willing to take his best game and completely reinvent it, to make it even better.
- Someone who is comfortable working with people from all different cultural, age, and ethnic groups.
- Someone who will be able to work across time, distance, and culture through and with technology.
- Someone who will work at developing others to be better at what they do, who can help them transcend their current abilities to achieve higher-level abilities, while developing shared leadership practices.
- Someone who is willing to be transparent, be vulnerable, embrace conflict, and work at achieving ground truth with others to build conditional and ultimately deeper levels of trust.
- Someone who enjoys other people being successful, as much if not more than their own success.
- Someone who will work with his or her most vulnerable followers to minimize the category of recoverable mistakes.

I realize that this leadership stuff is a lot of work, and it is a life-training program to cast oneself whole. I have tried myself to be transparent with you on this issue throughout the last seven chapters, as I do believe this is one of the most complex social phenomena to understand, let alone to develop. We are now going to add in yet another level of complexity, and that is how technology is going to impact on how you lead, helping again to ramp up the complexity of developing leadership. However, we also began our discussion with the analogy that once we understood the special effects, we could begin work on the development part. So, if you are unclear about the special effects, I still have some white space to fill before I am done. Sticking with this is all part of what constitutes exemplary leadership. Earlier in this book we called it persistence. Now it may be termed patience.

AN EXERCISE FOR BUILDING TRUST

One of the ways to build trust is to develop the ground rules for interaction and stick consistently to them. One of the main reasons why leaders lose trust is because of inconsistency, either perceived or based on actual variation in behavior. What I would like you to do is to build a Compact of Understanding with the people you work with in your organization. The Compact will include your most important core value and how that value is translated into actions or behaviors. When I say behavior what I mean is that it is something that you and others can see. For example, let us say the core value is openness. The behavior expected of everyone is to communicate a mistake that has been made as early as possible to everyone, and to agree to fix it. Or, if the core value is equity, then when rewards are distributed you will identify what the criteria were that you used to determine the award, and you will be able to justify that criteria to others. The Compact-building process is a shared leadership experience where you should take the role of facilitator to identify what is the core value and what are the actions and behaviors that will support it. Once you have generated a draft document, spend a week reflecting on its implications for behavioral change for you and your followers. Revisit the Compact a week later and discuss any changes you might all want to include in it. Then, agree to it by signing the Compact and also agree that after a certain period of time, you will debrief how well it is working. My recommendation is to debrief initially on a weekly basis and then over time, extend it to 2 or more weeks.

8

E-leadership Is Leadership Plus

It was a pleasant summer afternoon off the coast of Pensacola, Florida. All of sudden the calm is broken when a young boy is attacked by a bull shark. He screams for help as his arm is ripped off and held in the shark's mouth. His uncle enters the water, grabs the shark by its tail, and pulls it on to the beach where a game warden shoots it dead. As of this writing the boy has survived, and the doctors were able to sew his arm back on. All are waiting to see what type of neurological damage was done due to the loss of blood. His uncle refuses to do any interviews and is seen as a hero.

Roll forward 2 months—an article appears on the web indicating that in fact the uncle of this young boy was fishing for sharks. It was he who attracted the shark to the shallow waters where it attacked his young nephew. The bastard!! Hold on, this is all hooey, all made for the Internet hour. Someone decided to make up this story and soon it had spread around the world. This is an example of the awesome power of what we are now confronting in the age of the web and Internet. Imagine what a despot leader could do in terms of having a global platform to project his message. It is cheap, it is quick, and it can be devastatingly effective.

One evening we were visiting some friends to celebrate the ending of summer. One of our friends works as a high school teacher and had saved an e-mail for me that she had received from another teacher at her school. Essentially, the e-mail was written by the Superintendent and was supposed to be sent to another administrator. In the e-mail, the Superintendent described a question he received from this teacher that he was unable to answer. He asked this third party to write to the teacher so she would know that he and some other administrator were aware of the problem she had raised at the open forum. He then went on to say, "However, just give her a brief and concise answer .... Don't give her any other info. She is the type of person that wouldn't be happy no matter what plan we design." My friend received the memo along with the rest of the school district by accident. After reading it, I kept thinking about how many e-mails are sent too quickly to the wrong place, including some of my own. In this instance, I wondered what effect his statement: "Don't give her any other info" had on future questions and trust in his leadership. The obvious concern is over what he says publicly being consistent with what he says privately. I cannot imagine that he will be seen as being authentic any time in the near future.

EXAMPLES OF TECHNOLOGY CHANGING THE CONDITIONS FOR LEADERSHIP

There are help groups springing up all over the Internet who share information with each other to combat all sorts of maladies, both physical and emotional. These types of communities are spontaneously forming, or in some cases they are promoted by the medical community, pharmaceutical firms, other community groups, or all three, to help members help themselves.

The web has become the largest flea market on earth, and has created one of the most successful web-based companies, called e-Bay. It has connected literally millions of garage-sale buyers to share information, their passion for hobbies, and antiques around the globe. It has become a community unto itself, where people even receive reliability ratings so that others will know how candid and accurate they were in describing and delivering on their product.

Another example would be Jack Welch, the former CEO of General Electric, who spent time going to chat rooms that had been set up to discuss General Electric, General Electric products, and services. He spent time listening to what current or prospective customers said about General Electric, showing another example of what he termed the boundaryless organization.

In the spirit of being transparent, if I had written this book even 3 to 4 years ago, I could guarantee you this chapter would not have been included in that book. For the better part of 15 years, when I thought about leadership, I thought about either face-to-face leadership, or leadership at a distance that occurred when a leader influenced someone who then in turn influenced someone else and so forth down the line. However, the linking up of the world via the Internet, the increased flexibility in where and when people can work, and the rapid globalization of businesses have created a challenge for leaders today to lead teams that are virtual, work with colleagues who not only do not speak the same language, but are not up at the same time as their team leader, and work with people they have never met face to face.

Now keep in mind that leadership is always embedded in some context, and technology is changing that context in which we all lead. You will see there are some real positives to this change in terms of how you will be leading, and I will cover some of the pitfalls as well.

There is no doubt in my mind that you have or will lead others mediated through technology, if that has not already occurred in your work. At the present time, and back over the last 5 years, there has not been a time in my own work where I have not been working with someone or some group of people that I have never met face to face. The world we have created poses some fascinating challenges for us to lead through a whole new medium, which is helping leadership migrate south in many organizations. What I mean here is that leadership is going down to all of the right levels in organizations where decisions are being made at the point of contact with clients, customers, and between workgroup members.

There are so many questions to ask, it is hard to figure out where we should start in discussing this new mediating link in the leadership process. For example, revisiting a topic from our previous chapter, how do you build trust in leading a group that you have never met face to face? How can you understand and be sensitive to the needs of people if you do not know them in the sense that you get to know people when you see them each day at work? How are you going to get followers to buy into your vision, if you cannot be in their presence when you are presenting it and being able to read their nonverbal reactions? How are you supposed to be transparent, when there is no face-to-face contact? How do you disclose comfortably to people who you have never met, and who you do not even know? How do we stereotype people if we cannot see the color of their skin, or their gender? Well, there are some advantages to this technology, at least until we are all on broadband video-streaming.

Okay, if you want to, go ahead and unplug your computer and throw away the personal digital assistant. Why should we even mess with all of this stuff? Well, the truth is that we have to mess with it, since it is not going to go away. Indeed, it is very likely that many of us will work in more virtual teams than we do with face-to-face ones over the next 10 years and beyond. As technology becomes even more portable with screens affixed to contacts in our eyes, and voice-activated computer chips inserted into our vocal chords, virtual working with each other at a distance will become increasingly more commonplace. At some point the distinction between what is virtual and real will narrow to imperceptible levels.

The big questions I have in my own work on leadership include the following: What remains relevant to us from what we have traditionally learned about leadership and followership in this new emerging context? How do we prepare and develop both leaders and followers to lead in this emerging context? What is the next new context that we will have to lead in once we have addressed the beginnings of virtual leadership? I could add here, what will distance really mean when virtual work is the norm versus the exception? For example, as the world appears to grow smaller, does the psychological distance between us also change?

TWO SYSTEMS ON A COLLISION COURSE

Today, the failure rate for inserting advanced information technology into organizations hovers around 50–60%. Indeed, in one recent study, the author reported there was an inverse relationship between the amount of money invested in introducing new technology and the degree of failure. Okay, I am a medical doctor who just told you that you have a very serious condition that requires immediate surgery. Your chances of it working are around 30%. When would you like to schedule the surgery?

Most people would never accept a procedure on themselves that has as high a failure rate as we endure with the deployment of new technology. Yet, it must be working if so many people are becoming connected, but at what cost to organizations and society? In the United States, the cost is estimated to be about $100 billion per year in losses due to delays and failures in implementing new technologies. The finger seems to point to two interrelated areas causing the failure, which include leadership and culture. You may not be surprised to hear that, in a recent study conducted by Towers and Perrin and the Society for Human Resource Management Foundation, the major factor in failures of mergers and acquisitions, which also hover around 60%, was leadership and culture. When reengineering failed, and TQM failed, the reasons were leadership and culture. Learning from mistakes is great, but repeating the same ones over and over again is usually described by most 16-year-olds as "duh!" So how can we address issues of leadership and culture, as we enter into this new form of merger and acquisition where advanced information technology is assimilated into organizations?

I would like you to view leadership and technology as one of the greatest internal mergers of our times, if not all time. Let me explain what I mean here by an internal merger. Prior to the insertion of a total enterprise resource system into an organization, there is a social system that exists and hopefully is evolving over time. As part of this social system, there are communication systems, leadership systems, and cultural systems. The existing social system or culture in which the technology is being inserted, has certain dynamics, which might be captured generally in words like open, *collaborative, trusting,* or *supportive*. The social system contains much of what we have discussed in this book up to this point as context. Conversely, the leadership social system may be described as *autocratic, closed, untrustworthy, political,* and *self-interested*. Now which of these descriptions comes closer to describing your organization's leadership social system?

Now consider what the features of the information technology system are in terms of being attributes of a social system. For example, does the technology enhance open communication and collaboration? For advanced information technology applications to be successful, they must eventually merge and coevolve with those systems that are already in place within an organization. Here I mean social systems, although in some cases when we say one system must speak to another, we may also mean technical systems interacting with each other. The internal merger is a process that unfolds over time, whereby the existing social system adapts to, transforms, and evolves with the technical system that is being inserted. In the end, the adaptation may lead to a totally new social system, which now has to be led, and that is where work on leadership becomes critical. You will need to adapt how you lead to be able to adapt to the advantages provided by most advanced information systems. Realize that organizations were designed to handle and coordinate information flows long before the computer came along. Now, they still have the same function, but the technical processes available to make it happen have changed totally and so will how coordination is achieved in organizations. The move toward having information go south in organizations is a direct result and if led properly would demonstrate the benefits of properly integrating advanced information technology in organizations.

Organizations must adapt how they organize taking into consideration the features or spirit of the technology. Here is where leadership and culture play a very important role. For example, a lot of technology available today is geared toward increasing the exchange of information, levels of collaboration, and access to ideas needed to meet and exceed customer expectations. Most of this technology is still pull technology in that it does not anticipate your needs per say, but rather you can pull in the information you need if you know where it is located, which is no trivial undertaking in terms of knowledge management in complex organizations.

The bug in the system is not always in the software. To the contrary, in a culture that is not open, is not collaborative, and is not sharing ideas readily, a collaborative system is a virus that will be rejected by the host system versus merged and fully integrated. The sheer social force of a technology system can be used to change how an organization functions as a social system, but the resistance to that change will cost a lot and will no doubt create delays in implementation, as well as failures. Do you see where some of the $100 billion spent on problems with implementing technology is going now? If the spirit of the technology is collaborative and your boss is not, you might as well unplug for all it will be worth to your organization.

ROLE OF LEADERSHIP IN TRANSFORMING SOCIAL AND TECHNICAL SYSTEMS

What I have said about technology mergers with social systems is similar to almost any process in terms of the issues and problems one must anticipate and overcome. For example, many organizations that have flattened hierarchies and networked themselves talk about implementing a team system. However, what I have oftentimes found is that the leaders say they want teams, but their mental model is all about how to influence individuals. They may really want teams, but they do not have the models or practices down to a point where the technical system is enabled to merge with the existing social system. Teams would represent a new technology in a hierarchical organization where people are selected, evaluated, and rewarded based on who they are as an individual and what they do as an individual. The failure rate associated with inserting teams into organizations is very much in parallel with the problems we observe with the insertion of new technology. Both affect the leadership and cultural–social system and both will be rejected if they do not align themselves with those systems, or if they are not accommodated in some way.

In this time between times, we are recreating what was meant by organization, both structurally and in terms of process, but the software that is lagging behind is the mental models in people's heads of how this technology is supposed to merge with what we now have to do at work. How do we include technology in the possible selves of both leaders and followers in terms of enhancing the full range of their interactions?

Chester Barnard (1968) in his classic book on executives discussed one of the ultimate goals of what we are trying to accomplish in the design of organizations, which is to increase cooperation. Today, we refer to cooperation as knowledge sharing, learning organizations, and highly developed structural and social capital. Yet, without a culture of cooperation already in place, there is little chance that technology is going to simply change the culture and make it cooperative. This is a challenge for leadership, not technology, and a challenge that you can handle using the basic ideas already presented in this book. I return to this point shortly.

THE GREAT LEADERSHIP MIGRATION

In yet another famous title, yet to be published, I described the move toward introducing new technology as the "Great Leadership Migration" in organizations. In the Northern hemisphere during the early fall, the geese begin to head south (downward) during their yearly migration for warmer climates. Similarly, leadership is migrating south in organizations as a consequence of inserting new advanced information technology. More people know more, and as consequence are more responsible for leading themselves, or sharing leadership responsibilities. By having more information of higher quality we are positioning people at all levels of organizations to lead themselves.

Yet, as information and influence go south in our organizational hierarchies, it affects very directly the leadership social system and culture that exists within the organization and ultimately the relationships that emerge between organizations. It means that the total social system must become more transparent, that it must become more collaborative and it must adopt more of a shared leadership paradigm. I guess it is fair to say that 60–70% of those leadership social systems do not agree with the transformation, and have pulled out the shotguns to nip the migration once those geese cross the border. BANG!

Any cultural system can kill any technical system if it chooses to do so, and apparently many have made that choice given the high failure rates observed thus far with advanced technology implementations. From a strategic business perspective, and in terms of cost and benefits, by readying the social and structural context to receive advanced information technology, we are fundamentally building a new culture, where new conduits of information are evolving. These new conduits of information require leadership that knows its own values, whose behavior is consistent with their words, and whose system of justice is transparent. I hope this is all sounding somewhat familiar and redundant to you.

Organizations were formed to control and disseminate information with various systems and procedures that are expected to become part of the mental models in the heads of leaders and followers. In bureaucracies we call them standard operating procedures, and in organic, flexible organizations we focus more on the culture of shared information. Now, we have a new conduit for information exchange via fiber optic networks or radio signals, and that new medium will no doubt change the way we lead, follow, share, and learn from each other. This is easily supported as it already has changed the way successful companies are leading themselves and I would add successful leaders. Consider companies such as Federal Express, Dell, WalMart, Mrs. Fields Cookies, IBM, GE, Southwest Airlines, Intel, or Cisco and eliminate their ability to use technology to conduct business. They cannot do their business without advanced information technology, and that is how fundamental information technology has become to their operational models of business, their value propositions, and their positions in their respective markets. Now we must consider how fundamental technology is to the operational business of leadership and its development. We have a tremendous opportunity today to link development closer and closer to the execution of leadership. For example, we could use Short Messages Service (SMS) technology to signal through someone's cell phone that they should try to find some positive behaviors to recognize at work that day. This may be part of the leader's plan to be reminded by the coach to express more open recognition for followers' positive behaviors at work, after receiving feedback to the contrary. Imagine the possibilities, as we are better able to link training just in time with performance.

We now have the capacity to follow unobtrusively our trainees into the workplace following workshops to help boost the training effects over time, at a fraction of the cost that it would take for a trainer to come on site and meet with trainees after the close of a training program. A virtual coach can log on anywhere at almost anytime in the world to provide a manager with an ear to listen to issues or problems that are being confronted that he or she does not yet feel capable of handling.

Moreover, we can now develop more dynamic and intelligent systems where both trainers and trainees share information on what is working with their developmental plan and what is not working, by creating online libraries of knowledge based on each other's experiences. The whole field of leadership assessment, development, and evaluation is opening up to completely new ways of developing leadership using advanced information technology. Yet, since they are new, most ways are completely unproven and require a great deal of experimentation. For instance, what should the content be in an electronic coaching session? How long should these sessions last? How often should they occur? What type of advance preparation is required to make them most effective? How well must the coach and trainee know each other for these sessions to be totally effective? These are all good questions that have yet to be fully explored if at all. I have more to say specifically about new ways to design leadership development processes in the second to last chapter.

DETAILING THE COEVOLUTION PROCESS

Two people get married and think they know a lot about each other. Of course, all of you reading this book, who already know better, would say that as you coevolved in your partnership you learned more about each other's deep beliefs and values. You learned more about your respective desires, which may have also evolved over time. Marriages are mergers of two independent systems. Their failure rates are hovering in the United States around 50% and around the world we are witnessing a rising trend with such failures, as being divorced loses its social taboo in many cultures. People who do not coevolve with each other get divorced, or live together oftentimes in a culture of destructive conflict. As they go toward failure we also see some deevolution as well! Marriage is probably one of the best examples of shared leadership in its truest form.

When most organizational leaders decide to introduce new technology, the first-order effects they may consider are how these vast amounts of information that are now readily available can be accessed, by whom, and for what purpose. Ask Double Click about these second-order effects. Specifically, once we have access to these vast amounts of information on people, how do we use that information in a responsible manner, as well as for profit? Double Click had to back off on providing information they had acquired on the buying patterns of their customers, which they intended to sell on the open market, because it was not seen as a responsible use of information. As more and more people work online in a transparent virtual environment, monitoring performance will become easier and privacy will become increasingly more of an issue for organizations. That issue of privacy, we discussed earlier, will continuously rise up to become one of the major issues that leaders will need to deal with in organizations over the next 25 years.

Other second-order effects are that everyone knows more about your core business and competencies as information systems open up information to the outside world. What is proprietary information now versus in the past is clearly up for grabs. What is your competitive advantage in terms of knowledge and information is also up for grabs by your competitor. How will you lock up intellectual capital in a market where people regularly shift from one company to another? How do you lead people, who oftentimes know the consequences of a decision you have not even made yet?

Currently, the U.S. Army is struggling with the fact that troops deployed overseas often see on the web or via television news, what is going on around them before their officers tell them the news. Typically, these officers are not intentionally withholding information from their soldiers, but rather are trying to check the veridicality of the information before passing it along to them. Yet, top leaders in the military, as well as others, are concerned about the effects such changes in information availability are having on the credibility of their leaders and leadership. They are looking into how to project an array of information that is bogus, so that it will be even more difficult to discern which Trojan horse the real message lies within.

I spent some time lecturing at the United States Military Academy at West Point. During my time at West Point, we discussed the first and second-order effects of simply introducing e-mail to all cadets and giving each cadet a personal computer in the dorm room. The leadership considered the first-order effects of efficiency in communications, enhancing the ability of students to interact with instructors and other cadets beyond the walls of the classroom, as well as the access it provided cadets to relevant information that could inform their decisions more effectively. All of these first-order effects have occurred. Unanticipated was the impact that such effects had on the social system of West Point. First, some cadets and faculty felt that technology was substituting for personal contact with each other. Second, the cadets were remaining far more connected with their social networks at home than in the past, and it appeared this change in behavior might be affecting the levels of cohesion of the cadets at West Point. Third, the closed developmental system of the past, and I mean here closed in terms of who controlled information dissemination, was going away as more information was readily accessible to everyone.

However it should be kept in mind that the trickle down can be either positive or negative in terms of second, third and fourth-order impact. How the leaders behave and what they role model will in part determine whether it's a positive or negative trickle down effect.

There is an old adage, "information is power in organizations." If distributed systems are designed to distribute information, information is far more shared today than in the past. If shared information is still power, then leadership is moving to a new platform that will require collective and shared leadership, even in the steepest organizational hierarchies. This is something that you must become prepared to deal with as a leader and it requires a rapid alternating pattern of being a leader and follower, and leader, and follower, and so on.

The West Point Academy is perhaps a very small example of a much larger phenomenon occurring in organizations, society, and on a global basis. Let me again personalize this to my own social situation. There is rarely a day that goes by that my e-mails do not come from several different countries. I regularly work with people from different cultures, and oftentimes am aware of what happened in their lives before what happened to a colleague next door. On most days, there are a few e-mails coming from students that I have never had contact with before. They typically want to discuss some aspect of my work, asking for some support on a project, or simply connecting up with me because they read something that I published. I oftentimes think about those students who probably would never have contacted me by phone, feeling too inhibited to have a conversation with me due to differences in status, or language difficulties. Also, there are times that within 2 weeks, I may have 10 e-mail interactions, and all of a sudden, I have a new partner I am working with in research, whom I have never met face to face.

This new medium is changing people's access to me, it is changing the way I interact, and it is changing with whom I interact on a daily basis, including my own family who from time to time e-mail me on trips. It is creating tremendous advantages to be in contact with many different cultures around the world. It has also increased my work day significantly, and has made me feel that I am always working on yesterday's stuff, when I interact with colleagues in Australia, New Zealand, and Singapore, who are into the next day before I am midway through yesterday for them. It has accelerated the pace of my work to a very significant level, as more documents are passed back and forth by e-mail versus snail mail, and the expectations for turnaround have shortened, along with many people's attention span! It is, in my opinion, one of the great benefits of the information revolution and one of the great tragedies. We can no longer get away from our work easily.

What is happening in my life is a microcosm of what most leaders out there are now entering into and experiencing, or have been in the middle of experiencing for some time. If you are not, likely you are very unaware of the changing dynamics of work, and it is time you got connected. You may also be in some country where the Internet has not yet been deployed to the extent it has been in the United States. Yet I would say with some degree of confidence, that if they build it, it will change the way you interact with people. We are seeing this happen throughout the world in emerging economies that are going from no phones to cell or fiberoptics cable in one generation. As I previously mentioned, countries like Uganda have decided that all homes will have an Internet hookup and PC, thus they are investing in their infrastructure by connecting everyone throughout the country. They, as well as we, should be concerned about the digital divide that is being created between the have and have-not countries. This will be one of the major challenges for the developing world over the next 30 years, to stay connected and to be on the right side of the digital divide. Dissemination of information has always been a global concern from our earliest explorers figuring out how to circumnavigate the world, to our explorers in the information technology age. The conduit for information has changed, while its importance to development and advancing as a society has not.

We know from history that technology will rapidly advance, while behind it the social system will try to catch up. All of the evidence accumulated on failure rates with implementing new technology would support this statement. Here I am referring very specifically to the leadership social system in organizations. The compelling question for leaders is how will we adapt and coevolve with the emerging technology systems that are infiltrating organizations today? Let me pose some questions for your consideration to help you better frame the issues that you are or will be confronting in terms of your own e-leadership development:

- Where do people in your unit or organization hear about what is really happening in your organization?
- How would you characterize the transfer of important information within your organization from a vertical and horizontal perspective? What is the level of accuracy versus spin in the information and data provided?
- How much of your interactions with your fellow workers or followers involves assuring them of the accuracy of information you are communicating to them? How important is it for you to go down and meet with them to assure them what they heard was actually correct?
- When was the last time a fellow worker or follower directly challenged your position either in a one-to-one conversation or with others being present?
- If you are already working with some employees virtually or at a distance, how have you developed or maintained your relationships with them versus people whom you interact with face to face on a more regular basis?
- Where do you get your information from, and how accurate do you feel what you are hearing or picking up through electronic interaction is?
- How hard is it for you to get others to share what they know willingly with others either face to face or virtually?
- How have people you work with used advanced information technology to broadcast their agenda? Should there be any restrictions on how this medium is used? If so, what type of restrictions would you recommend?

Embedded in these questions is a basic idea that you need to consider now. How developmentally ready are you for an information system that allows just about anyone to know what you know either when you know it or even before you have learned about it? How ready are you to work in an organization where people will access you (whom you have never met), and expect you to be able to develop a relationship with them and to work with them to accomplish their objectives? They will expect creative ideas, individual consideration, and even some inspiration without ever shaking your hand or gazing into your eyes. How ready are you and your organization for this new reality that is already here?

We are entering into a world today where the CEO can communicate with everyone, everyday on whatever issue he or she chooses to discuss. One CEO recently sent out a heartfelt message on a long-time employee who had recently passed away. He shared with employees some personal insights and experiences that said something about the type of person who had just passed away. This was a person that was widely respected and the message appeared to have a very positive impact on a grieving organization. Consider the power of one message sent to everyone, at one moment in time. That is the power we are now examining in terms of how it is shaping what constitutes an organization today.

We live in a world where employees will quickly band together into a network to share information, because they judge the organization to be too closed, and they will seek alternative communication links to fill that void. Today, employees can see what other companies are doing, what customers want, and what suppliers need typically more quickly than anyone at the top of their own organization. When we used to teach strategic leadership in business schools, we would say the leaders at the top needed to look outside, while people in the middle of the organization were more internally focused. That is just not the case anymore in most organizations. Everyone at all levels is either looking out, or can look out, and should be looking out for critical information.

What happens when customers and clients can access your organization at any level, at any time and with any one of your employees? How do you assure that the interactions with your customers and clients will be equivalent and of high quality when those interactions can occur at any point of contact with the organization? Today, 80% of recruits in U.S. organizations come through the Internet door. The Web site is what they see first. What messages does your Web site send to the whole world? Are they informative? Interesting? Inspiring?

In a recent meeting in Washington, DC, I was part of a group discussing the impact of technology on organizations. One person in the group said to go to the federal Web site for jobs and then go to some of our top private corporations. The federal Web site lists jobs in very technical jargon, signaling to people you can be a very microoriented bureaucrat with limited discretion and a large amount of rules and regulations to wade through at work. The Web sites of our top corporations present their core values, they provide realistic previews of jobs—one is even in cartoon format to reduce download time—and they discuss how you will grow and develop in your job/career. Today the conduit for information about organizations is not necessarily the person, it is the story told on your Web site. To some extent, the leadership of your organization is reflected on what is there and what is not. From the examples I previously gave, do you think that a potential applicant might infer how much innovation and creativity is promoted in the two different job settings?

Many organizations are now moving strategically toward this change at light speed, in order to have everyone take a 360-view of their customers. What this means is that for any customer any point of contact in that organization should know you, what you have asked for in the past, what your last interaction with the organization was like, and what you typically purchased from that organization. Traditionally, such a knowledge repository was in the salesperson or supervisor's head, and today it is on your Intranet, or should be, in order to be competitive with world-class companies. Of course, the downside of information access is privacy, and this again is an area that leadership must begin to discuss how to balance.

What is the relevance of all of this for your development as a leader? Let me lay out what I think are the top five points of impact on your leadership development that you must now take into consideration to remain relevant over the next decade:

1. Is the spirit of your leadership consistent with the spirit of the functionalities available to your followers given the type of information technology in use or soon to be in use in your organization? If the technology has a spirit of collaboration, and you are directive as a leader, how will these two systems coevolve?

2. As more people know what you know, how can you help facilitate that they share their knowledge with others in a way that results in optimal performance? How will you add value to the exchange of information? We can build the best knowledge repository system in the world, but without a culture of sharing it will remain an empty shell. In one organization there were 2,000 Lotus Notes users, but only one team that used it for collaboration. Why? How does this all impact the knowledge repository you need to build to be a world-class competitor?

3. How prepared are you to move from being a content leader to a process leader? Most people around you will be experts in areas that you are not, and yet you will be the project leader leading typically face to face, virtually, or both. You will need to work with them to facilitate their work, even if you do not fully understand

it, and in many cases they will also lead themselves and you will do the same with your own work.

4. What sort of strategy do you have in mind for balancing face-to-face interactions with those interactions that occur at a distance via technology? Which interactions are better served face to face versus at a distance? Some leaders will resort to overusing technology because it is there, convenient to use, and efficient in terms of time. Some will use it to show massive amounts of individualized consideration, but will be perceived as disingenuous. How you balance the use of the technology and face-to-face interface will be important to building credibility with followers/peers, and more importantly, satisfying their needs at the point in time when they need to be addressed.

5. What type of learning plan do you have in place to help coach yourself and others on how to best use information technology to enhance each other's work and quality of life? You might want to start using technology for tasking others, disseminating information, and providing and receiving updates. You may even send a compliment or two, but as you get more into the personal realm, it is likely to require some face-to-face content. I would recommend that you use technology wherever you can to augment your face-to-face interactions. Where it substitutes for face to face is where you need to be very diligent to monitor its impact on your relationships.

In some ways, leaders have never been better able to be connected to their followers than they are today. In addition, followers have never been better able to feed back information to their leaders in a shorter period of time then they are able to do today. Yet, there is something that is stuffing up the system if we have so many failures with inserting new technology. Let me use one example around the issue of transparency to emphasize this point.

A HYPOTHETICAL SITUATION

In a completely transparent culture in which I lead, all information is made available to those who need to know, exactly when they need to know it. If the organization is tracking my conversations and abstracting and storing content for use by others, that is a good thing for all of us. In this organization, when a leader does something that has a negative consequence for some employees, the feedback they receive is usually very swift and direct. People take the issue to the source around here when they have a problem with that source. When important decisions are made we are well informed in advance, through the process of implementing the decision and afterward as we debrief our levels of success. I am quite aware of the resources that others receive to do their work and where I might disagree with a particular allocation, my manager is always prepared to justify her decision or to find out the justification for decisions made above her level. When people know things in other units that are important to what we do, they share that information readily and oftentimes without it being requested.

In the world that I described, the insertion of advanced information technology should be a relatively easy transition. To the extent that you feel comfortable in your own leadership style being in line with what was presented, you should have no problem with implementing the new more open systems technology from a social systems perspective. Indeed, what you have is an open system in terms of culture, matched to an open system in terms of advanced information technology.

Supporting what I described is a very key component in this transition process, which is replacing the structural glue of organizations that was previously based on formal hierarchies and procedures, to what is simply labeled trust. As we defined in the previous chapter, both conditional and more mature forms of relational trust represent the willingness of someone to be vulnerable to someone else without oversight or monitoring. Today, many leaders are being asked to be vulnerable by opening up the information channels to everyone about everything, and to support what they are doing openly. This is a huge challenge for any leader, who says my organization is somewhat political. Information is still power in organizations, even if it is transmitted in bytes. How you deal with the migration of information and power to your followers in this age of networking at all levels, both inside and outside of your organization, will determine how successful you are in leading others, along with other fundamental facets of leadership like integrity, openness, caring, innovative thinking, and perseverance.

To be successful in this new context for leadership, you must learn about shared leadership. In most leaders' mental models of leadership, this means being equal with others in how you influence a decision. In others it means to delegate responsibilities. In others it means to consult, but retain the final decision. What it means is what I said earlier: to be a leader you are often a follower, and as a follower you often have to take the lead. Technology has made this exchange even more dynamic and more rapid to the point where it is so rapid, it appears to the naked eye to represent shared leadership.

If leadership is comprised of followers, leaders, and context, as I have argued throughout this book, then as the context changes, so will the process of leadership. Today you are required to share or expand the boundaries of that role and to become in rapid sequence a leader, a follower, a leader, a follower, a leader, a follower, and a leader. Ironically, this is not something that is at all new, but it is quite different from the organizations that people like Chester Barnard talked about 70-odd years ago. Organizations had very clearly defined leadership slots and roles in the past. Today, the boundaries are being blurred in almost every organization. In high performing teams, such leadership has often been present in face-to-face form. Indeed, when members of teams in our research have described their leadership system they oftentimes have described it as a shared system. The cell we are referring to as a team now is being reproduced throughout organizations in virtual form. Our collective challenge is to share leadership in broadband space, which is becoming virtual in terms of interactions, each and every day. Like in all high performing teams, this will require developing conditional and ultimately unconditional trust, the new-age glue!

I would like to offer some steps for you to consider during this period of transition from a totally face-to-face type organization, to one that is at least mixed virtual. It seems pretty clear to me, that as we move away from strict hierarchical systems two things must occur. First, the intentions of leaders will need to be made much clearer, and processes will need to be put in place to assure they are understood by others, such as the AARs discussed earlier. Intentions will now be mediated much more via technology where interactions are virtual, potentially causing greater levels of confusion around "what I am supposed to do at work" or what was the leader's intent. Understanding the leader's intent through the whole implementation process will become increasingly more important as we interact with each other at a distance, as we share more in the responsibilities for task execution and as the context continually changes, forcing us to adapt to new contingencies.

The second area is developing a social system where people trust each other enough to share their most valuable information. Without trust, more information exchange is probably not better, in that people will flood each other with information that is irrelevant. Trust provides the basis for disseminating and understanding information that is sent at face value. Yet, even with high levels of trust, teams will need to be sure what was typed or said was actually heard accurately. So often, people will convey something on e-mail and not realize they have angered or offended someone. I recall working with a close colleague totally via e-mail, and finding him to be very strange. However, after I met him and got to know his style of humor, his messages did not seem all that strange to me, or maybe it was me, and not his messages.

The advantages of using technology to mediate our interactions are that we can get almost immediate feedback and give immediate feedback to others. However, as some of us have already experienced, sometimes a message sent in the heat of passion is a message one regrets the next morning. Placing a governor on the system to slow us down is probably not a bad idea after all. What has always applied in face-to-face conflicts in terms of trying to step back to revisit an argument is even more critical in virtual interactions where negative interactions can quickly spiral out of control.

What are the main messages that I wanted to convey to you in this chapter and for you to reflect on before we do another chapter together?

1. Technology is fundamentally affecting the balance of information in organizations, and that change is transforming the nature of the organizational social system.
2. Technology can coevolve with human systems if the spirit of the technology and people, particularly leaders, are consistent with each other. If not, they will not get along very well and technology usually loses, as does the investment made in technology.
3. Technology should be used to augment interactions, not substitute for them.
4. To create the type of knowledge repository that will add value to your work and others will require that you build a culture in which sharing information is normative.
5. Technology seems to be making everybody appear smarter than you, but do not worry, because everyone else is in the same boat!
6. We are at a point in time where we can enable vast numbers of people around the world to communicate with each other, and to do so at a very, very low cost. Through these information systems we can stamp out ignorance that oftentimes has been controlled by those most interested in controlling information.

7. Technology can be used to extend the leader's impact on others in many positive ways. For example, the leader can reinforce an important message periodically by sending to every follower who is connected, her or his observations, examples, a short article, a question to consider, a story about a particular event and so forth. The power of dissemination has been exponentially enhanced via technology, and needs to be captured effectively.
8. Leaders can also use technology to augment the face-to-face coaching that gets done each and every day. Again, they can reach out to people with examples, drop an insight into the person's pocket PC calendar, attach an interesting survey, finding, an article, and so forth.
9. Leaders or coaches can also form a group, let us call them Leader's Anonymous. These self-reflective development groups could be brought together any time or anywhere to discuss challenges and opportunities confronting members of this forum. Imagine the power of stretching this forum across a global organization or consortium of organizations, with proper facilitation for cultural differences.

A VIRTUAL TEAM EXERCISE

If you work with a group that is connected by e-mail, why not choose a project to work on that you only discuss by e-mail. In other words, restrict all interactions to only using e-mail on this project. Try out these steps:

1. Take the first session to discuss project goals and objectives. Also, discuss how the group should be configured to address the goals and objectives. If you can set up your system so everyone's input is anonymous, then try that out in this exercise.
2. Spend the second session discussing an ideal process and what a Compact of Understanding would look like for this team. Try to come to some agreements on what the Compact will contain including how responsibilities will be determined, scheduling, allocation of resources, etc.
3. Set up a leadership structure for the team, which can be included in your Compact.
4. Begin work on the project. Agree to debrief your progress each week and on ways to improve process.

5. Once you have completed objectives for this project, do a face-to-face postmortem of what worked and what did not work that required amendments. In this discussion, focus on how you could have been more effective in terms of leadership, communications, scheduling, allocation of resources, support, sharing of information, evaluation, and follow-up.
6. What did you lose in not meeting and discussing this project face to face?

9

Leadership Development: What We Know We Know So Far

In about 1994, I was conducting my first leadership development program for top managers at Fiat. The project would last nearly 4 years in order to train the top 250 managers. This was supposed to be a safe workshop where we would train managers who were more predisposed to such learning interventions.

People were slowly walking into the room following morning coffee. A gentleman from Germany came up to me before sitting down and said, "I have been to all of these types of leadership training programs, situational, Kepner-Traego, team-building stuff, etc ... I don't see any value in all of this, and doubt you can teach me anything new about leadership." I said, "the difference in this program versus the others you mentioned is that it never ends, and we teach each other." He looked very curiously at me, and sat down. I thought at that time, why am I responsible for teaching anyone? Why do I have to convince people to develop as leaders? At the very least, should their own managers make that case for them before arriving at leadership training? I can say yes, but it is more complicated than simply expecting them to be developmentally ready to soar with our program.

Based upon a lot of reflection, I now see this is a very important leadership responsibility that I hold, and I, like other leaders, must try to inspire people to abandon their old way of doing things differently and perhaps new ways of doing things better. I have to convince them to change, and to sustain that change over time. It has led me to view workshops on leadership as work projects. They are my project team, I am for the moment the project leader, and the project is their leadership development, and usually to some extent my own. In viewing leadership development in this way, it forces me to think about my responsibilities as a leader, theirs as followers, and together our shared leadership responsibilities.

Another thing has occurred to me in the process of doing leadership training over the last decade. If it is not difficult, if it is not challenging, if there is no engagement and sometimes even conflict, then very little development occurs. Thus, it is with the most challenging people that I have found the greatest successes, because they offer the tension that creates the kinds of breakthroughs where substantial development occurs. If we are polite to each other, and thank each other for a wonderful *x* number of days together, little if any development seems to occur. It is bringing people to a point of self-awareness with their self-images that provides the basis for self-development to occur.

Roll it forward 6 months from this workshop. The same German gentleman came up to me and said that he had rethought his model of leadership and it was still emerging in his mind. He became one of my toughest critics and one of the best developers of leadership in the workshop, as he took it personally, and he took it on, and it seemed to change his thinking, which is the precursor to changing behavior and actions.

Over the last 10 years, we have been examining what works and what does not work in terms of leadership development. The good news is that there are many things that work. The bad news is that we still have a special effects problem in terms of what actually constitutes leadership development. We do some of this or that, and it works, but why it works is still a special effect. Indeed, some might even argue that what worked were only some modest shifts in behavior versus fundamental change in the perspectives of individuals or their level of moral reasoning. More importantly, we have rarely if ever assessed what changed in followers as a consequence of their leader changing perspective and style.

Although there are certainly a lot of cures for leadership development out there that profess to work, I will tell you that very few of them have actually taken the test—the test being to systematically evaluate the impact of leadership development programs on at least behavioral change, as well changes in the way leaders think and in performance improvements. There are very few (less than 10%) leadership development programs that have been evaluated, regardless of claims to the contrary. If there is one fundamental point that I would like you to take away from this chapter, it is that you should always ask for the evidence supporting the efficacy of a leadership development program. You will be surprised at the answers you will receive to this question. Here are some of the more typical ones:

- We are presently working on a project that should be done this year.
- We know it works because clients tell us so.
- We have some faculty from the university who are looking into this with us.
- Good question!
- No one can demonstrate this specifically works in terms of what impacts leadership development. You just have to believe in our product.
- There are too many elements to consider measuring to find out whether it works or not, but we can build evaluation into our budget.
- We have some case materials we can send you if you are interested.
- I think you are being too academic!

Here is my view on all of these types of reactions, and it is quite biased. If you are asking people to change their perspective about themselves and behavior, which will ultimately affect and change others, since that is what leadership is all about, then know what you are messing with before doing so. We do not bring pharmaceuticals to market with the hope that they may have the effects we desire. I believe the very same standard ought to be applied to leadership development. Leadership is one of the most awesome human forces in the universe. Look what destruction it has caused and miracles it has reaped throughout history. We can help people a lot, or we can hurt people a lot with the wrong prescription.

Let me summarize in the following what has been shown to work in terms of leadership development interventions, which you can consider for your own leadership development and those people you are trying to develop into more effective leaders.

1. Leadership development unfolds over time based on one's developmental readiness, and where you are in your respective life stream. It will unfold more or less smoothly depending on the developmental support that characterizes the context in which the person now operates. As it unfolds it can be boosted with additional support mechanisms, such as when a peer or coach (or

both) provides periodic feedback on how well the person is progressing toward a leadership development goal.

2. It is difficult to imagine how someone can develop to their full potential as a leader without receiving some feedback, at least in terms of how others perceive an individual as a leader. Of course, as we said earlier, not all feedback will have a positive impact on one's development, but I am also confident that the absence of feedback will not help development either. In a third of the cases feedback has been shown to be positive in terms of impact, but we do not know why a third, nor what happened in the other two thirds of the cases.

3. Ultimately, for leadership development to take hold in terms of development there has to be a change that occurs in thinking, or to use our earlier phrase, the individual's mental model of what is possible—their possible selves. An individual may be ready for development, but how he or she views himself or herself, can keep them from taking on some challenge that can shape or adjust their thinking about how they can influence others. Generally, when people get feedback on an area needing improvement, they can intellectually understand the gap they need to address, but oftentimes they cannot translate that level of understanding into practice. I think there are several reasons why this occurs. First, and this may be the simplest explanation, they do not see how changing their way of leading can do any good in their type of organization. Second, they believe the organization or their leader will support change, but they cannot visualize themselves doing the new behavior. They oftentimes can describe it very accurately, but they are unable to see how it would look in terms of actually doing it. Third, they are able to visualize themselves as exhibiting the behavior, but it is not yet a natural tendency and they often seem very mechanical in their responses. Finally, they understand, they can visualize it, they can enact the behavior, and even know where to make adjustments to improve, and it feels quite natural to them. It is here that we have seen a fundamental change in leadership development take place, and frankly, most leadership development programs hardly come close to tracking someone to this point in their developmental cycle.

4. I believe a fundamental change in thinking occurs when people alter their mental model to accommodate a new model of leadership, which they have just learned and had some initial success in using. For example, in our own work on leadership, we use a model for leadership development called the full range model, which I describe in more detail in the last chapter. We chose the term *full range* to challenge people going through our training to continuously ask where they were along the full range of leadership, and to challenge themselves to see where they could augment their range of behavior. To some degree, we start out by saying that it does not matter where you are on the range; as long as you are on the range you can build up to higher levels of potential by demonstrating new behaviors that have a higher impact on performance. The whole idea is to get participants to think about how they distribute leadership behaviors throughout their day and to alter that distribution over time—a shift in both positive thinking and what they are doing. For example, at one end of the range is passive-avoidant leadership. This end represents a leader who tends to wait till problems go wrong before taking action, if any action at all is taken. Motivating such leaders to become more active and to take in greater inputs can change the range or distribution of behaviors such leaders exhibit. Another leader may display more critical behaviors, or be more pessimistic, and by shifting to seeing what can be done, versus what should not be tried, can begin to shape the range of behaviors exhibited by the individual to look more positive. Of course, there may be many complex reasons for their lack of optimism initially, which I fully recognize as being something one must address at the core of the leadership development process. How can someone lead who is pessimistic about the potential outcome, except to lead toward stagnation or to lead backward? The point I am trying to demonstrate here is that by offering people a mental model against which they can compare their own behavior, one has the opportunity to shift both the individual's way of thinking, as well as behaving. Also, part of changing the way people think is getting them to do things differently, which we can reinforce, and by doing so show how the new behaviors lead to better outcomes.

5. One mental model that the Gallup Organization work to change is to get people to consider focusing on building their

strengths, as opposed to remedial interventions. Their strategy is very intellectually stimulating, in that it releases people from focusing on what is wrong, and instead concentrating on what is right and building it out further. In many ways, their approach dovetails quite nicely with the higher end of the full range leadership model labeled *transformational*. Transformational leaders work to enhance their followers' full potential, and concentrating just on strengths may be a more focused way of accelerating leadership development.

6. Assuming we can shift behavior to line up with a new mental model, then reinforcing the change in behavior to stick, is critical to sustaining change over time. One of the inherent problems with leadership development programs is that the program typically has a better culture and support system than the real world participants return to after the close of the program. In such programs, we have referees called trainers or facilitators, we have clearer guidelines for interaction, we generally have more collective goals clearly articulated, the focus is primarily on development whereas at work it is primarily on task, and there is usually much more time afforded for reflection and AARs. Typically, the organization to which we are returning people represents at best what could be, versus the as is. In some better scenarios, the organization is willfully trying to change itself and is using the leadership development program as a vehicle for enacting the desired change. Jumping back into an organizational stream that is moving forward, rather than going against the current, is a tremendous advantage for individual leadership development. Many times, the leaders themselves are not aware of the types of changes that can take place in such settings, until they start to see behaviors that are unfamiliar to them. (These behaviors are part of that new distribution of behaviors that I previously referred to.) I find that many leaders will start to get nervous as people's behavior begins to change, as it introduces a level of ambiguity and unpredictability that is difficult for them to understand and to manage.

7. Part of the science of effective leadership development is to target what should be evaluated up front for change with top management, so that when the changes begin to occur they can celebrate their personal stock going up, rather then worrying about unpredictable turns in the organization's internal market.

One of the first things I typically discuss with senior management around the introduction of a leadership development program is for them to work with me to identify the metric or index they will use to measure successful change. Recently, I had an HR executive ask why this was important, and how we could measure such intangible change anyhow. My reaction to such queries is simple. In HR we need to be just like the other functional areas of management, so if we ask senior leaders to invest in leadership development, then they ought to have some idea of their Return on Investment (ROI) or maybe Return on Learning (ROL). Getting people in HR to think in these terms is a real challenge, however once you do that, they begin to see before them an enormous set of opportunities enabling them to begin to showing where investments in people produce a return. For example, one of the returns on learning how to be a more effective virtual leader would be how long it takes for virtual teams to achieve project milestones.

8. Generally, if senior management and HR are not at a point where they are asking for the ROI on training leaders, then it is likely they do not have the wherewithal to sustain the change. Why? They probably have no idea what they are investing in regarding leadership development, and therefore they do not know what to track. What stock should they focus on? Is it even in their portfolio? They typically do not know. If they do not know, we need to help them understand the magnitude of the investment they are making, as they will be more serious about the need for support to keep their investment growing. It is a lack of attention to this form of investment by senior management that usually kills the effects of leadership development efforts. Why not tie leadership development to specific projects that are driven by how effectively the leader and followers deploy what they have learned?

FOOL PROOF LEADERSHIP DEVELOPMENT: 100% RELIABLE

There is no such thing as fool proof leadership development. Anytime someone tells you there is, please ask him or her for the data, or politely ask them to leave your office. I recently attended a conference where a noted leadership developer spoke about the development work done at her premier training institution. After presenting an elaborate training model with lots of glitz and glitter, I asked her what evidence did she have that any of the development work her center did had a positive impact on leadership development? I added to my question the following: "on just one individual." Her response was, to say the least, disappointing but not surprising to me. She said, "I am aware of some work going on in that area, but that is going on in another department." She then said, "Now, did I answer your question?" I said, "Absolutely!" It was the same lame response I got from a colleague of hers a few years back, except absent the "other department" remark. They have collected no data to determine whether they truly have had a positive impact on someone ... anyone, and they are one of the premier leadership development centers in the world, at least according to the *Wall Street Journal*. I have a *real* problem with that, as I hope you will now have as well.

There are some questions that I would like you to routinely ask when someone says they have a program that can develop leadership. I would like you to consider that you are the FDA, like the prescription drug example I previously gave, and you are applying the same standards to the use of a leadership development cure as you would to a new drug. What can you ask?

- Tell me about the model(s) of leadership and learning approach that underlies your leadership development program. How has the model been validated, in other words, what has it been shown to predict in terms of processes (innovative behavior, collective efficacy), and outcomes such as production, sales, turnover, profitability, etc.?
- Most programs that have some model also have a way to measure the behavior and attributes comprising that model. This is usually done with some type of survey tool. Again, ask them to provide you with some background data on the instrument and how it has been validated. Ask them for the technical manual to see what type of studies have been done on this instrument. If there is no technical manual, forget using the instrument except for educational purposes. What I mean here is that there are a lot of interesting instruments out there, which can make you aware of things about yourself that you may not have thought about before. As far as that goes, they are fine, but they are over-the-counter stuff compared to the prescription-based cures. If there is a manual, look to

see the type of sample populations the measure has been validated on, and what type of performance indices have been used. I think there should be at least 10 separate studies done on any leadership survey instrument before it should be used for development purposes. After 10 times, items that did not work should have been eliminated and if it can predict performance in the majority of 10 cases, I would say it is probably a pretty decent survey. I say majority, because oftentimes, you have a great leadership survey and terrible organizational data. For instance, everyone on the performance appraisal survey is evaluated a 3, thus there is absolutely no differentiation among top, middle, and bottom performers. So the best survey in the world will fail to predict anything when there is nothing reliable to predict.

- Take a look at who has done the research on the instrument. If all of the research on the survey has been completed by its developers, then I would be cautious recommending it for use in developing leadership. The best test of any instrument, whether it is medical or psychological, is to have independent confirmation of its reliability and validity.
- Now moving to the leadership program itself, how do they measure its impact? There are five levels that are appropriate to include: How well the program was liked and how it might have changed attitudes toward leading and developing as a leader. What did people learn from the program and how was this measured? What type of behavioral change occurred and how was this measured? What impact did the program have on performance or in predicting performance? What was the return on investment in the program? Please refer to the end of this chapter for an extensive list of questions that you can use to assess impact of leadership development interventions.

You will find that only 10% of the leadership development interventions out there will be able to get past the first level of evaluation of programmatic impact. Noting the paucity of evaluation, you may want to also consider entering into a relationship with researchers to test a program that has been piloted with other groups. This is perfectly legitimate to do, and in fact, by measuring what impact the program has, it is very likely it will have an impact given all of the attention being allocated to change. I would be delighted to see more leadership developers conducting research on their models and methods in collaboration with organizations who intend to use their work.

Essentially, as we have discussed leadership development now, it can be viewed as a planned intervention in the life stream, where given a particular model, method, time period, and evaluation strategy, we expect to change the course in people's mental model, behavior, and direction of the life stream. Simply thinking in this way in designing the leadership development intervention will help to make it more successful. Leadership development, like leadership itself, is a process that is embedded in a context that is changing and emerging all of the time. Today, to discuss leadership development without considering how technology can enhance it over time seems in my opinion to be outdated. Clearly, we can use technology in many cost-effective ways to enhance leadership development. Here are some specific ways to do so, which we have played around with ourselves:

- We send articles in advance and after our first program intervention to stimulate reflective learning. We ask people to fill out STAARR reports to record positive and negative incidents of leadership. We later use their observations to help develop the model of leadership in use within their respective organization in a workshop.
- We collect survey data on the web to assess leadership, to do pulse surveys to feed back to leaders for furthering their reflective process, to assess the culture or climate for feedback in a second or third face-to-face workshop, etc.
- We use groupware technology to set up peer learning groups who can continue to support each other virtually by sharing ideas, examples, suggestions, observations, etc. These peer learning groups typically meet on a monthly basis following the close of a face-to-face workshop, and do so until the next workshop. We are also now introducing virtual coaches or facilitators who interact individually and with the peer learning groups to help facilitate the transfer of learning from workshop to in stream back in the organization.
- We provide copies of example developmental plans in virtual team rooms where people can come to look at examples they might incorporate into their own developmental planning process. We also provide cases that can help stimulate participants' thinking to try new strategies for working with colleagues, followers, or both.

- We are currently building a leadership knowledge repository that participants will be able to tap into, in order to see what other individuals and groups have generated while being at the same developmental point as the current participant in terms of his or her own developmental achievements. This knowledge repository will contain the goals set at particular points in time, obstacles perceived, support required, etc.
- We are connecting virtual coaches together via online groupware systems, so that they can work with each other to come up with the best strategies for developing others. With this strategy, the more experienced consultants are able to share their wisdom with less experienced ones either through online discussions or by placing helpful ideas and suggestions in a database accessible only to the coaches.

These are some of the economical ways we can use technology to support leadership development, over time, distances, and cultures. As with the Internet, we are at the very front end of using technology to enhance the continuous development of leadership. We now have the very best opportunity to develop leadership at work in a cost-effective way, with the support of advanced information technology.

In the next chapter, I move our discussion up to strategic leadership development focusing more specifically on leading at a distance and impacting larger groups and systems as opposed to individual followers. Then in the last chapter, I present the mental model that we have used and validated for leadership development over the last 15 years, along with some of the evidence to support its use. I use this model as one example and as a practical framework to help integrate many of the areas that I have discussed in this book. Then I am done and your work hopefully begins or continues in terms of your leadership development.

WHAT CAN YOU TRY TO BOOST YOUR LEADERSHIP DEVELOPMENT?

Select a particular area that you want to change in terms of the distribution of your behavior. Let us take a very fundamental aspect of your behavior. On a day-to-day basis, how positive are you with people you work with and how positive are they with each other? Let us set a goal of shifting the distribution of positive behaviors upward about 20%. Thus, if you have five positive instances per day, let us simply add one more behavior per day in your interactions with others that is positive.

First, let us define what positive means. Positive can be optimistic, supportive, encouraging, recognizing, complimenting, etc. Start with a definition of what you mean by positive.

Now for the next couple of weeks, I want you to record every instance of positive behavior. I am assuming this will not be a huge chore, if you have chosen it for change. At the end of each day, reflect on what you did that was positive, and then check it off. This will give you a base line of where you started before any intervention.

Recall, the intervention here is very simple. You merely have to add 20% positive behaviors to your distribution over the course of a week. When doing so, at the end of each day, reflect on what the reactions were to your change in behavior. Try to look at nonverbal and verbal channels. Do you sense the people you work with feel there is a change? Is it something noticeable to them? Do you get the sense they feel the change is genuine or that you are trying to manipulate them in some way? If you feel they feel there is some manipulation, you may need to back off on the positives and make sure you have complete transparency in your agreements, and in every transaction—recall our discussion of conditional trust-building, as it may be relevant to what you are trying to accomplish here.

What I am trying to demonstrate in this exercise is that by changing a single type of behavior, you can demonstrate to yourself that you can change and self-regulate your leadership. Moreover, by doing it in a systematic way, we can show that it is not all special effects, smoke and mirrors, or both. Finally, the best leaders are focused, disciplined, and persevering. I am trying to model each of these attributes with this rather straightforward exercise. Leaders are also positive, and being positive can become infectious and strategic and can have a very positive impact on performance. It raises the beliefs in our mind that we can have a positive impact, and beliefs drive behavior, and behavior drives performance. Indeed, one can now leverage technology to spread the positive behaviors throughout the entire world, with the press of a button.

SUMMARY OF QUESTIONS

These questions are designed so that you can look at leadership development at different levels of analysis. The levels start with you and go up to the strategic organizational level.

What Are Some of the Key Points of Impact for Leadership Development?

On Me as an Individual

- What I believe?
- What I have learned?
- How I think?
- What I know?
- How I behave?
- How motivated I am?
- How confident I am?
- How open I am?
- How transparent I am?
- How adaptive I am?
- How optimistic, hopeful, and resilient I am?
- How I choose to learn from others?
- How I challenge others?
- How I link to others?
- How willing I am to change?
- How able I am to change?

On Others

- What they believe?
- What they have learned?
- How they think?
- What they know?
- How they behave?
- How motivated they are?
- How confident they are?
- How open they are?
- How transparent they are?
- How adaptive they are?
- How optimistic, resilient, and hopeful they are?
- How able they are to lead?
- How able they are to be exemplary followers?
- How fairly they treat their peers?

- How they challenge me and others?
- How willing they are to change?
- How able they are to change?

On Collectives

- Degree of engagement?
- Degree of alignment?
- Degree of coherence?
- Degree of reserve potential?
- Degree of focus?
- Degree of renewal?
- Degree of knowledge acquisition, transfer, and diffusion?
- Degree of innovative actions?
- Degree of cooperation?
- Degree of collective energy?
- Degree of innovativeness?
- Degree of inclusiveness in social networks?
- Degree of centrality and balance in social networks?
- Degree of speed in execution?

Some Performance Metrics

- Per person productivity
- Market share
- Market penetration
- Market growth
- Client acquisition
- Build out of client services/products
- Rate of change in performance output/profits
- Shareholder/stock evaluations
- Peer evaluations of organizational reputation
- Quality of applicants
- Absenteeism & turnover
- Cycle time for new product development
- Customer engagement

DEFINING LEADERSHIP DEVELOPMENT AT AN INDIVIDUAL LEVEL

I assume in all of the following examples that we are talking about how one or more people influences one or more people to willingly move toward achieving a particular target goal or objective.

- I have a greater sense of awareness between who I am, what I am offering to others in terms of influencing them, and how I can apply my capabilities and strengths to be more effective in achieving targeted objectives.
- I have learned about specific ways that I can be more effective in influencing and engaging individuals, groups, and larger entities.
- I have learned what to focus on when attempting to develop followers into leaders.
- I am more energized to explore areas that I heretofore did not recognize as potential strengths that I can leverage to achieve desired outcomes.
- I am more efficacious in trying to use specific strategies to influence others to achieve certain directives, which I did not use before.
- I have developed a clear sense of what I want to build in terms of my own future development, as well as the development of my unit or organization.
- I have learned strategies to help identify the strengths in others that can be developed.
- I have a better sense of how to articulate my core message to groups to motivate them to work toward our common purpose and objectives.
- I know how to build a developmental plan for others to help accelerate the deployment of their strengths.
- I feel more capable of influencing my peers on how to work together to achieve common goals and expectations.
- I have learned specific strategies to work with peers of mine to get them to identify with our core beliefs and values.
- I have learned how to identify strategies for disseminating important messages throughout my organization to enhance identity with the message and alignment in moving forward.
- I know the difference between leading directly and leading indirectly in terms of using methodologies to assure that my

most important beliefs are conveyed accurately to my most distant followers.

- I am more confident in approaching my leader to get him or her to buy into the objectives that I feel are most important for us to be pursuing.
- I can deploy specific strategies with my leader to get him or her to champion efforts that I want to initiate.
- I understand the importance of my behaviors/actions being consistent over time with my beliefs.
- I have learned reflective strategies that help me to revisit and learn from important moments/events.

DEVELOPING LEADERSHIP AT A DYADIC LEVEL

- I consider the importance of critical moments/interactions with each of my followers (peers) in terms of developing a deeper sense of trust in each other's intentions.
- I know how to structure the rules of engagement with my leader in order to optimize the level of transparency that we have in our relationship.
- I can recognize that each of my relationships with followers has its own developmental trajectory, which I will work to positively accelerate using strategies to build alignment around our learning objectives.
- I have learned how to provide a safe context for my followers to offer me their most critical observations.
- I debrief with each of my followers after we have gone through a significant challenging event.
- I have asked my leader to work with me to develop one specific leadership development goal that he or she and I can work on over time to enhance my impact on others.
- I see the importance of matching each of my follower's strengths with mine, and figuring out the best way we can optimize each and every interaction.
- I now focus on developing my followers into leaders by addressing one of the demands of leadership and periodically assess how each of my followers is growing toward being a more effective leader with respect to that demand.

- We can link some of these points to the performance indicators previously identified.

DEVELOPING LEADERSHIP AT A GROUP LEVEL

- All of my followers now know what my core beliefs are and their relevance to our work together.
- My peers see me as someone who they can come to for authentic feedback on ways they can improve their performance.
- I have worked to create a sense of mission and alignment around our core mission.
- People who work with me are transparent in sharing the most essential information with others.
- My workgroup has a clear sense of its identity and what is important to achieve.
- My team feels efficacious to take on new assignments and challenges.
- All of my employees have a heightened level of engagement at work.
- People view me as taking the time to find out what they need to be their best at work.
- We have created a climate in our unit where everyone feels responsible to share the most important information they have about a project.
- People in my unit continually step up to the plate to help each other get better.
- We have a common developmental goal that we all are monitoring to assure that we collectively improve our performance over time.
- When we get together to work on new projects, my team members balance inquiry and advocacy to get the best possible solution.
- I am able to make the links between what we have done as a leadership team and the innovative products of our work.
- By establishing a clear sense of accountability and identification with our goals, we have sustained growth year over year by 10%.
- The Per Person Productivity (PPP) of members of my group have increased 8% since we began setting individual performance improvement goals in my team.
- We can link some of these points to the performance indicators previously identified.

STRATEGIC LEVEL LEADERSHIP DEVELOPMENT

- I have learned how to work issues through my top management team so they can articulate a clear and consistent message about priorities to their constituencies.
- We have elected to focus on one core value this year to drive what it means to achieve sustainable growth in our business.
- If you asked our customers what is our most important and core value, you would have 100% agreement on what is our core value.
- We have rolled out a new vision for our division and are able to track, over time, how each member translates that vision into changes in his or her particular work processes.
- After instituting the program No Ideas Left Behind, we have seen an increase in unsolicited ideas at all levels of our organization of 25%.
- If you examined the directives that come from the four levels of management below our Top Management Team (TMT), you would see a high degree of coherence in the messages we have conveyed from our team on our top three priorities.
- We have built a culture of transparency and trust over the last 2 years, which supports a much faster integration of new information technology into our work processes.
- I am confident that each and every manager in our organization knows one developmental goal for each of his or her respective followers, that he or she is tracking for improvement over time.
- We have developed a highly engaged work culture.
- People who work here describe our organization as being strengths-focused/based.
- We can also link some of these points to the key performance indicators previously identified.

10

Raising Leadership Development to Strategic Levels

I met the young CEO of a large healthcare management organization a year ago, which in the United States is hated about as much as the Internal Revenue Service. I have a good college friend who also works for one of the largest HMOs, and he said to me that working for the most hated organization on earth can be a little frustrating on your drive into work. The CEO had recently been picked by the Chairman of the Board to head up the organization of approximately 20,000 employees. He was completely homegrown and had spent his entire career within this one organization. Everyone knew him, some had grown up with him, and it appeared that he was well-liked by employees and generally trusted.

In our 1-hour interview, he discussed at length the importance of information technology and how it would transform their business operations over the next few years. He discussed the importance of having each and every employee literate in the use of technology and the type of investment required to accomplish this objective. In conversation, he referred to some cool sites he liked to visit and discussed a presentation he had heard a week ago on a product that informed call center employees on the mood of their caller. Specifically, when a call came in the agent could bring up the client's profile, and if there was a smiley face that meant the last interaction had gone well. If there was a neutral face, then there was nothing to write home about. If there was a sad face, then this client had not had a good interaction on the previous call, or had some problems with services and that was the reason for calling in to this center.

When I left the interview, I remarked to my colleague that I had rarely met a CEO so in touch with technology and how it would be affecting his future business. She looked at me and smiled but did not say anything else.

In the next interview, we discussed with one of the CEO's senior managers the CEO's leadership, the type of culture he was creating, and so forth. During the course of the interview, she remarked on his unsophisticated approach to technology, and how she was sure he had never turned on a PC! Throughout the day I probed on the use of technology in this business and the CEO's position on technology. Many of his closest senior managers had no idea that this CEO rarely made a purchase by going to a store anymore, did a lot of his personal travel by e-tickets, was part of several virtual chat groups related to his hobbies, and probably knew more about PCs than some of the people in his IT department.

The point of this story is that the CEO had not diffused his passion for technology, not even at the most basic level of understanding. Part of what CEOs must do is to strategically manage the message they want every one to hear and to live up to over time. In this simple example, the CEO was quite surprised and even amused to hear that many of his managers thought he used his PC as a paper weight on his desk!

It seems fair to say that much of our discussion about leadership and its development has focused mainly at the individual or small group/team level. This seemed a very natural place to work on together, since most people when asked to think about leadership think about it as an individual. Rarely do people consider leadership as shared, although that is changing as organizations become more horizontal in structure as opposed to vertical. Yet, to many people leadership is an individual-level phenomenon, in part because a great deal of the research on leadership comes from the most individualistic nation on earth—the United States.

In this chapter, I would like to raise leadership to another level, so to speak. At this level, leadership can be represented as a strategic process, obviously driven by the actions and behaviors of people, but nevertheless interpreted as a collective strategic process. For example, we have discussed the idea of creating greater openness in an organization to fuel the sharing of information and knowledge and also to stimulate innovation. I can walk into an organization somewhere in the world, and find a very high degree of openness versus walking into another organization where every bit of information is carefully filtered before being transmitted. Where does this sense of openness come from, and more importantly how can it be developed within people's collective mental model, culture, and ultimately individual behavior? Let us explore these two issues by examining how strategic leadership occurs, how it is diffused, and how it creates a sense of alignment around achieving an open environment for discussion.

WHAT IS STRATEGIC LEADERSHIP?

Traditionally, when people discussed strategic leadership they generally referred to very senior managers, the CEO, the senior management team, and so forth. It was the leadership of an organization that set the strategic direction for that organization. Personally I would agree with this definition, but would add that in today's world it is probably limiting to the notion of what constitutes strategic leadership. How? Although strategic direction is generally promoted from the top of an organization, its formation and dissemination now involves many more participants than just the top management team. To some extent, and given what I have already said about changes in information dissemination, more and more people have to be involved in strategic thinking in order to promote a strategic direction. Therefore strategic leadership now encompasses a much broader segment of an organization, if not the entire organization.

The challenge organizational leaders now have in front of them is to articulate the strategic intent that needs to be pursued and then to get others to interpret it, modify it as necessary, implement it, and then evaluate how close to intent they were able to achieve. To some extent, everyone in the organization now has a role in the strategic leadership process. Therefore each and every individual shares parts of the strategic leadership process that he or she must fulfill for the strategic intent to be actualized.

Let us start with a simple and perhaps traditional example. The top management team formulates an abstract but compelling future vision for the organization. That vision is communicated throughout the entire organization in e-mails, speeches, one-to-one conversations, departmental meetings, and in marketing campaigns. People at all organizational levels are asked to interpret and to translate the vision into action within their respective units. In other words, what does the vision mean for you and your unit? How does it change what is important and what is no longer important in terms of your work processes? How does it impact the way you work together in your unit or between units? What resource implications are involved, and how will this change the way resources are allocated. What can you do to help others understand the implications of the vision? What are some of the gaps that are in the vision that you need to fill? What is the part of the vision that most excites you and that you most identify with and are inspired to achieve? If there is no excitement generated, the vision is likely to be yet another wall covering with little meaning, except to create broader cynicism in the organization.

As you can see, this example is traditional in terms of where the vision began, but, subsequent to its initial point of dissemination, if everyone does not get actively involved in interpreting the vision it will not work. Indeed, it may not even be heard correctly at subsequent levels. Why? Let us take an extreme case where the culture of the organization is highly cynical. Top management puts forth a vision and people at the next level say no way. They say no way in terms of their words, actions, and behaviors. Soon afterward, the vision is lying dormant somewhere caught within the cynical culture cycle of this organization, or worse yet, it appears on the wall in each person' s office, as a reminder of how out of touch the top management team really is around here!

Let us try another extreme example. In this very different organization, the culture is one of active and positive engagement. People at all levels have a can-do attitude, and will work a vision through from its initial rough cut to complete execution. People at all levels go out of their way to communicate the vision as clearly as they can understand it, and then add in their own interpretation. They discuss with each other why the vision is important to their current and future work, even if it is not yet perfect. They try to support each other in learning about the vision's implications for current and future business. People send articles to each other related to the vision's content. You find people discussing it at lunch, and coming back to their supervisors with new ideas and directions built on the initial vision. There is an ownership of the vision, even if not fully understood, which was not achieved in the first organization. Ownership, deep ownership of the vision, is a critical component of strategic leadership. Ownership presupposes identification and identification presupposes understanding, and commitment.

Strategic leadership involves developing ownership and identification in a new vision or mission. It includes people at all levels of the organization, as not to include them would create a gap in alignment. Soon into its dissemination, it is not described in conversations as the boss' vision, or the top management team's vision, but rather it is our vision. That is ownership that eventually gets reflected in behaviors and actions. A great vision must have broad ownership to be successful in achieving its audacious goals.

From the examples I have previously given, it is clear that strategic leadership includes leaders and followers, it includes preparing the context for change, it includes openly communicating the intent of the vision and it includes a very active engagement of all parties in the vision's dissemination and ultimately the alignment of the workforce. We could even back things up a bit up stream, and say the active engagement also starts with the vision's creation. How? It can be from the accumulation of many good ideas over the years from all levels of an organization, which finally tip into a vision. Alternatively, it could be as the vision itself is under creation the top management team spends a lot of time discussing their ideas and potential future directions, soliciting input from all participants or stakeholders.

Imagine the competitive edge you can have if you have a workforce that gets charged versus shocked when one puts forth a new vision. Think how quickly you can get people aligned around and supportive of the new vision, if people are already engaged in the organization and are owners. Strategic leadership involves the advance preparation of the workforce's collective mental model, to be adaptive to new ideas and initiatives. This collective model, once sparked with new ideas, stimulates even more ideas, and builds on rather than burying what they heard. Strategic leadership works to build the network of mental models that allows people to test out assumptions, while also sharing assumptions that are fundamental to defining the organization, for example, we are an open organization that thrives on innovation. Or, we never know where an innovative idea will come from and we are always on the alert to see what new ideas are out there. Help everyone be heard!

Frankly, it is easy to tell when someone is in an organization where there is little sophisticated strategic leadership. First, as you talk to different managers, the message about what is important for the organization to consider and focus on varies dramatically. Ask them the question, "What is your most important core value?" and they look at you rather strangely. Talk to the newest member of the unit, and find out how they learned about what this organization stands for, and you will have a pretty good idea of the quality of the organization's strategic leadership system. If all conversations were coded in the organization, you might find there is more emphasis on what we cannot do, what they do not tell us, what we should be waiting to be told what to do, what is not worth doing, or all of the aforementioned. A great strategy always provides the organizing principle that underlies the very best an organization produces. For example, at West Point, the organizing principle is to develop leaders of character. Every great organization has a great organizing principle. What is the organizing principle for your organization? What is the organizing principle for some of our most venerable organizations, for example, Southwest Airlines, General Electric, Delta Force, Wells Fargo, IBM, Hewlett Packard, Harvard University, Mayo Clinic, Berkshire Hathaway, Johnson & Johnson, Merck, Toyota, Gallup and so forth.

Let us go back to the beginning regarding what constitutes strategic leadership is. It is the collective mental model developed in each person's head about the organization's vision, mission, culture, and climate. The model is engaged by everyone and is especially promoted and reinforced through words, behaviors, and actions by senior management. There is a consistency and alignment across levels about what is important to the organization. One unit looks for ways to coordinate more effectively with others, in that all units are aligned around the vision and mission. It is hardwired into every interaction.

Cooperation and engagement run high, even in cases where people disagree. By disagreeing everyone knows that they are simply trying to get to the best solution as opposed to destroying another unit's chances at growth, success, or both. The main competitors are not the unit across the hall, but the competitors in the open market. Drop a critical point or bit of information in one part of the organization and in short order it will be disseminated intact to all points of the organization. Information and knowledge are treasured assets, and yet they are generously shared for the betterment of the organization. I know what you are thinking, "What planet is this guy on?" If you are thinking that, however, you are already providing useful feedback on the status of effective strategic leadership in your organization.

SOME REALISTIC EXAMPLES

I worked with one company where the CEO had one particular vision that he would express, every opportunity he had, to his senior management team and to larger audiences. Unfortunately, his message was seen as being completely out of line with where the team felt the organization should be heading. Only one top manager really bought into it, and he did so for his own self-gain, not for the good of the organization. He provided support for the vision only in the hopes that he would get favors from the CEO, who was very frustrated with the resistance shown by his other senior managers.

In conversations with each senior manager, and their followers, it was evident that the organization had sent many inconsistent messages, that there was no alignment around key targets or initiatives, that information was poorly shared even when readily available, and that the CEO was dumbstruck by how little people in his organization knew about the vision he was pursuing. The reason why they did not know about his vision was because his top management team either did not tell them or told them something quite different. After a period of receiving so many mixed messages the workforce just decided to sit back and wait till the dust cleared. They did finally get going with some substantive discussion, long after the CEO was fired and half the workforce was laid off. Whether the layoff could have been avoided is a good question. However, not doing anything to change in an industry that was changing at light speed provided a much higher probability for the layoff to occur.

In a very different organization, a new CEO came in after the retiring CEO had built up a very successful organization. Her job was to build on that success and take it to the next level, which in some board member's minds was quite different from the previous successful formula. She spent a lot of time in her first 6 months referring to the reasons for past success, and also her charge by the board to raise this very successful organization to the next level. During her first 6 months, she went around and listened to people, had her senior managers listen, and told people "Just keep doing what your doing that made us successful." After gathering a considerable amount of information, she engaged a consulting firm to look at the emerging and future markets for her organization. She began to discuss what those markets were and what it would require to move into those markets in terms of changes in direction, resource allocation, employee competencies, and even structure. As time went on, she got more specific in her descriptions, and yet she continued to solicit input at all levels to reinforce the importance of having everyone's input. As you can imagine, taking a successful organization and asking it to change its formula is by no means a trivial task. Many would argue that it is easier to strategically lead an organization from a burning platform than to a dim light in the future, regardless of how appealing that light may be. Not all people are moths!

In this second example, we can see several aspects of effective strategic leadership emerging. First, getting the workforce to understand who they are and what are their core strengths will provide a baseline assessment to build new initiatives on. Second, by listening to employee concerns and their aspirations in the first 6 months, she was able to promote a more open exchange of ideas that provided the basis for some blue sky discussions. Third, she was creating a culture of sharing and ownership in a process that could have profound implications for setting significantly new directions for this organization. Fourth, looking to the outside for signals of what our focus should be helped to set the stage for a successful organization to not be so inwardly focused on their old program for success. Finally, getting her top managers to work with her in a coordinated way to achieve the next level of success for this organization is yet another example of strategic leadership. Keep in mind, this is the same management group that brought the organization to its earlier levels of success, and likely without their support she would be like the leader previously described, dead in the water.

In these two examples, I discussed the strategic leadership coming from a single individual in the beginning and then becoming more diffuse over time, as well as more widely disseminated. This does not mean that strategic leadership must start with an individual. In fact, with the second example, some might argue that it was a subgroup of the board of directors that set in motion the choice of the new CEO, who was then charged by them and with their support to bring them all to the next level. In reality, it is almost always both individual and group-based, particularly as it emerges and evolves over time.

Taking it from an individual perspective, you must consider how you reach others through the influence of people around you, indirectly through information technology, or both. As a senior leader where you place yourself, whom you interact with, what you emphasize and repeat, and what you acknowledge and reward all become part of the strategic leadership system that is created. When creating a new vision, you must consciously think of ways to spread the vision like a virus. There are many antibodies in bureaucratic organizations that will simply kill a good virus. You will need to be very clever in adapting the virus to the conditions of your organization. Sustaining a new direction is the ultimate measure of success at the strategic leadership level.

From a strategic leadership perspective nothing is more important, in my opinion, than the ethical tone a leader or leaders set and the moral perspective that supports it. Setting standards for what is right or wrong according to your own decisions, actions, and behaviors builds a very important facet of the strategic leadership system. That facet is what frames in people's minds what is acceptable and unacceptable behavior. Strategic leadership when it is most effective also clarifies what are the old and new boundaries for appropriate and inappropriate behavior. At the high end, strategic leadership must identify what are the high standards for aspiration. This is an extremely important responsibility, especially today as most people are more cynical about the ethics of leadership, given how many of our role models have been shot down publicly. One day a kid from the Bronx pitches a perfect game in the Little League World Series and the next day, we hear that his birth certificate may have been doctored to change his age. What seems like a minor incident in the grand scheme of things is part of a stream of incidents over the last 2 decades that takes our heroes for a day and then vilifies them.

Ideally, once a high moral standard is embedded in the mental models of the workforce, you will be able to trust that the interactions your managers and their followers have with each other, suppliers, clients, and other organizations are interactions that represent the highest moral character. By operating at this level, we can assure commitment to standards as opposed to compliance where we need to monitor each and every significant interaction. Again, this is where developing deep trust has enormous payoffs for an organization. Such developments also provide a competitive edge in one's organization that is exceedingly difficult to replicate.

Some organizations, like our military, spend an inordinate amount of time discussing moral and ethical conduct as part of their strategic leadership system's development. Why would they do so? Perhaps because it helps to makes them the best military system in the world. Today, the United States can likely win any battle with its advanced technological superiority. However, as with Vietnam, it can win any battle but lose a war that has no clear purpose, no clear moral standards, and no clear future direction. More specifically, the U.S. Army spends a lot of time discussing the proper and humane treatment of prisoners, even ones who have committed the most atrocious acts of war. Why? They have learned that if the opposing side believes they will be treated humanely as prisoners, then they are much more willing to give up when things look bad in battle.

During World War II, the Japanese and Germans wanted to convince their populations that if the Americans, or worse yet the Russians, took them prisoner, they would be immediately tortured and then killed. So either you die fighting for a cause you believe in, or you die an atrocious and less honorable death in a prison camp. They did not want their soldiers to have a choice, which in the grand scheme of things makes sense, doesn't it? By making us the best army to surrender to, we are doing the right thing, and we are taking the fight out of our opponents. One wonders why this is not applied more directly to industry. Let me give you an example of where it has been applied successfully.

One electrical contractor in Washington, DC told me that he has had to lay off employees during downturns in the economy. However, when he does lay off people, he treats them as if they are alumni, keeping them informed of all developments in the organization. Over time, he has found that by treating people humanely and with dignity, the word of mouth recommendations he gets from former employees is enough to sustain and even grow his workforce as needed. Indeed, he has been able to hire back nearly 60% of those laid off using this approach. Treating people with dignity and humanely even when you have to get rid of them is doing the right thing, and by doing the right thing strategically, it appears there are tremendous benefits. This is a clear example of strategic leadership in terms of building a human resource base and culture that can sustain an organization's standards through the worst of times. In fact, it is in the worst of times that cultures are oftentimes firmly rooted for good or bad. Yet, there is an alternative approach and that is to build strength into one's culture each and every day. The strength-based culture should be tied minimally to high ethical standards, an honest concern for one's workforce, a continuous search to discover the needs and aspirations of one's customers/clients, a driving vision that is positive and energizing, and a culture in which everyone's voice can be heard.

Let us try approaching strategic leadership through the lens of service quality. I stayed at a world-class hotel in New York City a few years back. When I came into the room with the baggage handler, he noticed there was an ashtray with a cigarette butt in it. It was a nonsmoking room. He asked if I could wait a minute before unpacking and then he called the front desk. Within a minute he was off the phone and asked if I would consider looking at an upgraded room. Sure! We went up to a suite overlooking the Stature of Liberty. He apologized for the inconvenience and asked if this room was okay. Sure! I asked him how he got permission to make the change. He indicated that it was his call, and that he had merely called the front desk to find out what was available in the hotel. He did not need permission to change the room under these circumstances.

This service example reflects the strategic importance this hotel chain places on service quality. One of the most important interactions with a hotel is either at the front desk or when you invite this stranger into your room with your bags. This is an incredibly important point of contact that the strategic leadership of this hotel chain firm had obviously thought about and had incorporated in their training. I saw the reflection of that the strategic thrust in the behavior of that hotel employee. It went from strategic thinking of top management, to strategic execution via training and support of employees, to a mental model in this employee's head that guided his actions and delivery to me, the customer.

Let me try one other service example. A large global consulting firm went through hundreds of applicants to find the one receptionist they wanted to hire. They decided they wanted someone who could recall people by their voice intonation. In that way, the person could answer the phone and hearing a voice say, "Oh Mr. Johnson, it is nice to hear from you." Imagine Mr. Johnson's reaction being recognized in such a manner, rather than being a nameless phone call. Someone thought about the importance of how this seemingly minor interaction made people feel when they called this consulting firm.

The point I am trying to make is that strategic leadership is all about how we collectively think and what implications that thinking has for each and everyone's reactions. So many interactions occur outside the purview of top management, but in an organization that is attentive to strategic leadership, every interaction represents some aspect of that organization. When you start to think in that way, you take control of the strategic leadership of your organization, as opposed to having it control your destiny.

What are some of the common points that make up strategic leadership in any organization?

- It requires the active engagement of leaders and followers sharing in leadership responsibilities at all levels.
- Engagement presupposes there is a common mental model that is constantly being developed, but has clearly articulated base assumptions, values, moral standards, direction, milestones, etc.
- There is alignment across and within levels around a common purpose and direction.
- That information is not compartmentalized nor is knowledge. Information is disseminated to all of the appropriate points to which it needs to be transmitted throughout the organization.
- If you poke into the organization at any level or in any unit, you will, by and large, get the same story.

- It can begin with an individual and/or a group, but without the group's support it will never get very far in terms of dissemination and alignment.

A STRATEGIC LEADERSHIP DEVELOPMENT EXERCISE

One of the goals of strategic leadership is to cascade through organizations' important messages and directives. However, in many organizations, there are considerable obstacles to disseminating strategic information throughout the organization that were previously mentioned. In this exercise, I would like for you to examine how successful your organization is in disseminating key information throughout the entire organization. Take a major initiative or directive that is now underway, and spend the next several weeks trying to confirm how well the directive or message has been communicated throughout your organization. You can do so in the following ways:

- How has the organization used formal channels of communication to disseminate the directive, such as newsletters, Web sites, or e-mail?
- How has your manager communicated the directive? How has he or she assured that people understood the intent underlying the directive?
- How have your colleagues interpreted the directive? What type of spin have they placed on it, if any?
- What do newer employees know about the directive?
- What would you do differently to assure the message had been communicated more coherently, consistently and effectively?

Take a look at some directives that are or will be coming out of your unit. If you are not in charge of the unit, talk with your manager about evaluating how effectively key messages are communicated and diffused through the unit and to other units. Discuss what type of strategy you could use to optimize the diffusion of the message and to assure the message is accurate and fully understood. The directive could be about something that is going to happen, something that did happen, something that you might want to happen and are brainstorming around, or all of the aforementioned. What type of communication strategies would you employ? How could you use strategic redundancy to assure people get the message and interpret it as you intended? How can you use debriefing or the AAR process to deepen your unit's understanding of the message?

A second part of this exercise is to examine how organizations portray themselves to the world via the web. Take a look at what Levering classifies as the top five companies to work for versus the bottom five out of 100. How does each of these sets of companies communicate what they value, what they intend to accomplish, how they intend to accomplish it and what role you would play if hired? Examine each of their Web sites to see how appealing the message is that the company is conveying to you. How well does the company articulate what it is striving for in the future? Is there a clear and exciting vision presented? How does the vision get translated into what employees do, and the benefits they can expect to receive? What kind of future does the company present to the outside world?

You can approach this exercise as a stock analyst. What is it about this company that makes it appealing to invest your money in? How consistent is the message if any, that you pick up when reading the Web site? Would you be more or less prone to investing in the top five and bottom five organizations? If so, why? Also, instead of picking the bottom five organizations out of the top 100 best, you may want to pick five that did not make the list at all and use them as your bottom five comparison. Another strategy is to pick public sector Web sites and see what type of message they project out to future employees. How did they differ in terms of a focus on core values, vision, and mission? How are opportunities for advancing in one's career presented in the public versus private sector sites?

The point of this latter exercise is to determine how strategically aligned the organization is around its core values and vision, based on what it projects to the outside world via the web. As noted earlier, nearly 80% of the recruits coming to an organization have their first initial contact via the web. Thus, a company's Web site has become a strategic vehicle for portraying who they are and why you might want to considering coming to work for them. It is a form of electronic strategic leadership.

11

Down Stream Along the Full Range of Leadership

When I was growing up, I rarely saw myself as a leader. To be perfectly honest, I was afraid to be in the lead. I was very adept at using humor to get myself out of tough jams in high school. In our school, by the end of the spring, if you had not been called out for a fight, you would be! It was late spring and I had entered the cafeteria and sat down next to someone I knew. He was angry about something, and my mere proximity to him annoyed him for some reason. Before I realized it, he was calling me out to fight. I had almost made it through the year, and now it was my turn. Word spread like wildfire, even faster than the Internet! All of these upstanding middle class kids did not want to miss a pummeling. Whether I could take this guy or not, I was scared … scared all afternoon. For the first time in my life, I was not able to wiggle out of a dilemma.

I was reaching inside myself, thinking about my hero, Muhammad Ali. He never was afraid. Damn it, I didn't want to be afraid anymore. I still was. By late afternoon we were in our last study hall when something miraculous occurred, which I would have to say was divine intervention. The skies darkened, it got really cold, and first it started to rain and then to hail. You could see the disappointment in people's eyes. One sunny spring day gone sour, and who in their right mind would want to stand outside in the rain and hail watching a stupid fight, especially one that was by no means the top contenders in the school, an undercard billing at best!

Kenny approached me and I could see the fight was not in his heart. He said, "Let's drop it for now, and we'll take it up on Monday." Monday never came, and I skated through high school never again being called out.

So how do we create the challenges that you must confront to develop into the full person you can be and to achieve your full potential? I am still searching for that in myself, and I hope you will do the same each and every day, because that is the way to develop leadership—each and every day we emerge, we get better, we know more, and we can influence people more effectively.

I will refer to these challenges as trigger events in our lives that oftentimes have a profoundly positive effect on our development. In Fig. 11.1, my colleague Fred Luthans and I have tried to capture the whole process of personal and leadership development in a simple model. Let me explain. The top left-hand part of the model represents what we come into the world with our talents and strengths. Building on those capacities or attempting in some cases to break them down, we have life experiences that shape our development, that comprise our life stream. On the bottom

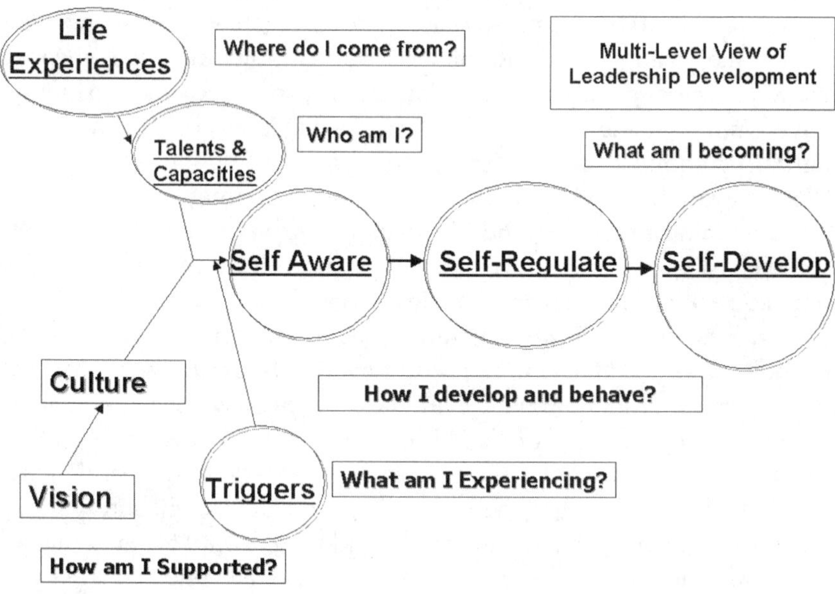

FIG. 11.1. Multi-level view of leadership development.

left, we have the context in which we are currently operating and there we specify the importance of the vision and culture to nurturing leadership development. If you work in an organization that values developing each person's potential and supporting that development each and every day, you know exactly what I am talking about. Someone in the organization, or many, care about you and your development, which we have labeled in the full range model *individualized consideration*. For those who work in an organization that has no vision for development or support, you also probably understand what I have described here.

Now we turn to the planned trigger events. These events are planned either because we choose to engage in them or someone decides they would be helpful to our development. Life takes care of the other events. A planned event may be simply taking on new job roles. It may be going back to pursue an advanced degree. It may involve taking on certain challenges in order to build on strengths that you have as an individual. Ask yourself the following question: "Have you planned any trigger events for the next 2 years, to accelerate your leadership development?" If not, you are allowing life to develop your leadership as it sees fit. I believe exemplary leaders take more active control of their development.

The rest of the model represents what we typically focus on in terms of leadership development, including enhancing our self-awareness of where we are and where we should focus our energies, then focusing those energies by regulating our development and then finally being consistent in our efforts to call it self-development. A number of important individual and contextual factors feed into self-awareness, but we must go beyond simply being aware to enhance leadership development.

Throughout the last 10 chapters, we discussed leadership development from many different perspectives. During the course of our discussion we covered the importance of the context in shaping development, using the metaphor of the life stream, and I shared with you some points in my own life stream, which have had an influence on my development. We have also gone on the inside, so to speak, and discussed the importance of an individual's mental model to shaping development. This internal focus included a discussion of the individual's perspective-taking capacity and how they defined for themselves their possible self. In the chapter on leadership development interventions, I mentioned the importance of having a model as a core aspect for training and development. In this last chapter, I would like to present a model that we have been testing over the last 15 years. During those years we have demonstrated how it predicts performance and how it can be effectively used for development. The model is called the full range of leadership. If you asked the questions I coached you to ask about the model and methods associated with it, my answers would be Yes ... Yes .... Yes. Yes, the model has been validated. Yes, we have been able to reliably measure its components. And yes, we have shown in very sophisticated field experiments that its application can enhance leadership development.

We chose the term *full range* to accomplish a specific purpose. We wanted to challenge our colleagues and ourselves, as well as anyone else wanting to be a more effective leader, to identify where they were along the full range of leadership and then work on developing to the next level. It did not seem very inspirational to us to refer to it as effective or exemplary leadership, but to be somewhat bold in our labeling it to really challenge whether we had explored the *full range* of leadership potential. Of course, the answer to that question thus far is absolutely not, but nevertheless the challenge is now out there for us all to explore.

On a personal level it has kept me questioning over these last 15 years, have we expanded the range of leadership enough to continue to be relevant? Have we gotten into leadership at a deep enough level to understand its essence? Have I challenged myself enough to keep moving up the range, to the very top, which we have labeled, perhaps for obvious reasons now, *idealized leadership?*

I feel I can answer those reflective questions with a yes. In fact, after moving from my position of 20 years at SUNY-Binghamton to the University of Nebraska, I have now begun work with my colleagues to explore what we feel is a totally unexplored root construct at the base of the highest end of leadership, which we have labeled *authentic leadership,* and authentic leadership development. Authentic leadership means to know oneself, to be consistent with one self, and to have a positive and strength-based orientation toward one's development and the development of others. Such leaders are transparent with their values and beliefs. They are honest with themselves and with others. They exhibit a higher level of moral reasoning capacity, allowing them to judge between gray and shades of gray. We refer to authentic leadership as the root construct that is necessary, but not sufficient to be transformational.

The authentic leadership development process is what we have been discussing throughout the chapters in this book. Authentic leadership development takes into account that life and planned trigger events shape leadership development. It represents an honest and transparent look at leadership development. It assumes that we must evaluate leadership development to not only understand what we have achieved, but to also reinforce development. Authentic leadership development is my challenge to the field of leadership development to get authentic or get out of the way. You are part of this process, as I have now told you what questions to ask to determine whether leadership development is or is not authentic.

When working with people who want to develop their leadership, one of the more difficult starting points is getting a common definition or model of leadership to start with. Our approach is that leadership is a social influence process that is comprised of a number of different style orientations and perspectives that fall along what we have labeled the full range of leadership. In terms of styles, we include at the bottom of the range avoidant, passive, or laissez-faire leadership. Above passive-avoidant is corrective leadership, which is represented by waiting for things to go wrong before taking any action to correct the problem. Above that point on the range representing passive-corrective leadership are leaders who look for mistakes all of the time in order to take corrective action. Such leaders monitor the situation very closely looking for any deviation from standard. Where a deviation does occur from standard, they are quick to correct it and get things back in balance.

The next part of the range moves from a corrective exchange to one where the leader constructively transacts with people to clarify expectations, achieve agreements, provide goals, and offer recognition. The primary perspective or motivation underlying this orientation to leadership is to get something done, and to do so in the most effective manner possible. The focus is on task accomplishment as opposed to developing people, unless the development of people is seen as integral to accomplishing the task.

The next four styles are qualitatively different from the previous ones described, and have been labeled *transformational*. These style orientations represent a cluster of interrelated styles that characterize leaders who change situations for the better, develop followers into leaders, overhaul organizations to provide them with new strategic directions, and who inspire people by providing an energizing vision and high ideal for moral and ethical conduct. The fours styles have been called *individualized consideration, intellectual stimulation, inspirational,* and *idealized.* Let me talk about each one relative to some of the other topics we have passed through in our discussion of leadership development.

IDEALIZED LEADERSHIP

Idealized leadership at its core represents the highest levels of moral reasoning and perspective-taking capacity. Such leaders are willing to sacrifice their own gain for the good of their work group, organization, and community. They set high standards for work conduct and are a role model for those standards. They build trust in people because those who work for them know they are working toward the common good, and their sacrifices along the way are evidence of that, along with the consistency of their actions with their values. These are people who see the good in others first, and when it is not obvious they work to bring it out through development.

INSPIRING LEADERSHIP

Leaders who have expanded possible selves are likely to be more inspiring leaders. They see there is something yet to accomplish in who they are and what they want to become. They typically have the courage to take the necessary risks to achieve their audacious goals. They have their feared selves in check, which allows them to explore new possibilities. They are also not so bound by rules that they cannot go beyond them or even break them to accomplish great things. Through their energy and vision of a more desirable future, they are usually able to get others to come along with them on a journey toward achieving the vision. They are persistent, focused, and aligned around a common purpose, which they work to get others excited about and energized toward achieving. They are positively driven leaders who create a positive expectation for success in followers.

INTELLECTUAL STIMULATION

As organizations restructure and move toward sharing a wider band of leadership responsibilities, there is an even greater need for the third style, called intellectual stimulation. As markets change and transform, the need to continuously question our most sacred assumptions becomes essential to developing a knowledge-based and learning-oriented culture. To be adaptive, this style gets people to think about alternative ways of approaching opportunities and problems. It is not a leader being smart, but rather the leader tapping into the full intellectual smarts of her followers. They do so by encouraging followers to be keen observers of future trends, to support each other in learning new approaches, and in listening hard to what others have to say before passing judgment. Leaders who are intellectually stimulating see the advantages of creating unity through diversity. By bringing together and integrating a diverse range of perspectives, they are able to create genuinely new ideas and initiatives. The goal of intellectual stimulation is to continuously generate the highest levels of creativity from one's followers.

INDIVIDUALIZED CONSIDERATION

The hallmark characteristic of this style is getting to know exactly who the people are who work with you and for you, and helping them to develop to their full potential. This leader spends a lot of time concentrating on the best ways to develop his or her people to their full potential, providing the necessary support to accomplish this objective. They are sensitive to the needs of others, but also challenging, to get others to not accept where they are but to question where they can go in terms of their full development. They engage people at work by knowing their likes and dislikes. They are not simply considerate people by any means, but rather *individually* considerate. They can be extremely challenging with people who need to be challenged, and completely supportive and facilitative with those who require that style, who may be the same person at different points in his or her respective development.

The main idea underlying the full range model is that we exhibit behaviors throughout the day, week, and year with others. By getting leaders, teams and followers, to move up the range in terms of the frequency of behaviors emitted, we have shown that more transformational leadership relates to higher levels of satisfaction, engagement, commitment, potency, effectiveness, and performance. So, the goal is to first get a picture in people's heads that there are four main overarching styles: passive-avoidant, corrective, transactional, and transformational. Each of these style orientations can be associated with a different perspective: What can I avoid or leave for handling later on? What must I correct? What must we agree on and execute? What must we strive for, develop, and achieve?

Now, what I would like you to do is to take a look at this full range model (Fig. 11.2, 11.3), and describe the most frequent style you observe in other leaders in your organization. Which perspective best characterizes your supervisor? Which perspective best characterizes your workteam? Would you say there is more emphasis at the top, middle, or bottom of the range?

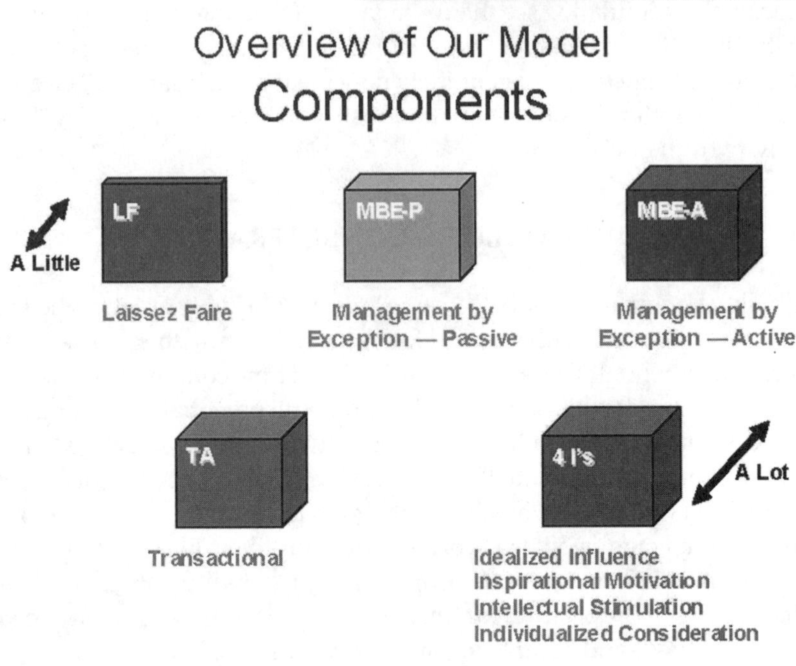

FIG. 11.2. Full range model.

The depth of the box represents how frequently the leader exhibits behaviors associated with a particular style orientation of leadership. In this more optimal model of leadership (Fig. 11.3), the leader exhibits laissez-faire leadership relatively infrequently. Going up the range, the leader exhibits more passive management-by-exception than laissez-faire. Similarly, in the middle range, the leader is exhibiting active management-by-exception more so than passive, but less than transactional leadership and transformational. Near the top, the leader exhibits transactional leadership fairly often, but exhibits transformational leadership more frequently. This is considered an optimal model because the distribution of leadership behaviors exhibited by this target leader is more towards the higher end of the full range. Leaders who exhibit this pattern of leadership styles would generally be seen as relatively if not highly effective by their followers.

My purpose in asking these questions is to begin to use this model as a lens for interpreting the behaviors and perspectives of people around you,

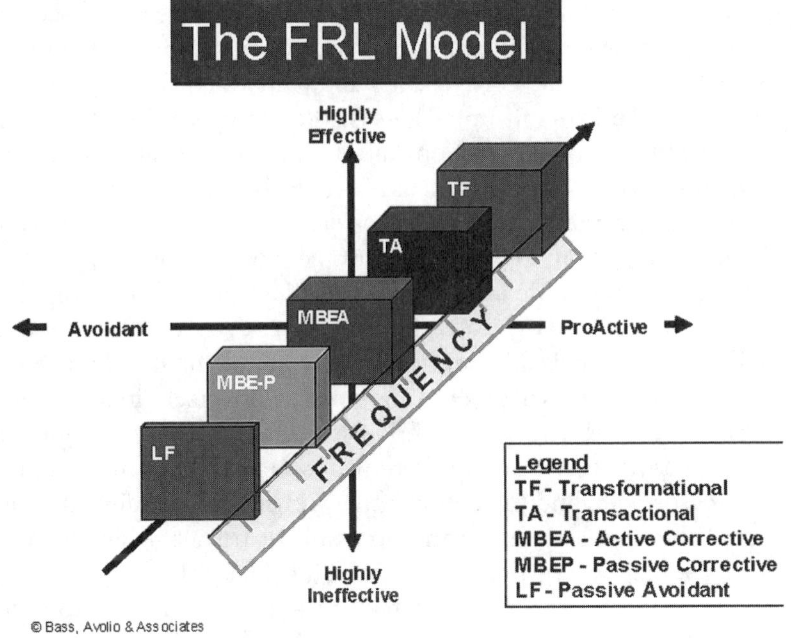

FIG. 11.3.

and then to decide how you can change the distribution of behavior toward the upper end of the full range. If you have already described the upper end of the range, I suspect that you are pretty satisfied with how you are treated and being developed. Great! If not, then we have some work to do, both in terms of your own leadership, and the leadership of those around you.

Let me describe the use of this model in more detail, but do so from what would be a unique vantage point in the leadership literature, the follower. We so often discuss leadership from the leader's point of view, but fail to consider how uninteresting leadership would be without followers. So, I thought I would end my discussion of leadership development, spending time talking about the recipient of all of this leadership training or the follower. I do this at the end, so that you start thinking about the follower as you lay this book down.

To lead, someone must follow whether in a steep hierarchy or a self-managed team where leaders and followers oftentimes are the same person stretched over time. Indeed, if all leaders put their follower's lenses on more often, we would likely have less of those communication problems in organizations.

So, from a follower's perspective what does each of these perspectives mean? For the passive-avoidant it means to me that, "I never hear from you until something has gone wrong, and sometimes it has to be very wrong for you even to show up!" There is little if any attention to development and to sharing of information, data, or knowledge that can advance our system's development. The focus is usually on what one can do to do the minimum acceptable level of performance. Your radar screen, so to speak, does not pick up many hits except the most obvious ones!

Moving up to the more active and corrective form of leadership, as a follower, I am delighted my leader finds mistakes even as they are emerging, as it reduces my risk of failing, which can be costly financially, in terms of risk to life, or in terms of other forms of risk. Conversely, in other situations, this type of leadership can seriously retard creativity and innovation. Simply put, no one around here wants to deviate from standards, procedures, or both, and to be innovative and creative requires that one deviates. When we deviate and are successful we do not get any recognition and if we fail, we certainly hear about it from our leader.

In its constructive and transactional form, it is easy for me to know what I am supposed to do, what is my scope of responsibilities, the resources I will have, and what I will receive when I am successful. Every aspect of the contractual arrangement is clear to each of us, and the quid pro quo for accomplishing our tasks are well laid out in our agreements. In its less exchange and reward orientation, my leader helps to clarify expectations and to specify the support he can provide for us to achieve our agreed upon objectives. It is reassuring to know what we need to do, and I trust my leader more as a consequence of her telling us what we need to do, when we need to do it, and how we can get our work done. My trust is borne out of her consistency in dealing with us fairly and equitably.

If my leader is transformational, he is completely interested in my development. He spends a lot of time observing and coaching me on my performance. He seems to know things about my capability that I myself do not understand. He provides goals for me that stretch my capabilities, and oftentimes my energy and patience. Each time I achieve a particular milestone, we celebrate the accomplishment, but yet there is soon another goal we have set to achieve. He helps me to understand why people relate to each other and to me the way they do. Each person is different, has different needs and competencies, and he believes that is one of the most important starting points for leading people to achieve their full potential.

My leader brings in different articles and books for us to look at that point to new ways of thinking. She oftentimes asks me to think about the assumptions underlying a particular course of action. What were you thinking at the time that led you to that conclusion? What were others thinking, and how might you have questioned their assumptions? Frequently, she gets us to look at industry leaders, to see what they do best and how they do it. It does not matter whether they are in our business or not. She asks us to look at the deeper perspectives underlying their success and to see what we can borrow and use ourselves. In my mind, she is a consummate thinker and teacher, because I always come away from our interactions knowing something I did not know before we met.

I am energized to be around my leader. He is constantly optimistic and positive about our future around here. He talks about what could be versus what is or what was. He demonstrates through his own words, actions and behaviors, his belief in our vision. He is a dreamer and a doer. He ignites our energy through his persistence and belief in what we are working toward in terms of our mission and vision. He is the most dedicated to the cause we follow, and his dedication has become infectious. When he is not around there is a sense of energy loss among us, although we all keep working hard, because we know that is what he would encourage us all to do.

My leader is someone I totally admire. He is someone who always goes to bat for us, is the last one in line for perks, and makes sure we all know why we are part of this organization. I have never trusted a leader as much as I trust him. He has earned my trust each and every day, by his willingness to sacrifice his own gains and desires for the good of our group. He talks about us when we accomplish something, but never about himself. Whenever recognitions are handed out, he walks to the back of the room and places us on center stage. Recently, we had a very difficult situation arise, where one of our employees took advantage of a customer. He was clear on the standards that we all follow from both an ethical and legal perspective. What this individual did was perfectly legal, but certainly was not of the highest moral standard. He was clear that this type of behavior was not acceptable, and would never be acceptable. He was willing to forgive this individual's transgression, but was very clear that it would not happen again without severe ramifications. We all knew he made a sacrifice here believing this person had made an immature mistake in judgment. Over time, we saw he was absolutely correct in his decision, even though he took a lot of heat at the time from his supervisor for not firing this person.

The descriptions that I gave you in the followers' eyes are ones that I have heard time and time again around the globe. Whenever anyone in any culture describes his or her ideal leader, invariably they describe what we have come to label the four I's of transformational leadership. They are universal in application across cultures, even though in different cultures what builds trust, or develops others may not be the same identical behavior. These concepts are universal, even though the actual behavior will vary from the most to least individualistic culture.

So here we are in your life stream, and nearly at the end of our discussion about leadership development. Let us say you understand the full range model and believe the points at the higher range of the model are associated with higher levels of performance. What then can you do to incorporate this model into your mental model of thinking and perhaps some planned trigger events? Here are some strategies to consider:

1. Think of someone in your life who had a profoundly positive impact on your leadership development. Generally, people describe this individual, be it a coach, priest, rabbi, minister, teacher, parent, etc. as representing the four I's of transformational leadership. Now, think about someone in your life who is looking for the same type of leadership at this current point in his or her life stream. What can you do to provide such leadership from a behavioral point of view?
2. Take the next week and complete a STAARR report on the leadership of your organization. Now record every incident that represents each of the full range of styles. What does your distribution look like at the end of the week? Is there a higher frequency of behaviors clustered at the lower, middle, or upper end of the range?
3. Talk to your colleagues, teammates, followers, supervisor, spouse about the full range model. What does it mean to you and the relationship you have with them? How can you be a transformational parent, team member, follower, or all three?
4. I would like you to choose a developmental goal for yourself, based on feedback on what you believe to be your primary and secondary style of leadership. You will need to discuss this with others who know you to acquire a more comprehensive view of your feedback on leadership. However, realize based on our chapter concerning feedback, that if you are an autocratic, dominating leader, it is likely that most people will give you bogus

feedback. If you judge yourself to be more corrective in orientation, people will not risk telling you what they really see, as you may not yet have their trust. So you may have to develop a transactional agreement with them, that you are asking for feedback to improve development and here is the agreement you will have with them to assure it is only used for that purpose. You likely may have to use a third party to gather the feedback anonymously if you really want to get an accurate picture of who you are as a leader.

5. Ultimately, I want you to set up a developmental plan that includes the following:

- A clear, specific goal on one particular leadership style that is measurable.
- A timeline for implementation and follow-up where you might revise the goal/objective.
- The specific activities and trigger events you will engage in to achieve the goal and objective, including keeping a STAARR report that you can go back and debrief over time.
- Specify the type of support you require to achieve this goal/objective including from followers, peers, supervisor, friends, etc.

By getting you to lay out clearly what you want to accomplish, how you are going to accomplish it, and during what time period, I am confident, based on what we have learned in research, that you can be successful in moving the leadership development meter up a notch, and then another, and another and another. Leadership development can occur in very brief trigger moments. It can occur when someone has simply said, "Have you stopped to consider what is possible here, in terms of our impact on the community?" It can occur when someone says, "Let us train a thousand leaders to be totally authentic and then give them the challenge to develop a thousand followers, and now we have 1 million enlightened individuals." It can occur almost anywhere if you stop to take the time to reflect on what just happened, and to think about what you want to happen next, and then after next.

Let me now close our discussion with one final thought on leadership development. The next time someone tells you about some born leader, just smile, knowing that maybe some day you will learn something about that person's life stream that will help make the special effects of leadership development not so special. If our streams cross somewhere in life, I will be most interested and deeply appreciative to hear what you have done to achieve your full potential as a leader. Have a safe and profoundly interesting trip down stream, and may all of your rapids be planned trigger events!

12

Research Supporting What Has Been Said

CHAPTER 1

Development is geared toward helping one build the intrapersonal competence needed to form an accurate model of oneself (Gardner, 1990). Zaccaro (2001) noted that there are certain individual attributes, which early on in one's development, help provide seeds for later development. For example, responsibility to others, an ability to inspire others to larger purpose, an ability to adapt to changes, and mentoring and coaching skills are considered important to shaping the emerging process of leadership development. All of these attributes are affected by how we are developed within our life streams, arguing in favor of the numerator as opposed to the denominator.

Zaccaro (2001) went on to suggest that we need to nurture individual cognitive complexity, social intelligence, openness, tolerance for ambiguity, and self-discipline in order to develop full leadership potential. Leaders generally view how things fit together in broader and more systemic ways than people who do not take the lead. They work at making sense of things that make no sense. Social intelligence is comprised of understanding how people relate to each other and to you as the leader. It is being sensitive to the differences that people bring to the relationship, whether those differences are based on personality, intelligence, attitude, culture, experiences, or some combination.

Great leaders are always open to new experiences, ideas, and perspectives. They encourage people around them to explore and to discover. Coupled with a higher level of comfort with ambiguity, such leaders have developed a discipline to stay focused and to persist toward the goals they intend to achieve. One can be a very creative artist and revel in ambiguity, but not necessarily become a leader of any sort. It is the focus and persistence to a cause, coupled with the openness to explore new avenues and perspectives that generally makes up effective leadership, among other elements as well.

CHAPTER 2

Lewis, Forsythe, Bartone, Bullis, and Snook (2001) indicated that experience does not simply happen to us; it is what you do with it and how you interpret it that effects one's development. How do people think and draw significant experiences in their lives? How is meaning attached to significant life events? The literature on moral reasoning suggests that we construct an internal and meaningful representation of the world and then respond to our interpretation of that worldview. The meaning we attach to events is shaped by our capacity to interpret those events and our own stage of moral reasoning. This helps to explain why some leaders always seem to take actions for their own benefit, versus others who are willing to sacrifice for the good of others.

For example, according to Kegan (1982), people who are Stage 2 thinkers identify with their own achievements and others as being a threat to what you want to do. Their framing of events is based on a what's-in-it-for-me perspective, that guides their own actions and interpretations of others. Thus, they view all relationships as being based on an exchange, or quid pro quo. Consequently, developing trusting relationships with others is extremely difficult, as a Stage 2 thinker is always wondering what is it that he or she wants from me?

Someone who is at Stage 3 can make another one's experience part of his or her own. It is at this stage that the person's perspective allows for empathy and understanding. Only with this capacity can your sense of self include the sense of how others experience you and therefore you can reflect on what they think about your behavior. In a sense, you can go outside yourself and see yourself through the eyes of others. You are not so consumed by yourself that you cannot search for what is good in others, or what they might see as problematic in your behavior and actions. This shift in frame of reference leads to every relationship not being simply categorized as being an exchange, which allows such leaders to consider what is good for the group as opposed to what is good for their own mentality.

CHAPTER 3

Markus and Nurius (1986) examined the importance of different relationships at different points in one's life stream to an individual's identity development due to an activation of alternative possible selves. In other words, the people we meet help to shape how we view ourselves in terms of what we fear, what we believe we ought to do, and what we desire in our future or possible selves. Markus and Nurius (1986) referred to possible selves as, "individuals' ideas of what they would like to become, and what they are afraid of becoming" (p. 954). Many parents encourage their children to try on different possible selves. There is relatively little cost, and a lot of gain to such a process of exploration. Yet, once we enter adulthood, such explorations become more expensive as they come with greater sunk costs in careers, family life, financial investments, etc. There is simply more to risk in redefining ourselves. Evidence clearly indicates that social interaction with significant others, such as role models or parents, helps to shape the exploration of different possible selves (Higgins, Tykocinski, & Vookles, 1990). This evidence is directly in line with what Weick (1995) meant when he indicated that to know our own identity we consult others through social interactions (Weick, 1995).

Lord, Brown, and Freiberg (1999) argued that our bosses can produce both short-term and long-term changes in followers' self views, possible selves, and goals. Clearly, as we have previously argued, they can restrict the range of possible selves or they can enhance what is considered possible even if improbable.

One of the ways to challenge what is our possible self is to distinguish between sense breaking and sense making in the process of creating meaning through dream building (Pratt, 2000). Sense making is how we go about interpreting the events that we go through in the as is or here and now. The sense making we do is based on our perspective-taking capacity, and as previously noted, stage of moral reasoning development. Sense-breaking is where we can envision a future that is inconsistent with our actual self. This sort of personal envisioning creates points of tension between the possible and current self. We need to challenge the basic assumptions of our identity to change, or to break what makes sense.

Sense breaking can lead to a recategorization of self into a different self-identity (Ashforth & Mael, 1989). Sense giving reinforces the identity once established.

In sum, there is a growing body of evidence to suggest we can confirm and disconfirm the way we define ourselves and that challenging the definition of our self is a very powerful mechanism for addressing change. However, to do so, usually requires a multitude of perspectives, which in the more fully developed person comes from their own self-reflection. However, for most of us, such reflective learning requires, as John Lennon once said, "a little help from our friends."

CHAPTER 4

Allport (1955) suggested that learning is a disposition to form structures such as moral conscience. What I have previously described is various learning regimens to enhance your perspective-taking capacity, which can enhance your moral conscience. People want to follow leaders and are willing to sacrifice for leaders who they trust have a high moral conscience.

On the negative side, object beliefs, negative life themes, and outcome uncertainty all made a unique contribution to the prediction of the harm done to society by a leader's policies (O'Connor, Mumford, Clifton, Gessner, & Connelly, 1995). Those leaders who saw the world as being, what's in it for me object belief, historically did the most damage to their organizations, communities and entire societies. They are leaders such as Idi Amin, Joseph Stalin, and Benito Mussolini.

Day (2001) described leadership development the following way, in line with the arguments presented in this chapter. Leadership development is integration: it represents a unique understanding of oneself versus other constructs; it is a strategy helping people understand others, to coordinate their efforts, to build commitments, and to develop a broader constituency and social network.

How can employees take charge of their own learning? We need to understand self-determined learning in organizations. By providing an empowering culture they can promote self-determined learning, especially if someone is predisposed to be a self-determined learner (London & Smither, 1999). London and Smither (1999) argue, "Employees must prepare for tomorrow today. This suggests that employees need to seek information to identify skill gaps, recognize areas to improve current performance, keep up with advances in their profession, and anticipate how changes elsewhere in the firm and the industry may affect work demands and skill requirements" (p. 4). In order to understand the intent of the leaders in the organization, all employees need to develop insight into organizational strategy and goals to know what areas would be most profitable to develop. Disseminating strategic intent and goals is a key component of building the developmental potential of one's workforce. Also, providing employees with work that is more complex and challenging than their day-to-day routines, with support from supervisors to explore alternative strategies has been shown to produce more creative outcomes over time (Oldham & Cummings, 1996).

CHAPTER 5

Feedback from oneself or provided by others is probably one of the most important ways to develop leadership, so taking time to understand it is well worth the investment of energy. However, although over 90% of Fortune 1000 corporations have used multisource feedback, the available evidence for its effectiveness is limited (Church & Bracken, 1997; London & Smither, 1995). To a large degree, we do not have evidence to support the idea that multisource feedback improves behavior. Indeed, as noted in chap. 4, feedback interventions led to a reduction in performance over one third of the time (Kluger & DeNisi, 1996).

What does feedback do in terms of development? Feedback activates self-awareness, and then we must design training interventions that build on that awareness and target behavioral change (London & Wohlers, 1991). Not only must the training intervention target specific change, it must also motivate the individual to want to invest the effort to make the change stick, which is self-regulation.

Feedback can direct attention to appropriate behaviors that may be substituted for ones that are keeping a leader from achieving his or her full potential (Reilly, Smither, & Vasilopoulos, 1996). Atwater and Roush (1995; confirmed by Johnson and Ferstl, 1999) found that feedback had an impact on overraters' self-ratings, bringing them more in line with follower ratings over time.

Besides the feedback itself, the context in which feedback is given has been shown to affect whether it has any impact on improving performance. Walker and Smither (1999) showed that managers who had follow-up meetings as a first step in the goalsetting process with their followers, demonstrated greater improvements in performance versus managers who did not have such meetings. It may be that the meetings helped to clarify the goals for these managers, or by meeting with followers, they were able to get their support or to feel more accountable with change.

Also in terms of the impact of the context, upward feedback has been shown to have less impact on individuals who are more cynical about the organization (Atwater, Waldman, Atwater, & Cartier, 2000). Moreover the cynicism level in the organization itself can impact on the motivation the leader has to try and change their behavior. In the more cynical context, the leader might ask, "Why should I change, when everyone around me is out for themselves, and will do everything they can to subvert my actions." Facteau, Facteau, Schoel, Russell, and Poteet (1998) showed that perceived organizational support enhanced the usefulness of follower feedback above and beyond the level of favorability of the feedback.

Kluger, Van-Dijk, Kass, Stein, and Lustig (1999) explored whether both positive and negative feedback could have a positive influence on performance. Specifically, negative feedback may help to improve performance where an individual needs to fulfill certain obligations, and without the negative feedback he or she would be prevented from accomplishing the objectives. Feedback information on failure and feedback information on success did not differ dramatically in terms of impact on performance. According to Higgins (1997), when people are under prevention focus they are sensitive to punishments. Negative feedback indicates a threat. Receiving positive feedback under prevention focus likely will have no effect as people have no reason to change. Under promotion focus, people have incentives to change to achieve maximum performance, and therefore will be motivated to change. Thus, both negative and positive feedback can increase motivation to perform, depending on whether one is under prevention focus or promotion focus.

Higgins's theory is based on the notion that people will regulate their behavior for different reasons and therefore, the type of feedback that is received may or may not be effective depending on what is the focus of self-regulation. Moreover, regulating ideals and obligations are not the only antecedents of a regulation focus. For example, when people imagine they can do things because they want to, their motivation seems to increase in response to positive feedback and decrease in response to negative feedback. Positive feedback can be both a motivator and demotivator depending on task obligation. For example, Walderesse and Luthans (1994) reported that groups receiving positive feedback showed no gains in performance, whereas the groups that received more negative feedback showed the highest performance gains. Similarly, Atwater, Rousch, and Fischthal (1995) demonstrated that U.S. naval midshipmen who had higher self than other ratings, and received negative feedback, showed the greatest improvements.

Walker and Smither (1999) indicated that almost no attention has been given in the literature to whether the leaders are accountable to using feedback in their own development. Forty percent of programs only provide feedback once. London et al. (1997) argued that by committing publicly to feedback by meeting with followers, the evidence points toward improvement in performance. Over a 5-year time span in which they followed the leader's development, these authors showed that improvements were greater each year for managers who had discussed feedback with followers. Also, improvement was greater for managers who initially received less versus more favorable ratings. One key question left unresolved by this research is whether self-imposed accountability or that imposed by others has the greater impact on improvement? For example, will asking managers after the close of a workshop to build in meetings with their followers to discuss their feedback, have any significant impact on improving performance? At present, this question remains unresolved.

CHAPTER 6

Pioneering studies in the early 1980s discovered that many senior executives believed they grew the most as leaders based on the variation and depth associated with their job challenges (McCall, Lombardo, & Morrison, 1988). These unplanned instream developmental opportunities occurred as job demands would tax or exceed a leader's capability, forcing them to confront areas of weakness requiring further development. This work was supported by work at AT&T by Howard and Bray (1988) who showed significant relationships between the breadth and diversity of challenging job assignments early in a manager's career and rapid career progression. Based on this early research more attention has now been given to identifying challenges and learning opportunities that are linked to an individual's developmental needs and aspirations (McCauley, Eastman, & Ohlott, 1995). Data is now being collected on the types of skills and capabilities learned in particular assignments to help inform individual developmental counseling and succession planning programs.

A classic form of using in vivo developmental assignments is known as job rotation. Job rotation has been used as a technique to enhance leadership skills (Druckman, Singer, & Van Cott, 1997). Some of the specific benefits of job rotation include seeing problems from another unit's perspective, knowledge about the interdependent linkages between units, and frameworks for understanding problems from multiple perspectives.

Executive coaching using on-the-job challenges and reflection is a fast-growing trend globally. Work is one-to-one tailored to the leader's skills and developmental needs, and generally takes place over an extended period of time (Kilburg, 1996). Coaching can vary in focus in terms of examining immediate and concrete problems for reflection to deeper aspects of examining style, character, and how one relates to others over extended periods of time. Reflection can be based on the decisions one makes, how one communicates to others, how one addresses conflict, how once enlists the support of others, etc.

As part of the move toward action learning, more and more organizations are bringing their managers into short seminars to teach them concepts, and to plan out projects, after which they return to their jobs to work on the projects. Such action learning projects are being used in companies such as General Electric, Motorola, and Ford Motor Company as a methodology for developing leadership skills in individual and group interactions (Cohen & Tichy, 1997).

Debriefing

Baird, Holland, and Bacon (1999) discussed the debriefing process and how organizations can modify the AAR process used by the U.S. Army for their own use. The idea of using AARs and debriefings is to bring learning and change as close to performance as possible. Too often, we work on fixing things that help improve the past, or as General Gordon Sullivan once said, "making the past perfect." The purpose of an AAR is to get the plan and action steps approximately right. You apply skills you already have, then learn where the gaps exist, get on with it and try it again. AAR is a way an individual or team can reflect and learn while it is performing. Learning why objectives were not fully met, what lessons can be learned, and how those lessons can be applied quickly to drive up the performance process is essential to the AAR.

CHAPTER 7

Levels of trust in organizations are at an historic low point; there are a number of things that relate to trust-building or that can enhance trust in organizations. These include enhancing the quality and transparency of communications (Muchinsky, 1977; Whitener, Brodt, Korsgaard, & Werner, 1998; Yeager, 1978). Trust stems from the fact that we believe that another party will act benevolently. It involves a willingness to be vulnerable to the expectation that the other will act benevolently without oversight. Blau (1964) argues, as we have above, that trust is developed through repeated exchanges between two or more parties. According to Blau's Social Exchange Theory, by habitually discharging one's obligations, trust develops that may mitigate the risk of opportunism inherent in most organizational contexts. Leaders develop trust in others by engaging in actions and behaviors that would be considered "trustworthy" behavior, that would be considered a social reward for followers. By engaging in such trustworthy behaviors, leaders can increase the likelihood of followers reciprocating with such behavior. The five categories of behavior that have been identified as building the foundation for trust by Whitener et al. (1998) include:

- *Behavioral Consistency*—Leaders who behave consistently over time and situations become more predictable, which leads to followers being more willing to take risks in their work and their relationship with the leader. Predictable, positive behavior reinforces the level of trust in the leader and this comes about by becoming more familiar with each other (Graen & Ulh-Bein, 1995; Orlikoff & Totten, 1999). Underlying the consistency in behavior is the ability and motivation to stay in touch with yourself by linking your behaviors to your underlying values and attitudes. Consistency breeds familiarity, predictability, and trust (Orlikoff & Totten, 1999).
- *Behavioral Integrity*—Employees observe the consistency between a manager's words and deeds and then make attributions about their integrity, honesty, and moral character. People trust others who are willing to take personal responsibility for their own actions and behavior. They are willing to be accountable and to not shift blame.
- *Sharing of Control*—Including followers in decision making and delegating control is seen as a social reward and can enhance trust building.
- *Communication*—The accuracy and openness of communication, as well as how well decisions are explained to followers, builds trust. Also demonstrating concern for others' welfare contributes

to developing trust in leaders (McAllister, 1995). Showing consideration and sensitivity to employee needs/interests, acting in a way that protects follower interests, and refraining from exploiting followers all can contribute to building trust in leaders. Also, demonstrating your willingness to discuss controversial issues and problems openly and sensitively helps to build trust, and to reduce any misunderstandings or false assumptions about you or your actions (Orlikoff & Totten, 1999).

- *Procedural Justice*—Where the policies and practices are seen as fair and equitable by all. Simply valuing people, being inclusive, and allowing for risks to be taken without arbitrary punishment can all contribute to building trust. When trust has been breached, demonstrating a willingness to admit a mistake was made, being willing to deal with the consequences, and demonstrating a willingness to move from the past into the future consistently can build trust.

Overall, trust makes us feel as if we are part of a larger whole. It makes people willing to put in extra effort beyond that which has been contracted for in terms of the exchange of rewards.

CHAPTER 8

A recent study was completed by Weisband, Schroeder, and Connelly (1995) that compared student virtual teams that were more or less successful over a period of a month of interactions. What the group reported was that teams that interacted significantly more often during the first periods of contact did significantly better. These results parallel results reported a few years back by Jarvenpaa, Knott, and Leidner (1998, 1999), who concluded that the first few hours of an MBA project team's interactions were critical to its success 6 months later.

Although quite preliminary, it appears that virtual teams that spend time creating their process structure up front are far more successful downstream in their interactions. What this means, is the team discusses the type of team it wants to be, how it intends to interact, who is responsible for various interactions, setting times to meet, objectives, etc. These are all critical elements to building any team, and they appear to be even more critical early on in the development of virtual teams.

In some recent work of our own on virtual teams, we found that virtual leaders who helped facilitate the specification of goals, objectives, and expectations had teams that viewed themselves as more effective and were more satisfying to work in over time. What was also interesting was that if the members of the team were more disposed toward trusting each other, versus less disposed, the effects were much more significant. In other words, the predisposition of members to trust one another (we assigned people to groups based on high and low disposition to trust others) affected how well the teams got off the ground virtually. Again, trust is the new-age glue that helps pull virtual teams together.

CHAPTER 9

Since 1994, my colleagues and I have been involved directly, indirectly, or both in testing the efficacy of leadership development interventions. In four separate studies, with sample populations ranging from high school students, community leaders, military officers, and bank managers, we have been able to demonstrate that leadership development, in terms of what people have learned and how they behave, can be significantly enhanced. We have been able to show that leaders can show more individualized consideration for followers after training interventions are completed. Leaders going through training have also been shown to be more intellectually stimulating, creating opportunities for innovative thinking and questioning of the status quo. We have found that leadership development can impact the culture of an organization's unit to be more transformational and less transactional. We have also shown in two instances that leadership development can impact positively on objective measures of performance. Characterizing the most successful efforts to develop leadership are the following attributes: a training regimen based on a well-validated leadership model, individualized feedback from multiple sources, a focus on building a concrete developmental plan that includes specific behavioral goals and potential obstacles to overcome, and training that is boosted over time with repeated interventions. For a review of this work go to Avolio (1999) or Dvir, Eden, Avolio, and Shamir (2002).

CHAPTER 10

The type of competition that is emerging today, and the speed of changes in markets, is creating strategic discontinuities, which places greater pressure on organizations to be strategically aligned and adaptive (Hitt, Keats, & DeMarie, 1998). Information technology and globalization have effectively blurred boundaries within organizations, across organizations and even across industries. Identifying who your competitors are today is a constant strategic challenge. New technologies are now forcing television companies, telecommunications, and utility companies to be in competition with each other. A software company acts like a bank, the airlines are getting into mutual funds, and auto makers are now in the financial services business. In terms of strategic leadership, the challenge is to provide enough stability to maintain focus, while also allowing for enough flexibility for rapid adaptation to discontinuities in markets.

Hitt et al. (1998) argued that many of the profoundly interesting changes going on are not linear changes, but rather nonlinear and discontinuous. Moving to control organizations more in periods of disequilibrium may simply not work anymore, as it has in the past. Today, top management must get everyone to continuously rethink current directions, while also thinking about how best to pursue current directions. Leaders must have the competence to balance flexibility with stability. The organizations that maintain strategic flexibility can position themselves to adapt to discontinuous changes in their markets.

To accomplish the type of strategic leadership required for transforming organizations, Hitt et al. (1998) recommended the following:

- Develop dynamic core competencies that you periodically revisit to determine their relevance.
- Focus on developing human capital, as the human element is fundamental to adaptive and creative change.
- Integrate new technology so it coevolves with structural and human technology.
- Articulate and support strategies that are clearly focused on short- to medium-term opportunities.
- Be able and willing to develop new structures and to alter the culture as required.

The strategic leaders of organizations can now help shape strategy formulation and execution in ways that were not feasible even 5 years ago, prior to the introduction of information technology and the web. Getting commitment to a solid vision, and respect for leadership and the culture of the organization are essential ingredients to organizational success (Canella & Monroe, 1997). Kotter and Heskett (1992) provided evidence that organizational cultures that enable organizations to anticipate and adapt to environmental turbulence are associated with higher performance. They define such cultures as having a common set of shared values and ways of behaving, being more risk-oriented and receptive to innovation, candid communication, integrity, teamwork, leadership, and enthusiasm throughout all levels.

The relationship of the CEO to the top management team is even more critical today, as the team needs to reflect the shared mental model and values of the organization and be able to consistently project the model out across time, distance, and cultures oftentimes through technology versus face to face. Strategic leadership must consciously consider the type of role models, behaviors, and values it wants to cascade across all levels of an organization and into all units. They need to create a contagious process that spreads the values and behaviors to each and every individual. Cascading through role modeling can now be considered a core leadership competency for top management teams (Kotter & Heskett, 1992).

A good example of how core values have been cascaded in an organization is the Body Shop led by Anita Ruddick. Ask employees about the vision and ask customers and likely they will say it is an organization that has been focused on social change. Specifically, this CEO models and cascades throughout her organization a focus on social change, although recently questioned by activist groups (Waldman & Yammarino, 1999).

CHAPTER 11

Over the course of the 1990s, the most researched model of leadership has been transactional and transformational leadership (Avolio & Yammarino, 2002; Lowe & Gardner, 2000). Consistently, with almost every positive outcome measure, transformational leadership has had a more positive impact on performance outcomes as compared to transactional leadership. Avolio (1999) covered much of the research on the full range model of leadership as does Bass (1998) and Avolio and Yammarino (2002). A recent meta-analysis of the full range model relationship to performance presented in Avolio and Yammarino (2002) confirmed the results of three earlier meta analyses of the literature.

Evidence to support the development of transformational leadership has also been provided by Dvir, Eden, Avolio, and Shamir (2002), as well as by Barling and his associates (1996) in a series of studies on developing transformational leadership.

Overall, the evidence accumulated thus far indicates that transformational leadership can be developed for greater positive impact on performance with leaders coming from both military and industrial settings.

References

Allport, G. W. (1955). *Becoming; Basic considerations for a psychology of personality.* New Haven, CT: Yale University Press.

Ashforth, B. E., & Mael, F. (1989). Social identity theory and the organization. *Academy of Management Review, 14,* 20–39.

Atwater, L., & Roush, P. (1995). The influence of upward feedback on self- and follower ratings of leadership. *Personnel Psychology, 48*(1), 35–60.

Atwater, L. E., Waldman, D. A., Atwater, D., & Carter, P. (2000). An upward feedback field experiment: Supervisors' cynicism reactions and commitment to subordinates. *Personnel Psychology, 53,* 275–297.

Avolio, B. J. (1999). *Full leadership development: Building the vital forces in organizations.* Thousand Oaks, CA: Sage.

Avolio, B. J., & Yammarino, F. J. (2002). *Transformational and charismatic leadership: The road ahead.* Greenwich, CT: JAI.

Baird, L., Holland, P., & Bacon, S. (1999). Learning from action: Imbedding more learning into performance fast enough to make a difference. *Organizational Dynamics,* 27(4), 19–31.

Barling, J., Weber, T., & Kelloway, E. K. (1996). Effects of transformational leadership training on attitudinal and financial outcomes: A field experiment. *Journal of Applied Psychology, 81*(6), 827–833.

Barnard, C. J. (1968). *The function of the executive.* Cambridge, MA: Harvard University Press.

Bass, B. M. (1998). *Transformational leadership: Industrial, military, and educational impact.* Mahwah, NJ: Lawrence Erlbaum Associates.

Blau, P. M. (1964). *Exchange and power in social life.* New York: Wiley.

Cannella, A. N. Jr., &. Monroe, M. J. (1997). Contrasting perspectives on strategic leaders: Toward a more realistic view of top managers. *Journal of Management, 23,* 213–237.

Cascio, W. F. (1995). Whither industrial and organizational psychology in a changing world of work. *American Psychologist, 50,* 928–939.

Church, A. H., & Bracken, D. W. (1997). Advancing the state of the art of 360-degree feedback: Guest editors' comments on the research and practice of multirater assessment methods. *Group & Organization Management,* 22(2), 149–161.

Cohen, E., & Tichy, N. (1997). How leaders develop leaders. *Training & Development, 51*(5), 58–71.

Cooper, R. J. (2000). The five virtues of Kofi Annan: Drawing on his days in the classrooms of M.I.T. and on the playing fields of Ghana, the U.N. leader pursues a moral vision for enforcing world peace. *Time, 156*(10), 42.

Day, D. V. (2001). Understanding the performance imperatives confronting today's leaders. In S. J. Zaccaro, & R. J. Klimoski (Eds.), *Assessment of leadership outcomes: The nature of organizational leadership* (pp. 384–410). San Francisco: Jossey-Bass.

Day, D. V., & Lance, C. E. (2001). *Understanding the development of leadership complexity through growth modeling.* Paper prepared for the U.S. Army Research Institute's Consortium Research Fellows Program.

Druckman, D., Singer, J. E., & Van Cott, H. (1997). *Enhancing organizational performance.* Washington, DC: National Academy Press.

Dvir, T., Eden, D., Avolio, B. J., & Shamir, B. (2002). Impact of transformational leadership on follower development and performance: A field experiment. *Academy of Management Journal, 45*(4), 735–745.

Facteau, C. L., Facteau, J. D., Schoel, L. C., Russell, J. E. A., & Poteet, M. L. (1998). Reactions of leaders to 360-degree feedback from subordinates and peers. *Leadership Quarterly, 9*(4), 427Œ448.

Frankl, V. E. (1985). *Man's search for meaning.* New York: Washington Square Press/Pocket Books.

Gardner, J. W. (1990). *On leadership.* New York: The Free Press.

Gladwell, M. (2000). *The tipping point: How little things can make a big difference.* Boston: Little, Brown.

Graen, G. B., & Uhl-Bien, M. (1995). Relationship-based approach to leadership: Development of leader-member exchange (LMX) theory of leadership over 25 years: Applying a multi-level multi-domain perspective. *Leadership Quarterly, 6,* 219–247.

Grundstein-Amado, R. (1999). Bi-lateral transformational leadership. *Administration & Society, 31*(2), 147–161.

Higgins, E. T. (1997). Beyond pleasure and pain. *American Psychologist, 52,* 1280–1300.

Higgins, E. T., Tykocinski, O., & Vookles, J. (1990). Patterns of self beliefs: The psychological significance of relations among the actual, ideal, ought, can and future selves. *Self-inference processes: The Ontario Symposium on Personality and Social Psychology, 6,* 153–190.

Hitt, M. A., Keats, B. W., & DeMarie, S. M. (1998). Navigating in the new competitive landscape: Building strategic flexibility and competitive advantage in the 21st century. *Academy of Management Executive, 12*(4), 22–43.

Howard, A. & Bray, D. W. (1988). *Managerial lives in transition: Advancing age and changing times.* New York: Guilford.

Jarvenpaa, S. L., Knoll, K., & Leidner, D. E. (1998). Is anybody out there? Antecedents of trust in global virtual teams. *Journal of Management Information Systems, 14*(4), 29–64.

Jarvenpaa, S. L., & Leidner, D. E. (1999). Communication and trust in global virtual teams. *Organizational Science, 10,* 791–815.

Johnson, J. W., & Ferstl, K. L. (1999). The effects of inter-rater and self–other agreement on performance: Improvement following upward feedback. *Personnel Psychology, 52,* 271–304.

Kegan, D. (1982). A profile of the OD practitioner. *Group & Organization Studies, 7*(1), 7–14.

Kilburg, R. R. (1996). Toward a conceptual understanding and definition of executive coaching. *Consulting Psychology Journal: Practice & Research, 48*(2), 134–144.

Kluger, A. N., & DeNisi, A. (1996). Effects of feedback intervention on performance: A historical review, a meta-analysis, and a preliminary feedback intervention theory. *Psychological Bulletin, 119*(2), 254–285.

Kluger, A. N., Van Dijk, D., Kass, R., Stein, O., & Lustig, H. (1999). *Positive (negative) feedback: Encouragement of discouragement?* Unpublished paper, Hebrew University of Jerusalem.

Kotter, J. P., & Heskett, J. L. (1992). *Corporate culture and performance.* New York: The Free Press.

Lewis, P. M., Forsythe, G. B., Bartone, P., Bullis, R. C., & Snook, S. (2001). *Promoting identity development in young leaders.* Unpublished manuscript.

London, M., & Smither, J. W. (1995). Can multi-source feedback change perceptions of goal accomplishment, self-evaluations, and performance related outcomes. Theory-based applications and directions for research. *Personnel Psychology, 48*(4), 803–840.

London, M., & Smither, J. W. (1999). Career-related continuous learning: Defining the construct and mapping the process. In G. R. Ferris, (Ed.), *Research in human resources management* (Vol. 17, pp. 81–121). Stamford, CT: JAI.

London, M., & Wohlers, A. J. (1991). Agreement between subordinate and self-ratings in upward feedback. *Personnel Psychology, 44*(2), 375–391.

Lord, R. G., Brown, D. J., & Freiberg, S. M. (1999). Understanding the dynamics of leadership: The interaction of self-concepts in the leader / follower relationship. *Organizational Behavior and Human Decision Processes, 78,* 167–203.

Lowe, K. B., & Gardner, W. L. (2000). A decade of the Leadership Quarterly. *Leadership Quarterly, 11,* 459–514.

Mandela, N. (1994). *Long walk to freedom: The autobiography of Nelson Mandela.* Boston, MA: Little, Brown & Company.

Markus, H., & Nurius, P. (1986). Possible selves. *American Psychologist, 41,* 954–969.

McAllister, D. J. (1995). Affect- and cognition-based trust as foundations for interpersonal cooperation in organizations. *Academy of Management Journal, 38*(1), 24–60.

McCall, M. W. Jr., Lombardo, M. M., & Morrison, A. (1988). *The lessons of experience.* Lexington, MA: Lexington Books.

McCauley, C. D., Eastman, L. J., & Ohlott, P. J. (1995). Linking management selection and development through stretch assignments. *Human Resource Management Journal, 34*(1), 93–116.

Muchinsky, P. M. (1977). Organizational communication: Relationships to organizational climate and job satisfaction. *Academy of Management Journal, 20*(4), 592–607.

O'Connor, J., Mumford, M. D., Clifton, T. C., Gessner, T. L., & Connelly, M. S. (1995). Charismatic leaders and destructiveness: An historiometric study. *Leadership Quarterly, 6*(4), 529–555.

Oldham, G. R., Cummings, A. (1996). Employee creativity: Personal and contextual factors at work. *Academy of Management Journal, 39*(3), 607–634.

Orlikoff, J. E., & Totten, M. K. (1999). Building and maintaining trust: The role of leadership. *Trustee, 52*(7), 12–16.

Pratt, M. G. (1998). Identity in organizations: Building theory through conversations. In D. A. Whetten & P. C. Godfrey (Eds.), *To be or not to be: Central questions in organizational identification* (pp. 171–207). Thousand Oaks, CA: Sage.

Reilly, R. R., Smither, J. W., & Vasilopoulos, N. L. (1996). A longitudinal study of upward feedback. *Personnel Psychology, 49*(3), 599–613.

Walker, A. G., & Smither, J. W. (1999). A five-year study of upward feedback: What managers do with their results matters. *Personnel Psychology, 52*(2), 393–424.

Walderesee, R. & Lufhans, F. (1994). The impact of positive and corrective feedback on customer service performance. *Journal of Organizational Behavior, 15,* 83–95.

Waldman, D. A., & Yammarino, F. J. (1999). CEO charismatic leadership: Levels of management and levels of analysis effects. *Academy of Management Review, 24,* 266–285.

Weick, K. (1995). Crisis & renewal: Meeting the challenges of organizational change. *Harvard Business Review, 73*(4), 1.

Weisband, S., Schroeder, S. K., & Connolly, T. (1995). Computer-mediated communication and social information: Status salience and status differences. *Academy of Management Journal, 38,* 1124–1151.

Whitener, E. M., Brodt, S. E., Korsgaard, M. A., & Werner, J. M. (1998). Managers as initiators of trust: An exchange relationship framework for understanding managerial trustworthy behavior. *Academy of Management Review, 23,* 513–530.

Yeager, S. J. (1978). Measurement of independent variables which affect communication: A replication of Roberts and O'Reilly. *Psychological Reports, 43*(3), 1319–1324.

Zaccaro, S. J. (2001). *Nature of executive leadership: Conceptual and empirical analysis of success.* Washington, DC: American Psychological Association.

Recommended Readings

Ackoff, R. L. (1999). Transformational leadership. *Strategy & Leadership, 27,* 20–25.

Atwater, L., Rousch, P., & Fischthal, A. (1995). The influence of upward feedback on self- and follower ratings of leadership: Errata. *Personnel Psychology, 48,* 562.

Atwater, L., & Waldman, D. A. (1998). 360 degree feedback and leadership development. *Leadership Quarterly, 9,* 423–426.

Atwater, L., & Yammarino, F. J. (1997). Self-other agreement: A review and model. *Research in Personnel and Human Resources Management, 15,* 121–174.

Atwater, L. E. (1995). The relationship between supervisory power and organizational characteristics. *Group & Organization Management, 20,* 460–485.

Atwater, L. E., Ostroff, C., Yammarino, F. J., & Pleanor, J. W. (1998). Self-other agreement: Does it really matter? *Personnel Psychology, 51,* 577–598.

Austin, J. E. (1998). Business leadership lessons from the Cleveland turnaround. *California Management Review, 41,* 86–106.

Avolio, B. J., Bass, B. M., & Jung, D. (1999). Re-examining the components of transformational and transactional leadership using the Multifactor Leadership Questionnaire. *Journal of Occupational & Organizational Psychology, 72,* 441–462.

Bass, B. M. (1998). *Transformational leadership: Industrial, military and educational impact.* Mahwah, NJ: Lawrence Erlbaum Associates.

Bass, B. M. (1999). Current developments in transformational leadership: Research and applications. *Psychologist-Manager Journal, 3,* 5–21.

Bass, B. M. (1999). On the taming of charisma: A reply to Janice Beyer. *Leadership Quarterly, 10,* 541–554.

Bass, B. M. (1999). Two decades of research and development in transformational leadership. *European Journal of Work & Organizational Psychology, 8,* 9–33.

Bass, B. M., & Steidlmeier, P. (1999). Ethics, character, and authentic transformational leadership behavior. *Leadership Quarterly, 10,* 181–218.

Conference Board (1999). *Developing Leaders HR Executive Review* [on-line] 7(1). Available www.conference-board.org.

Conger, J. A., & Benjamin, B. (1999). *Building leaders: How successful companies develop the next generation.* San Francisco: Jossey-Bass.

Domagalski, T. A. (1999). Emotion in organizations: Main current. *Human Relations, 52,* 833–853.

Emrich, C. G. (1999). Context effects in leadership perception. *Personality and Social Psychology Bulletin, 25*(8), 991–1006

Fulmer, R. M. (1997). The evolving paradigm of leadership development. *Organizational Dynamics, 26,* 59–72.

Gardner, J. W. (1990). Leadership and the future. *Futurist, 24,* 8–13.

Golembiewski, R. T., & Yeager, S. J. (1978). Employee surveys and a revolution of rising expectations: Do the wrong people ask for too much? *Group & Organization Studies, 3,* 24–30.

Jensen, S. M, & Luthans, F. (2002). Positive Organizational Behavior (POB): A new approach to global management. *Nanyang Business Review, 1,* 17–29.

Kegan, R. (1994). *In over our heads: The mental demands of modern life.* Cambridge, MA: Harvard University.

Kelly, G. G., & Bostrom, R. P. (1997/98). A facilitator's general model for managing socio-emotional issues in group support systems meeting environments. *Journal of Management Information Systems, 14,* 23–44.

Koza, M. P., & Lewin, A. Y. (1998). The co-evolution of strategic alliances. *Organization Science, 9,* 255–264.

London, M., & Smither, J. W. (2003). Feedback orientation, feedback culture, and the longitudinal performance management process. *Human Resource Management Review, 12,* 81–101.

Luthans, F. & Avolio, B. J. (2003). Authentic leadership: A positive developmental approach. In K. S. Cameron, J. E. Dutton, & R. E. Quinn (Eds.), *Positive organizational scholarship* (pp. 241–258). San Francisco: Berrett-Koehler.

Muchinsky, P. M. (1977). A comparison of within and across-subject analysis of the expectancy-valence model for predicting effort. *Academy of Management Journal, 20,* 154–159.

Muchinsky, P. M. (1977). The interrelationships of organizational communication and organizational climate. *Academy of Management Proceedings,* 382–387.

Muchinsky, P. M., Friedman, H. L., Borus, M. E., & Ullman, J. C. (1977). Work performance and satisfaction. *Industrial & Labor Relations Review, 30,* 424.

Mumford, M. D., O'Connor, J., Clifton, T. C., Connelly, M. S., & Zaccaro, S J. (1993). Background data constructs as predictors of leadership. *Human Performance, 6,* 151–196.

Neck, C. P., & Manz, C. C. (1996). Thought self-leadership: The impact of mental strategies training on employee cognition, behavior, and affect. *Journal of Organizational Behavior, 17,* 445–467.

Offermann, L. R., Hanges, P. J., & Day, D. V. (2001). Leaders, followers, and values: progress and prospects for theory and research. *Leadership Quarterly, 12,* 129–132.

Ron, N., Popper, M., & Lipshitz, R. (1999). *Post-flight reviews in the Israel Defense Forces Air Force as an organizational learning mechanism: A functional analysis.* Unpublished manuscript, The University of Haifa, Israel: Department of Psychology.

Rooke, D., & Torbert, W. R. (1998). Organizational transformation as a function of CEOs' development stage. *Organization Development Journal, 16,* 11–28.

Ruvolo, A., Markus, P., & Rose, H. (1992). Possible selves and performance: The power of self-relevant imagery. *Social Cognition, 10,* 95–124.

Saunders, C., & Miranda, S. (1998). Information acquisition in group decision making. *Information and Management, 34,* 55–74.

Seibert, K. W. (1999). Reflection-in-action: Tools for cultivating on-the-job learning conditions. *Organizational Dynamics, 28,* 54–65.

Smither, J. W., & London, M. (1995). An examination of the effects of an upward feedback program over time. *Personnel Psychology, 48,* 1–34.

Smither, J. W., London, M., Flautt, R., Vargas, Y., & Kucine, I. (2003). Can working with an executive coach improve multi-source feedback ratings over time? A quasi-experimental field study. *Personnel Psychology, 56,* 23–45.

Smither, J. W., London, M., & Vasilopoulos, N. L. (1995). An examination of the effects of an upward feedback program over time. *Personnel Psychology, 48,* 1–34.

Smither, J. W., Wohlers, A. J.,& London, M. (1995) A field study of reactions to normative versus individualized upward feedback. *Group & Organization Management, 20,* 61–89.

Stewart, W., & Barling, J. (1996). Daily work stress, mood and interpersonal job performance: A mediational model. *Work & Stress, 10,* 336–351.

Torbert, W., & Fisher, D. (1992). Autobiographical awareness as a catalyst for managerial and organizational development. *Management Education Development, 23,* 184–196.

Weisband, S. (2002). Maintaining awareness in distributed team collaboration: Implications for leadership and performance. In P. Hinds & S. Kiesler (Eds.), *Distributed work* (pp. 311–333). Cambridge, MA: MIT Press.

Zacharatos, A., Barling, J., & Kelloway, E. K. (2000). Development and effects of transformational leadership in adolescents. *Leadership Quarterly, 11,* 211–226.

Index

H

I

J

K

L

M

N

O

P